Teen Brain, Teen Mind

24.95

Teen Brain, Teen Mind

What Parents Need to Know to Survive the Adolescent Years

Dr. Ron Clavier

KEY PORTER BOOKS

Library and Archives Canada Cataloguing in Publication

Clavier, Ron
    Teen brain, teen mind : what parents need to know to survive the adolescent years / Ron Clavier.

ISBN 978-1-55263-527-8

    1. Parent and teenager.   I. Title.

HQ799.15.C53 2005   649'.125   C2005-901589-6

ONTARIO ARTS COUNCIL
CONSEIL DES ARTS DE L'ONTARIO

The publisher gratefully acknowledges the support of the Canada Council for the Arts and the Ontario Arts Council for its publishing program. We acknowledge the support of the Government of Ontario through the Ontario Media Development Corporation's Ontario Book Initiative.

We acknowledge the financial support of the Government of Canada through the Book Publishing Industry Development Program (BPIDP) for our publishing activities.

Excerpts from John Steinbeck's *East of Eden* and *American and Americans* appear with the permission of Penguin Group, USA. Excerpts from Barbara Strauch's *The Primal Teen* appear with the permission of Random House. Excerpts from *The Health Effects of Cannibis* (1999) appear with the permission of The Center for Addication and Mental Health (Ontario).

Key Porter Books Limited
Six Adelaide Street East
Tenth Floor
Toronto, Ontario
Canada M5C 1H6

www.keyporter.com

Text design: Jack Steiner
Electronic formatting: Heidy Lawrance Associates

Printed and bound in Canada

08 09 10 6 5 4 3 2

To my parents, Minnie and Dave Clavier,
for their courage, wisdom, and love.

Acknowledgments

I used to think that writing a book would be easy. After all, my lectures to parents about their teenagers were always pretty articulate and well received. But a book is not just a series of lectures, and I needed the confidence, patience, and hard work of three women to transform those lectures into their present form. Daphne Hart, my agent, saw the work's potential and convinced Key Porter to publish the manuscript. Wendy Thomas spent countless hours helping me reformat and clarify the contents. And Key Porter editor Linda Pruessen brought the book to its final form. I am grateful to each of you.

So much of this book is based on the strength, ethics, and love of my wife, Lita. I thank her not only for her support and encouragement, but also for her leadership in our own parenting efforts. I also thank our daughters, Jessica and Gillian, who have always been my true joy. They have matured into wise and independent women, with whom I continue to seek life's challenges and explore its treasures.

Table of Contents

"When a child first catches adults out—when it first walks into his grave little head that adults do not have divine intelligence, that their judgments are not always wise, their thinking true, their sentences just—his world falls into panic desolation. The gods are fallen and all safety gone. And there is one sure thing about the fall of gods: they do not fall a little; they crash and shatter or sink deeply into green muck. It is a tedious job to build them up again; they never quite shine. And the child's world is never quite whole again. It is an aching kind of growing."

—John Steinbeck, *East of Eden*

▌Introduction:
Around the Moon

Most parents want to be good parents. But what does that mean? I've asked hundreds of parents that question. They say they'd like to see their kids happy and fulfilled as adults. They say they'd like to see their sons and daughters able "to stand on their own two feet," in control of their own destinies, without them or anyone else telling them what to do. If I could condense it all down to a single word, the thing parents want most for their kids is for them to be *independent*.

So what do *teenagers* want? Well, I've asked hundreds of them that question too. What do they say? "More independence!" "We want to be able to make our own decisions, and not have anyone else telling us what to do."

So where's the problem? Parents sincerely want their kids to have *exactly what the kids themselves want to have!* There should be bliss and harmony! And yet raising adolescents seems to go along with so much tension and anger. What's going on?

If you go back and ask the parents what it is about their teenagers that drives them crazy, they'll tell you: "They're so damned *independent*! You can never tell them anything. They always have to make their own decisions!"

Wait a second! Did I miss something? Didn't you just say that's what you wanted from your kids? "Well sure," the parents say. "We want them to be independent … but they want it *now*. We want it *later*!" A dad might say: "I think my son *ought* to be driving the family car any time he wants … when he's 42 years old." A mom might say: "Sure I want my daughter to enjoy lots of great sex … after I'm dead, so I don't have to worry about it!"

We're getting somewhere. The problem is not with differing objectives. The problem is with *timing*. And that leads directly into the next question for parents:

How will you know when your kids are ready for more independence?

To answer that question, I use the analogy of human space exploration. In fact, I originally wanted to call this book "Around the Moon" because it brings to mind exactly what raising adolescents can be like for so many parents.

On December 24, 1968, I was 20 years old and I was listening to the radio with my friends. It was the height of the space race, and for the first time in history, human beings had thrust themselves out of the Earth's orbit. They were on their way to the moon! As they approached their destination, we were *terrified*. What was about to occur had never happened before. When the spacecraft went behind the moon, all communication with it would be cut off until it reappeared 34 minutes later. All we knew was that all sorts of things could happen to it while it was back there: it could crash! It could miss the orbit and slip into deep space with no hope of returning! The man in the moon could reach out and grab it! And no one would even know it was happening, let alone be able to do anything about it.

That's what raising teenagers feels like for many parents. Our kids leave our orbit and move away from our gravitational pull. They are naturally curious and they need to explore new and mysterious places. And sometimes, when they get to their destination, they go out of communication and appear lost to us. Parents know that the kids have to make this journey. But like those of us who had to wait back on Earth in 1968, the teenagers' parents are often terrified. Who can blame them? So many bad things, known or unknown, might happen. Only one thing is certain. For the kids there's no turning back. They must do this.

And yet some teenagers seem inexplicably unwilling or unable to leave the comfort of their parents' "orbit." Others seem to be so eager to get going that they leave too soon, without their parents' consent or approval, and without proper training or equipment.

In many cases, parents feel unqualified to prepare their kids for so important and dangerous a voyage. All too often, irresponsible parents let them go, unprepared, simply to avoid open hostility in the family. Perhaps they themselves were never trained for that task. Worse, they might have been the victims of really bad training—the result of poor experiences they had at the hands of their own inept parents. And when parents hold their kids back, it's usually because they have no confidence in their own handiwork. It's why kids rebel so much. The virtual anthem of the typical adolescent is "You're too overprotective!" or "You don't trust me!" And they're right.

More responsible parents know that trying to delay their departure or going along with them to protect them would be foolish. So what's a parent to do? We must provide them with the best survival training and the best life support system available.

I can remember the cheer that went up at Mission Control when the astronauts came out from behind the moon. They were safe! And yet they were transformed. They'd experienced things that only they could understand. No one could explain it for them, any more than they could hope to convey it to anyone else.

By making sure that our teenagers are well equipped, we can expect them to return from their voyage, transformed, but safe. This book gives parents the knowledge, the tools, the courage, and the comfort to prepare their kids for their journey "around the moon."

Part I:
The Brain-Mind
Connection

1 One Brain, One Mind?: Dualism, Monism, and the Drive to Survive

Let's get something straight right from the start: Parenting teenagers is a tough business. If you've bothered to buy this book, you're likely concerned or even devastated by the seemingly incomprehensible and sometimes dangerous beliefs and behaviors coming from the minds of your teens. You want to protect your kids and help them, but you don't understand them. What goes on in their brains is beyond you.

This curious relationship between the teenage mind and the teenage brain is a mystery that I will make less mysterious in the pages that follow. Understanding the changes in your children's brains as they develop from infants into adults goes a long way toward explaining what goes on in their minds—and toward helping you to cope. Think about that for a minute: understanding the *brain* can help you understand the *mind*. This statement makes an important assumption about the relationship between the brain and the mind—an assumption that we need to explore before we go any further.

Two Halves of One Whole

Historically, people have approached the brain-mind relationship in one of two ways. According to the theory of *dualism*, the mind is a separate entity from the physical brain—or at least something that is bigger than the sum of the brain's physical parts. In this view, the mind is elevated to the level of something that resides within us, but which can be added to or removed from the physical realities of the body. For example, the ancient Greeks, who believed in this theory, used the term "psyche" to mean both "mind" and "soul."

An opposing view—and the one on which all of my neurological research has been based—is *monism*. In this theory, the brain and the mind are one and the same. Monism reduces the mystery of "the mind" to a complex but humanly comprehensible set of biological events. This point of view has some interesting implications. For example, things that might have been labeled "psychological" in nature (for example, certain forms of addiction) must now be viewed as having biological or physiological roots. Furthermore, anything identified as being "mental" (literally, "of the mind") must also be biological in nature. Thus, mental illnesses are recast as biochemical imbalances and physiological anomalies.

This monistic approach does not deny the existence of spiritual forces and entities—including "God" and "soul"—but these concepts remain outside the realm of the mind and are for philosophers and people of faith to describe and debate.

The Hunger Analogy

Here's a crystal-clear illustration of this one brain/one mind approach. Certain brain cells (neurons) are fitted with tiny appendages (cilia) that reach into the passing blood supply and sample it for sugar content. These neurons have evolved in such a way that they become active and fire when the blood sugar level falls below a certain threshold. This firing is perceived or experienced by the neuron's owner as hunger. Her brain is telling her to eat; she *thinks* she's hungry. When she does eat (thereby adding sugar to her blood supply), the neurons stop firing and she doesn't feel hungry any more. Simple, no?

This brings us back to where we started: If the brain and the mind are one and the same, then in order to understand the mind, you must understand the brain. And my entire purpose in writing this book is to convince you that, by extension, *in order to understand the teenage mind you must understand the teenage brain.*

Of course, this is much easier said than done; for although the brain can be seen, photographed, examined, and documented, it still holds many mysteries. What is the brain? What is its function? How did it come into being? How does it work? Many of these questions can be answered by examining the development of the brain itself.

The Purpose of the Brain

When my kids were little, I used to drive them crazy with "learning moments." In one of these, I taught them the biological "truism" that "ontogeny recapitulates phylogeny." Confused? So were they! What this really means is that the human brain develops from its embryonic origins (ontogeny) in much the same way (recapitulates) that simpler life forms evolved over millions of years into more complex forms (phyla). We can therefore understand a lot about the purpose and function of the human brain by examining much simpler forms of animal life.

I Will Survive!

The simplest animals consist of only one cell. They are called protozoans; the simplest of the protozoans is the amoeba. Amoebas live in water. They have no brain, no way of knowing where they are and no capacity to do anything about it. Despite this lack of sensory awareness and motor control, amoebas consume nourishment when they have the opportunity to do so. They also reproduce by mitosis (meaning that they divide into two genetically identical organisms), thereby ensuring the survival of the species.

According to the theory of evolution, the amoeba is not only our simplest animal, but also the first to appear on earth. The theory holds that over millions of years, and through a process of random changes (mutations) in their DNA, some amoebas transformed into new species. This new species had features that the original organism lacked. Specifically, it had sensors that enabled it to detect chemicals in its environment. It was even able to differentiate between chemicals that signaled the presence of food and those that signaled the presence of something dangerous—either a predator or a toxin. This remarkable creature also developed motor capacity—the ability to move itself toward things that were good for it and away from things that were bad (scientists use the term "sensorimotor" to describe organisms that have achieved this level of development). Another way of saying this is that the organism's reactions to the stimuli in its environment were strictly reflexive. Without knowing it (remember this is still only a one-celled animal) it had evolved in such a way as to approach food and avoid danger. And in doing so it dramatically increased its chance of survival. We call this sort of behavior "adaptive" and use the word "maladaptive" to refer to behavior that goes against an organism's best interest, which is to survive.

This simple paradigm governs all of life and explains the *raison d'être* for the human brain: It is the evolutionary end-product of our animalistic drive to survive and reproduce by seeking out and accepting what is good for us, and by avoiding and rejecting what is bad for us. But what happens if we confuse the two?

The Maturation of Beliefs

What happens if we can't tell what's good for us from what's bad? After all, our behavioral decisions are based entirely on what we believe at the time. Just imagine what would happen if that one-celled animal mistakenly *believed* that a predator was food or that food was a predator. Disaster! In order to survive, we need our belief systems to be accurate. And since the accuracy of our beliefs still relies on that ancient biochemically mediated detection system, its malfunctioning results in inaccurate beliefs and consequent human disasters. For example, an anorexic girl perceives herself incorrectly and rejects the food that will keep her alive, and a smoker perceives nicotine as something that he needs, and embraces the tobacco that will kill him.

Why does this happen? Neuroscientists debate whether the human brain ever really finishes developing. However, they do agree that, unlike many other organs, the brain is not finished its development at birth. It is simply too complicated to be "ready" in nine months. This means that it undergoes significant anatomical and physiological changes *while a child is growing up*. It makes perfect sense, then, that children arrive at their beliefs in a much more neurologically immature way than adults. It also makes sense that these very significant changes in brain development and function have major implications for teenagers.

The Menstrual Analogy

Perhaps the most significant of these implications is an overwhelming sense of confusion. Not only is the emerging teen beginning to feel and think differently, he's doing so without understanding why, and without the least bit of instruction on how to handle the changes.

We can get a feel for the confusion and fear this must generate if we imagine what it would be like for a young woman to get her period without having been prepared. *Terrifying!* Imagine feeling a kind of pain you'd never felt before. Now imagine that pain followed by days of bleeding. Wouldn't you come to the conclusion that something was horribly wrong? Certainly this couldn't be normal! Perhaps you'd even think you were dying. That's why we take our daughters aside and talk to them: "I know this is going to sound weird, but pretty soon, something is going to happen to you. You're going to feel a sort of pain that won't feel exactly like any pain you've ever felt before. And you're going to bleed for several days. Now here's the thing: As perverse as this is going to sound, this is normal. In fact, it means that you are healthy." Talking to our daughters certainly won't take away the pain that comes along with menstruation, but it will go a long way toward preventing the fear.

Of course, like all the other changes we see at puberty, menstruation is merely a physical manifestation of the brain's maturation. As such, these changes can be thought of as the tip of the iceberg—the part we can see. But what about the rest of the iceberg, the vastly more significant part that is not so easily seen? In most cases, these cognitive and emotional manifestations of the brain's maturation are neither recognized as normal by adults nor explained as normal to teenagers. This is unfortunate. As I've said, a better understanding of the teen brain can go a long way toward a better understanding of the teen mind. So if you want to cope more effectively with the turmoil of the teen years, there are things you need to know about how the brain changes at the onset of puberty.

2 Changing Brain, Changing Mind: The Evolution of Thought

How do teenagers come to think the way they do? To understand that, it will help if we start with how infants and children view the world.

When parents are worried that their infants aren't thriving physically, they can consult a developmental chart that shows what's "normal" for various ages. Using that chart, they are usually gratified and reassured to see that their kids' heights and weights are within the expected range for their ages.

Jean Piaget, a Swiss developmental psychologist who died in 1980 at the age of 84, did something similar when he researched the cognitive functions of children. In his experiments, he delineated the process of how children's ability to think becomes increasingly complex as they get older. It should be noted that while Piaget's developmental scheme is fascinating and widely accepted, his is only one of several different "stage" theories. Another well-known, but less well accepted scheme is Sigmund Freud's description of oral, anal, and genital stages of development. This book will not discuss the relative merits of these different views. The main point to be made here is that as kids get older, the way they see the world changes. Parents need to recognize that these changes in perception are a direct result of normal developmental changes in the brain. The latest scientific foray into this field of study is the radiological imaging (magnetic resonance imaging, or MRI) of live brains in live people. For the most part, the data provided by these techniques confirm what the stage theorists have known for years—that kids' brains (and, therefore, kids' minds) undergo tremendous changes as they enter the teenage years.

This book focuses on the biological transitions that take place as the brain changes from that of a child to that of an adult. It is my belief that the reactions to these transitions—transitions that take kids from a pre-adolescent brain-stage to an adolescent brain-stage—underlie many of the confusing (and sometimes scary) attitudes and behaviors that we refer to as "typically teenage."

From Infant to Child

Piaget referred to the first two years of human life as the "sensorimotor" period, reminiscent perhaps of that primordial protozoan described in Chapter 1. The sensorimotor infant reacts directly to objects in his environment. Of course, the infant is not a one-celled animal, and while he is capable of rudimentary learning, he is not capable of using language to symbolize the things in his environment. In other words, the primary characteristic of the infant is to act without too much thinking.

When infancy is left behind, at around two years of age, the child enters what Piaget called the concrete operations period of development—a stage that will last roughly until the age of 11. To further clarify the developmental changes that occur during this crucial time, Piaget broke the concrete operations period into two subperiods: the preoperational stage (which occurs, with wide variations, between the ages of 2 and 7) and the concrete operational stage (which occurs, with wide variations, between the ages of 8 and 11).

Perhaps the most noticeable development in the preoperational stage is the use of language. But despite this outward sign of sophistication, the preoperational child is still working with a relatively immature brain. While he may be able to describe the world around him, there are plenty of basic concepts that he still can't grasp. Take reverse logic, for example. Ask a four-year-old if he has a brother, and he'll tell you yes. Ask what his name is, and the child may answer "Jim." Then ask, "Does Jim have a brother?" The answer might be no.

Conservation and Concrete Thought

TRY THIS Another illustration of preoperational thought is the inability to grasp what Piaget called "conservation." One of Piaget's simplest experiments on this front can be performed by anyone. Here's what you'll need:

- 2 equal-sized lumps of Plasticine
- a child between the ages of 2 and 7 (preoperational)
- a child between the ages of 8 and 11
- a child between the ages of 12 and 15
- someone older than 15

While the kids are watching, roll the Plasticine lumps into balls and show them to the kids. Next, ask the kids which ball contains more Plasticine. All the kids will probably say that each lump has the same amount.

Now, take one of the balls and roll it into a sausage shape (again, make sure everyone is watching). Then ask the children which shape contains more Plasticine. In most cases, preoperational children will tell you that the sausage has more. The older kids (beginning with the one between the ages of 8 and 11) will almost always argue that the amount of Plasticine has not changed, regardless of the shape. The older kids might also ridicule the youngster. If they're not very polite, they might call her stupid! But stupidity is not at work here. That preoperational youngster is wrong, but she's not stupid. Her brain is just relatively immature; consequently, her belief about the amount of Plasticine is wrong because of that immaturity.

Piaget used the term "conservation" to describe the ability to understand that the amount of Plasticine does not change with its shape. In other words, the preoperational brain is fooled by the change in shape. The brains of those who are older than seven are able to hold onto (or "conserve") the *belief* that the amount of Plasticine remains constant. When this becomes possible, it reflects a shift from a lower, preoperational functioning to a slightly higher level of functioning in the brain. This new level of functioning marks a transition into Piaget's "concrete operational" phase, the second of the two subperiods in the concrete operations period.

This simple experiment demonstrates that, no matter how hard you try, you simply cannot convey an understanding of "amount" to someone whose brain is not ready. It would be like trying to explain "red" or "green" to a color-blind person: they aren't stupid, but they won't get it. The best you can hope for is an awareness that other people are capable of understanding something they are not. But even that can be asking a lot.

Proverbs and Literal Thought

Another way psychologists test for concreteness of thought is by asking individuals to interpret proverbs or sayings. In the Plasticine experiment the seven-year-old kid was able to see that the amount of Plasticine remained constant despite a change in its shape. This is the one who might have felt so superior to the preoperational child. Ask her to tell you what it means to "not to put all her eggs in one basket." She'll probably not be able to break away from the exact, literal meanings of the words. She'll tell you that if you have a bunch of eggs, you better not carry them all in one basket. If you say, "Yes, that's one way to say what it means, but what else does it mean?" she gets confused. She's just told you what it means, and she has only one way—the literal way—to interpret the world. (At this point, if they haven't run away yet, the kids above the age of 11 might be tempted to ridicule the 7-year-old, and think of her as stupid, when she isn't stupid at all. She's just in a less mature stage of brain development—she's still thinking in a concrete way.)

I remember I once asked my then six-year-old daughter what she was painting. She said, "It's a bird in a tree." I asked why she had painted the bird in that particular way. She said, "Because." I asked, "Why because?" She said, "Just because!" It took me a while to realize that, for the concrete brain, "because" is a terrific reason. This is an essential concept for parents to understand, since it gives a very useful measure of what kids can and cannot grasp. There's no point giving an abstract explanation to a child with a concrete brain. She simply won't get it.

TRY THIS Here's a great way to utilize this new understanding. Parents of concrete-thinking children are forever entering endless debates over bedtime. It usually goes something like this:

"Johnny, it's time for bed."

"Why do I have to go to bed now?" (To get a real feel for this conversation, try saying that "now" out loud, in the whiniest voice you can muster!)

"Well, if you don't go to bed now, you'll be tired in the morning. You won't be able to do well in school, you'll be too tired to play with your friends after school, and you'll need to go to bed early tomorrow night, so you'll miss your favorite television show."

But "in the morning," "after school," and "tomorrow night" are all in the future—and to Johnny, the future doesn't really exist beyond the next few minutes. When you use abstract rationalization to tell Johnny why he has to go to bed now, this is what he hears:

"You have to go to bed because … blah, blah, blah, blah, blah, blah, blah."

So why not take a lesson from your concrete kid and simply say: "Because." To the concrete mind, "because" is a very satisfactory answer.

Beyond Concrete Thought

Have your teenagers ever said something like this?

- ▐ "If you stopped bugging me so much, I'd do better in school."
- ▐ "I'm not going to smoke forever, you know. I'll stop before I get addicted."
- ▐ "My teacher sucks. She doesn't like me. She wants me to fail."

When your teenagers talk this way, you might find yourselves losing patience; you might even find yourselves thinking of them as stupid. But remember the preoperational kid who couldn't grasp that the amount of Plasticine remained the same. And remember the seven-year-old girl who could see only the literal meaning of putting all her eggs in one basket. Those kids were not stupid; your teenagers are not stupid either.

To characterize them as such will result only in hurt feelings, anger, and rebellion. Please understand this: It's not stupidity in evidence here; it's brain immaturity. The owner of a teen brain is simply too immature to perceive that his beliefs are incorrect, and he certainly cannot grasp the full implications of his incorrect beliefs. You cannot convey the subtle implications of social situations like those listed above to someone whose brain is not ready for it.

So what is going on in the brains of kids aged 11 and older—after they leave the concrete stage of development, and enter what Piaget called the formal operational period? To me, it is the most fascinating phase of human cognitive growth, characterized by huge advances in the maturity of thought. Paradoxically, the most visible evidence of those advances takes the form of decidedly negative and seemingly immature attitudes and behaviors.

At this point, I'm sure many parents are dying to ask how old kids need to be before they start acting like mature adults. Well, it's a process, not an event, and it doesn't happen overnight. Moreover, there is great variability. And while the process generally begins at around 11 years of age, it's important to note that many people remain concrete throughout their lives.

As parents, you may find solace (and retain a modicum of sanity) by clinging to the knowledge that even the most seemingly immature teenage behavior is almost always a reflection of normal brain development.

Inability to See Consequences: The Future Is Now

Remember the purpose of the brain? Survival. As animals advanced through the various phyla, they developed more complicated ways of knowing what was out there and more sophisticated ways of dealing with it. Similarly, because we have such advanced brains, humans have devised elaborate ways of securing a food supply and protecting ourselves from social, environmental, biological, and political predators.

The most important factor in our ability to protect ourselves is that *we have brains that allow us to remember past experiences*. What's more, our brains allow us to have free will, meaning that we can make choices about our behavior. We can make judgments based on sophisticated concepts such as empathy and morality and ethics. Because we are aware of the probable consequences of our behavior, we can inhibit or stop ourselves from acting impulsively.

Now let's think about teenagers for a moment. Teenagers often seem oblivious to the possible dangers associated with their behavior. Whether they are cutting class, using drugs, or becoming sexually active, it's as if the adolescent is unable to see the future consequences of their actions. As a result, they are unable to use that information to avoid the associated danger.

In fact, that's exactly what's going on! The future is part of that pretty complicated fourth dimension—time. Teenagers who appear unable to grasp a full measure of comprehension of time are not unlike the younger kids who were either unable to "conserve" the amount of Plasticine, or to escape the literal meanings of proverbs. In the same way, the time-challenged teenager is being asked to grasp a concept—a dimension really—before her brain has matured sufficiently.

The Prefrontal Cortex

The part of the brain that allows us to "see into the future" and inhibit impulsive behaviors is the prefrontal cortex. It's a thin sheet of neurons that lies just behind our foreheads, and it's proportionately larger in humans than in all other species. Many scientists and clinicians call this structure the brain's "executive center" because it is so instrumental in how mature humans make decisions.

Here are some examples of how the prefrontal cortex allows mature adults to "see into the future." In our daily lives, we all have things that we want to do. Sometimes, these are things that we *could* do, but we don't. For example:

■ Some guy cuts you off in traffic. You want to get him back by being similarly rude and dangerous. You want to … but you don't.
■ It's a great spring day, and a woman would love to call in sick to work and spend the day on the golf course. She'd love to … but she doesn't.
■ A beautiful woman sits down next to a man on the bus. He'd like to take her in his arms and have sex before the next stop. He'd like to … but he doesn't.

When we stop ourselves from doing something that we shouldn't do, we're inhibiting our behavior. We can do this thanks to a simultaneous awareness of time: past, present, and future. Consider the man on the bus.

USE 'EM OR LOSE 'EM?

Recently, scientists at the U.S. National Institute of Mental Health began using computerized imaging technology to examine the prefrontal cortex. They discovered that at puberty (approximately 11 years for girls, 12 years for boys), the prefrontal cortex begins an anatomical process that changes it from that of a child to that of an adult.

Gray matter consists of the actual brain cells (called neurons), as well as their communicating links with other brain cells (called synapses). In the time leading up to puberty, the amount of gray matter in the prefrontal cortex proliferates to nearly double the levels found in adults. At puberty, a gradual pruning process begins, and it can take four or more years for the gray matter to return to normal adult levels.

Though no one really knows why this occurs, one theory holds that neurons that are not actually used are lost. While there is some evidence to support this theory, it would be very premature to suggest that encouraging teens to engage in activities that are deemed by some to be beneficial in adulthood would result in more successful adults. For example, a teenager who regularly practices piano (to the delight of his parents) might maintain gray matter thickening in the area related to finger movement. But the teenager who regularly uses a controller to play violent video games (to the horror of his parents) would maintain the same sort of thickening in the same part of the brain. Each behavior might produce a successful adult, and each might produce an unsuccessful one.

On the other hand, it is easy to see that during this period of brain reconfiguration, any deviation from normalcy in the chemical and physiological environment could cause lasting damage. This is precisely why parents, scientists, and educators worry about the alteration of those environments in adolescents who expose their brains to alcohol and other drugs.

His prefrontal cortex is working overtime to remind him about everything he's learned (and believed) in the past. "You're married," it's telling him. "You love your wife. Guys who take women they don't know in their arms on buses are creeps." The same prefrontal cortex is looking to the future as well: "The best-case scenario is that you'll embarrass yourself; the worst is that you'll get arrested. You'll frighten and anger this woman. You'll hurt your family and yourself."

All of this "chatter" makes it pretty easy for the man on the bus to stop himself, which is definitely a good thing. In most cases, adults who are able to delay or prevent an impulsive act—and inhibit their initial desires—are better off for having done so. Their awareness of probable negative consequences acts as a powerful deterrent. It is often easier to defer acting on impulse if the person in question can see himself experiencing some form of similar gratification in the future. For example, the man knows that sex with that good-looking woman on the bus is just a fantasy; he also knows that he has a real wife whom he loves and who loves him in return.

Unlike the man on the bus, however, a teenager does not have the advantage of comprehending time, and the future is only a vague word with little consequence. Telling a teenager that smoking may lead to cancer (in the future) simply has no meaning. And telling a teenager that sex without intimacy may make relationships less rewarding (in the future) will fall on deaf ears. To them, being without gratification now means being without gratification … period.

Parents must avoid labeling their not-yet-developed teens as "stupid" for smoking, cutting class, or becoming sexually active. That's not to say that those things should be condoned or even accepted. It simply means that by maintaining an atmosphere of communication and respect, parents will have much more power to intercede in such behaviors than if they begin the process by confusing, shaming, and blaming their kids for behaviors that the kids, because of their brains' immaturity, see in a very different way.

Adolescence: The Dawn of Abstract Thought

As I have said, when children begin to understand that there are several ways to interpret a saying such as "Don't put all your eggs in one basket," and that "because" is not really an answer to the question "why," they are entering what Piaget called the formal operational phase of development. The cognitive abilities that reflect their changing brains cause kids to emerge from concrete childish egocentrism into a more abstract, adult way of perceiving the world and defining beliefs. It's worth repeating that this change doesn't happen overnight. But not surprisingly, it appears to correspond quite nicely with the changes that have been described in the prefrontal cortex—beginning (generally) around 11 years of age. Above all else, it is essential for parents to understand that this is a tremendous and often painful process.

The New Computer Analogy

When a child's thought processes begin to change from the concrete phase described earlier to a more abstract way of seeing the world, it's as though the brain changes from a familiar, but old, slow, and relatively weak computer with few features to a fancy new (and much faster and more powerful) computer with lots of new programs and features. And that comparison is a good one.

Many of us remember our first computer. I got mine to replace the two instruments I had used previously: a pocket calculator and a typewriter. My first computer cost $6,000. I sold it ten years later at a garage sale for $25. Someone wanted to use it as a doorstop. (To sweeten the deal, I threw in a dot-matrix printer.)

Anyway, all of a sudden I had this computer sitting in my office at the university where I taught. More correctly, it was sitting *in its box*, in my office. That's when my colleagues told me I'd have to take it *out* of the box. So I did—and for the first three weeks I used it very effectively … as a paperweight. Finally, I was embarrassed into plugging the damned thing in!

But I had not been raised in the computer age. Despite my position as university professor (meaning that I was supposed to be "smart"), this was the moment I dreaded, because that was the moment my stupidity was to become manifest. I don't *mind* being stupid. And I don't mind my family and good friends knowing that I'm stupid. I just didn't want *the whole world* to know! But that's what happened when I plugged the computer in.

The first thing to appear was a flashing cursor in the upper left-hand corner of the monochromatic screen. It didn't matter what buttons I pushed; the cursor just kept flashing. It even appeared to get brighter and

(I know this is going to sound crazy) more *demanding*. I imagined that computer was becoming increasingly aware of my stupidity. I continued to push buttons, finally realizing that the keyboard was my enemy. Meanwhile, the computer's demands had turned to disdain. It was now openly scornful, ridiculing my every attempt to get it to make my life easier.

I felt stupid, defeated, depressed, angry, demoralized, and humiliated. What I wanted most was to go back to the time when I had my old pocket calculator and typewriter—a time when things were simpler, easier. If only someone had prepared me, or told me that what I was going through was normal!

When adolescence begins, kids are rather suddenly stripped of their comfortable child's brain (think of my old calculator)—a brain that had presented to them a simple world in which there was pretty much only one way to see things. All of a sudden, in its place is a much more powerful brain (think of the fancy new computer). This brain is able to envision an incredibly complex world—a world in which there are many different ways to see things. Unfortunately, unlike my situation, in which I was aware that I was dealing with a new instrument, most teenagers are never informed that their old computer has been switched. This intensifies their frustration because they think that what used to work just fine is no longer working. Moreover, this new brain doesn't come with a manual, and its owner has no way of knowing which point of view or interpretation (if any!) is correct.

In order to function with this new brain, a teenager must embark on a pretty intense learning process. And while she's learning, she's going to make mistakes. She's going to make poor choices. She's going to feel like she's never on the right track. She's going to feel useless, and angry, and depressed, and humiliated, and self-conscious, and defeated, and demoralized. *She's going to be in pain.* She's going to want to go back in time (psychologists call this "regression"), to a simpler world. But she can't. Whenever she tries, someone is there to say: "Just look at you! You're acting like a child!"

Armed with the correct knowledge, parents can interpret their teens' regressions in a more effective way—as indicators that a wrong button has

PAIN MANAGEMENT?

Parents would do well to remember that most teenagers have been shown that a good way to treat pain is with medication, i.e., drugs. Why the surprise, then, that many kids turn to drugs at this crucial phase of their development? This kind of effort at pain management is especially likely if the kids have not been warned about the normalcy of the pain they are enduring. And drug use at this critical period of neural development can, as I've said, be disastrous.

just been pushed. At times like this, it's important to step in and help rather than be critical. Remember the menstrual analogy from Chapter 1? When you recognize that your child is turning into an adolescent, the best help of all would be to take that kid aside and tell him or her something like this: "Look. Something is about to happen to you. You're going to feel a sort of pain that won't feel exactly like any pain you've ever felt before. Now here's the thing. As perverse as this is going to sound, this is normal. In fact, it means that you are healthy. I can't take away the pain of growing up, but I can try to prevent your fear."

Beliefs Revisited: A New World View

When your children enter the formal operational period of development, they will begin to realize there are many different ways to see the same thing, just as most adults do. Your children's thinking will become more abstract in nature. As wonderful as this sounds, parents must realize that it can be quite upsetting to learn that a world that used to have only one concrete way of being is suddenly complex and unpredictable. Moreover, often when we thought we were right about something, we turned out to be wrong.

Think about this for a minute. Although in most cases it's true that there are many different ways to see the same thing, there are some things we all agree upon, right? For example, all drivers know to go when the light turns green, and to stop when it turns red. Another way to say this is that drivers stop when they *believe* the light is red. According to the survival model of the brain, it would clearly be in the best interest of those drivers if what they believe about the light turns out to be true. If they get it wrong, disaster!

The way we experience the things we see is called perception—and perceptions form the basis of our belief system. This is pretty important because absolutely everything we do, including what we do as parents, is based on what we believe to be true. Here are a few things that you, as parents, might believe:

▌ Parents should never argue about rules in front of their kids; instead, they should provide a united front.
▌ Parents should intervene when their kids get into trouble at school.
▌ Parents have a right to search their kids' rooms when they suspect the presence of drugs.

I'll get to my own *beliefs* about these and many more specific issues soon enough. I'll also provide the clinical and experimental arguments supporting my beliefs. For now, it's enough to say that of all the beliefs you have, you are truly aware of only a tiny fraction. What's more, in very many of these beliefs, you are wrong.

If you think I'm crazy, keep reading.

The Setting Sun

Let's say I ask you and a roomful of people if you've ever seen a sunset. Well, of course you have. Now I ask all of you if you have any particular *beliefs* about the setting sun. Chances are, you'd say you did not or at least you'd be hard put to name any. Now I'll ask you all to give me a description of the setting sun, as it compares visually to the same sun when at its zenith (its highest point in the sky). I'd likely get all sorts of answers: "It looks bigger when it's setting," "It looks more orange or red when it's setting," "It's not as intensely bright when it's setting," "It looks more romantic when it's setting," etc. If I ask if everyone in the crowd agrees with these descriptions, you'd probably all say yes.

If I stop the exercise right there and send everybody home, you'd all be perplexed. You have discovered that everyone sees the setting sun in the same way. But let's say I ask you to make the following mental comparison: Imagine a setting sun and a flat horizon; then picture the sun just touching the horizon. Now imagine taking a familiar circular object (a coin, baseball, basketball, dinner plate, pizza, beach ball, orange) in one of your hands and holding it *at arm's length* next to the setting sun. Now I ask: What familiar object would have the same visual diameter as the setting sun?

Let's say I ask you all to think about it for a few minutes while I leave the room. And let's say that, when I get back, I find the room in pandemonium. Some guy is strangling an old lady; a mother of three is belting a teenager with a stick; some middle-aged man is jumping up and down on a high school principal. "What's going on?" I'd scream. I get all sorts of answers: "She said it's a beach ball! What an idiot! It's obviously a grapefruit!" "A grapefruit?" someone else shouts. "You're both crazy! It's a quarter!"

Luckily, the debate over the size of the setting sun is an "empirical" question, which means that its answer can be determined by experimentation. "Listen," I say, "the sun sets today at 6:30 p.m. Why don't we just wait and see who's right?"

Let's stop for a moment and make a few abstract generalizations. First, I chose the setting sun for this experiment because it's something everybody has seen many times. Still, it's not something you might have thought you had an opinion about. By following through on this exercise, though, you've discovered that you *do* have an opinion about the setting sun—specifically about its size. This is what I meant when I said that most of us are unaware of our beliefs.

Second, until you were challenged about your belief, you simply assumed that everybody saw the setting sun in the same way as you. Now you realize that not everybody who looks at the same thing sees it the same way. In other words, they don't *perceive* it the same way as you. It's extremely important to recognize this, but most of the time, we don't; we just assume that everybody is in agreement with us.

Third, we assume without question that our perception is the correct one. Now we see that everybody sees things differently. That often results in our denigrating the views of others, rather than looking at things from their point of view. Look at the terrible fight that broke out over the setting sun. Okay, that was just an example, you say. After all, the size of the setting sun is such an inconsequential issue. What does it really matter? Who really cares?

But, what if I had asked a *theoretical* question instead: "What is the true nature of God?" Let's say I gave you a few minutes to think about it while I went to the bathroom, and when I returned, I found the room in chaos again, with each person defending his or her belief—"The only true God is the Christian Trinity!" "No, the only true God is Allah, and anyone who disputes that is an infidel!" "What! How can a devout Jew be an infidel?" "You're all wrong! It's the Hindu way!" "No, the Buddhist way!" And the denigrating begins all over. Only now, it's not an empirical question. We can't do any experiments or read any definitive writings to tell us who is right.

Who was right about the setting sun? Do you remember what object you thought would equal it in size? Here's the answer: a regular-strength headache tablet, which is less than half the size of a dime. Surprised? Check it out for yourself the next time you get the chance. Since it's an empirical question, we don't have to argue about it.

Now think back to the moment you read the correct answer. Unless yours was the same, you must have experienced a moment in which you realized that you'd been wrong. This meant you were forced to recognize and accept the fact that something you always believed to be true was, in fact, false. At that moment, you might have said, or thought, "Hmmm!" And that was truly momentous because that was the sound of you changing your mind! This is one of the most important and sophisticated capacities of the human brain.

I'll remind you again about the dangers of seeing things (like the color of the traffic light) in a way that's different from reality, but for now, remember this exercise, and remember the feeling you had when you realized that one of your beliefs just might have been wrong. *Try to remember that your teen may be feeling this type of confusion on a daily basis.* Remember, also, that this debate was an easy one: It could be settled by simple experimentation. Most questions don't let us off so lightly: They are theoretical, not empirical, and they revolve around issues that are social, or familial, or spiritual, or political, or moral. And that's when things get really tough.

3 Teen Brain, Teen Mind: The Implications of Abstract Thought

By now, you should be comfortable with a few key concepts. First and foremost, your teenagers are coming to grips with a very startling fact: Not everybody sees things in the same way they do. They are also beginning to sense that their long-held beliefs may be inaccurate. Together, these realizations have far-reaching implications, especially for young teens who "didn't see it coming" and who weren't offered any strategies for coping. It turns their worlds upside-down. It makes them feel stupid and insecure. It makes them believe that something is wrong with them. And it hurts. But that pain is a good thing. It teaches them that there is such a thing as the future, and it helps them to understand how they ought to behave in that future.

Questions and More Questions

The turmoil that comes from a changing and expanding world view is indispensable, and it leads kids to ask a very normal and predictable question: "If I am wrong, then who is right?" Another way of saying this is "What or whom should I *believe*?" And because all our behavioral decisions are based on what we believe *at the time*, the companion question must be "What should I do?"

When these teens were children, there was no need for such questions. Kids believed that their parents were right, and that it was their parents they should believe. This belief was naturally (and with the best of intentions) perpetrated by the parents themselves. After all, who else had their kids' best interests at heart?

For kids, this knowledge of whom to believe and whom to trust is reassuring. But as adolescence kicks in, they begin to face legions of lobbyists—including parents, but now extending to friends, teachers, coaches, pop culture personalities, and many others—each demanding that *they* be trusted and believed.

"Why?"

Later on, I'll identify curiosity as the most human of the motivations that drive us to do things. Like the rest of us, teenagers are naturally disposed to resolve problems by finding answers. As they try to sort out the increasing number of viewpoints, opinions, and entreaties to "be believed," teenagers begin to ask the one question that best expresses their turmoil: "Why?"

Before going any further, let me remind you that when preadolescent *children* ask this question ("Why do I have to go to bed now?") a concrete answer ("Because") is often the best approach. Problems arise when parents fail to acknowledge that their kids are growing up. As they mature, usually (but remember this varies a lot) around the age of 11 or 12, their questions—and the answers they deserve—will mature as well. Consider the following examples of abstract questions:

- "None of my friends has to be home before midnight. Why do I?"
- "*You* drink alcohol and that's a drug. Why shouldn't I use drugs, too?"
- "You always say we should care about less fortunate people, so why did you get angry when I stopped to talk to that homeless man?"

If your kids are asking questions like this, it means they are beginning to question the status quo. They are ready for—and they deserve—mature answers. Things start to go wrong when parents fall back on their old standards. Instead of thinking through this issue and finding age-appropriate answers, many parents fall back on that old standard: "Because." Be careful. "Because" takes on many disguises, but it always means the same thing: "Those are the rules. No questions. I don't want to discuss it. Just do what I tell you to do." Is it any surprise that teenagers respond angrily? "You're treating me like a child!" they might say. And, of course, they are right.

CASE STUDY

Julie was an only child. She was 14 when her parents divorced. It didn't really come as a shock; there had been lots of fighting, though most of it had nothing to do with her. After the divorce, she split her time between her mother and her father, and the fighting continued. She soon came to see that her parents had two very different approaches to child-rearing. What's more, they each felt strongly that their approach was the best and that the other's was harmful. They were very vocal and very competitive about it.

Her mom had always argued that Julie's dad was away from home too much, and that, perhaps out of guilt, he was too lenient with his "little girl." She said that he hadn't had to deal with the day-to-day issues (such as homework, curfew, allowance, friends). After the divorce, her mom continued to enforce strict rules. Her father recognized that rules were essential, but he continued his more permissive approach.

Julie had her own ideas about how she ought to be raised, based on what she saw happening with her friends, as well as on what she saw or read in the media. For example, she felt that she should be able to study at her own pace, and set her own curfew and allowance, based on peer behavior and her own needs. When she told her parents that their rules were stupid and asked why she had to live with them, they always answered with some variant of "because" ("That's for us to decide, not you!" or "Don't talk back!").

Neither parent asked Julie for her views. Instead, they each tried to get her to side with them, catching her uncomfortably in the middle. In order to establish harmony in two households, Julie had to conform to what she saw as a stupid, arbitrary, and wrong set of rules.

This situation was worsened by the fact that Julie was still very sad and angry about the divorce. She also still felt pressured to perform well in school, in her sports, and in her artistic hobbies. When she saw that many of her friends did not have to put up with the added stress of combative parents, she began to suspect her parents' real motives (getting back at each other and claiming Julie's loyalty). When Julie received no good answers to her questions about why this was going on, she began to *demand* answers. And the more she demanded, the more she was frustrated by non-answers.

Frustration led to rebellion. Julie let her studies slide. She spent more time on the phone with sympathetic friends. She disobeyed rules and sneaked out of the house to meet friends. Not surprisingly, her grades began to suffer. To make herself feel better about those poorer grades, she began to cut class. Soon, she found the only place she could feel comfortable was away from both households. She began to spend more time with those friends who could empathize—the friends who were also going through some sort of family turmoil, and who were also cutting class and were generally seen by adults as rebellious. Slowly and surely, Julie's friends became transformed into the infamous "Wrong Crowd."

Only when the parents sought counseling, began to deal with their own competitiveness, and invited Julie into the rule-making process, did her need to rebel lessen. ■

Dealing with the Questioning Process

This questioning process is likely playing itself out in your household on a daily basis. In order to help you both recognize the process and respond effectively to it, let's look at its implications in three important arenas: the global arena (issues that face us all), the social arena (issues that are specific to one individual but still involve interactions with others), and the personal arena (an individual's relationships within himself).

Global Implications: An Imperfect World

The world is a terrific place. It is full of wonder and love and opportunity. It's a place where humans not only can feel inspired to take on great challenges but also through hard work can accomplish great things. But especially in the newly maturing minds of teenagers, this same world can appear to be a pretty unfair and dangerous place. As caring and loving parents, you've probably found that protecting your children from all kinds of troubles was easiest when they trusted your wisdom completely ("My mom is smarter than your mom") and in your competence ("My dad can beat up your dad"). What can feel safer and be more comforting to kids than being able to fall asleep in the back seat of the car while mom or dad drives home in the dark? Or to have a parent speak to the teacher about an incomplete assignment? Or to be soothed by parental assurances that "everything is going to be fine"?

While some of the world's dangers stem directly from things that are under our control, some certainly do not—like disease, violent weather, and death. We sometimes call these acts of God. As long as kids remain "concrete" in their way of looking at the world, they don't bother to question much about such troubles and it's easy for us to protect them. But as soon as their more abstract brain allows them to realize, for example, that God *could have* decided to create a world *without* such disasters, some teenagers become rebellious by questioning the validity or even the existence of God.

Then there are those troubles that are undeniably created by humans. As kids develop into adolescents, they can't help but notice global inequities such as poverty, racism, war, environmental decay, global warming, child labor, sexism, and so forth. And they begin to ask some pretty tough questions: "If we don't like the existence of things like poverty, racism, war, etc., then why do we put up with it? Why can't you (the parents) change a world that you yourselves have made scary and unlivable for yourselves and for us?"

If your kids haven't already asked these difficult questions, they will. What will you tell them? "Because"? For an adolescent, this just won't do. Neither will trying to make "because" more valid by adding an explanation: "Because that's how it was for me" or "Because that's what I was brought up to believe."

This is how that infamous "teenage rebellion" can begin. For example, consider the teenager who comes home from spending a weekend with a much wealthier friend's family. While there, she overheard her friend's father bragging about a tax loophole. The teen thinks this is dishonest but is too polite and frightened to say so in his presence. Later, when she asks her parents why such things go on, the parents might be at a loss to explain it. They might resort to "The world isn't a fair place," or "I guess that's what they mean by 'the rich get richer and the poor get poorer.'" Of course, neither of these provides a real answer.

Another teenager might learn that his country's government is providing financial support to a country that seems to be run by an oppressive

DISAPPEARING BOUNDARIES

Most parents, educators, and clinicians agree on the need to have limits or boundaries in our lives, and to set these out wisely and consistently when we're raising our kids. In today's world, however, due largely to the tremendous leaps in knowledge that flow from science and technology, old boundary lines are disappearing. Here are a few examples:

- When does life begin? When does it end? As parents, we were taught that you came into existence when you were born, and you ceased existing when you died. Now, we need to consult the Supreme Courts for rulings on these issues.
- What's human? With the publication of the human genome and with human cloning and other genetic engineering within our grasp, boundaries that a generation ago were unchangeable are now indistinct.
- Where's home? Technological innovation has made it essential for individuals to operate in a much more global way. Many kids choose to travel far afield for education and work, forgoing traditional ties with grandparents, siblings, and cousins.
- What is truth? Many of us grew up in an era when we relied on the media (printed and electronic) for our information. When "opinion" was being offered, it was identified as such, and we could choose to accept that point of view or not. Today, information is available on unedited and unscrutinized websites. How do we know what is fact and what is merely opinion?

If this isn't confusing enough, there is much disagreement over where new boundaries should be placed. Put most simply, not everybody sees the same thing in the same way. Today, everybody's got an opinion. And for the adolescent to accept the opinion of one means that he must reject the opinions of the others—something that can easily lead to arguments and rebellion.

dictator. If that teen comes to his previously all-knowing and all-powerful parents for an explanation but receives only shrugs and mumbles, he will go away disillusioned and will continue to seek answers elsewhere. Those answers will often lead him to confront and challenge his parents in ways he would never have dared when he was a child. He does this because, suddenly and without much warning, the world seems to be asking him to accept a lot of things "on faith," but his newly abstract brain is telling him this isn't such a great idea.

So what *should* we answer when our kids ask tough questions about global concerns? My advice is simple: Be honest. Many parents think that kids need them to be certain of everything. I think that's why many of us are reluctant to appear baffled by the same things that baffle our kids. If you, as a parent, think that you always have to be right or in control, I'm going to be blunt: You're wrong. In fact, kids feel reassured when they see that their parents share their doubts and insecurities. When my kids asked me why my generation had not put an end to war or poverty, I simply told them that I didn't have a good answer, and that while there had been some progress in that area (the end of the Cold War, for example, and the dismantling of many nuclear weapons) I was still disappointed in my generation for not doing more. If they asked me about why a man cheats on his taxes or why our government seems to support an unpopular dictator, I'd encourage them to voice their questions, perhaps by addressing those matters in a school essay or drama assignment. I'd encourage them to become active in school politics where they can do something about things that bug them. I'd help them get started; I'd see that they get involved. These things teach kids to feel "empowered," and empowerment is often a great consolation to those who see the world as a confusing and unfair place (see Chapter 5). Above all, I'd encourage them not to become cynical, but to remain idealistic, and to never let themselves be called naive for trying to make things better.

Social Implications: Introducing Democracy

We've seen that when true adolescence begins, teenagers are awakened to the new reality that not everybody sees the same thing in the same way. This understanding is soon extended to the realization that different societies will also have very different sets of beliefs and values about the same issues.

We define a "society" as two or more people who have decided to approach things together. This could be a family, a school, an athletic team or league, a corporation, a church, a peer group, or a nation. All these examples are societies, and no society has ever existed without rules. What's more, no society can survive if it allows its members to disobey the rules. The trouble for all of us, but especially for the newly abstract teenager, is that we each belong to a number of societies simultaneously. This is fine as long as the rules of one society (our family, for example) don't stray too far from the rules of another (our church). A major problem for many teenagers is that the rules of one of their societies (the peer group) often clash with the rules of another of their societies (their family). Again the unfortunate teenager must choose. In doing so, she risks alienating the group whose rules she must break in order to maintain membership in the other.

Further confusion can arise when kids see that other families, schools, and employers often set very different rules from their own families, schools, and employers. Even concrete thinkers may have recognized this, but it's unlikely to have caused the conflict it can with the abstract thinker who's now ready to flex her new mental muscles and challenge "the system." Usually, these observations come out sounding something like this:

❚❚ "Janet's parents let her stay home alone when they go away for the weekend."
❚❚ "Ben's parents offer him beer when he's eating with them."
❚❚ "None of my friends has to do two hours of homework every night."
❚❚ "The teachers are so strict. They won't let you hand in anything late."
❚❚ "How come I have to be at work so early?"
❚❚ "My boss docks my pay if I get there ten minutes late."

Since teenagers often see that other people's families, schools, and employers are pretty normal, happy, and successful, their underlying question is really "Why can't *mine* be more like *theirs*?" Remember, if the question is "Why?" and it comes from the brain of an abstract thinker, you must avoid answering "Because."

A far better answer is that rules *can* change. But wherever possible, this change should be made within the context of a participatory democracy. If participation and representation are not available to the aggrieved teenager, trouble is coming. The prototypic reply within a nondemocratic family/ school/job is: "This is *our* house/school/business, and as long as you want to be part of that family/school/job, you're going to have to obey the rules *we* set!" The problem with this is that it often turns into "it's *our* way or the highway!"

In the family, this kind of response makes the kids feel as if they have no place. They feel alienated and cornered. Doors slam, and they find themselves on the outside wondering how it all happened. And parents find themselves on the inside, wondering how it all happened. The only thing known for sure is that everybody is scared and miserable. You don't have to go there.

This business of setting rules in the family is a key topic, and I will return to it in greater detail in Chapters 5 and 7. For now, I will restrict my advice to this: *Be prepared to amend the rules whenever superior ones present themselves.* If parents adhere to the status quo out of convenience, lust for power, or arrogance, they threaten the lifeline of their own families. Rule changes should *not* be made, however, if the new rule threatens the health or safety of its followers, or if it is unethical. It becomes incumbent on the governing authorities to show those being governed the wisdom of the hated rule.

Let's focus on how this plays out in the family. Perhaps your teenage daughter isn't applying herself to her studies, and her grades are suffering. Or your son is using drugs. You worry about the destructive nature of these behaviors, but haven't been able to change them. Assuming there is no mental illness involved, how do you get these people to recognize that their ways of perceiving things and going about them are fundamentally wrong and that, as a consequence, they are in danger?

The Babysitting Analogy

If your teenager has never babysat, I strongly urge you to lead him in that direction. If he has, ask him if he's ever had to babysit for a three-year-old. Assuming the answer is yes, ask him what the three-year-old is like. He's likely to say that three-year-olds are cute, but curious; they're independent and hard to control; they always want to touch everything and to explore. These traits are all results of a neurological development that permits the child's brain to control his bladder and his bowel, and to exercise fine motor control. This, in turn, results in the leaving behind forever the definitive attributes of babies—diapers and bottles. To three-year-olds, there are only two kinds of people in the world: the ones who wear diapers and the ones who don't. A quick look at the pelvic area proves that these kids are no longer babies, and they don't want to be treated like babies any more.

Now ask your teen to imagine that while he was babysitting, the phone rang, and he told the kid to stay in front of the TV and not to move. But when the phone call was over, and he returned to the family room, the kid was gone! And the front door was open! And the kid was toddling down the front path toward the busy traffic in the street!

Instead of asking your teenager what he'd *do*, ask him what he'd *feel* at that moment. Here's what teens usually say: "scared; panicky; angry; in trouble." Now ask him what he'd *do*. Teens usually say: "I'd go get them and bring them back to the house." Ask: "What if the kid doesn't want to go back to the house? What if she cried, and yelled at you, and called you a lousy babysitter, and said she was going to tell on you, and that if she gets her way, you'll never work that street again!" Teenagers usually say that they'd take her back to the house anyhow, regardless of the flak.

But what if the three-year-old demanded to know why she was being stopped? The teenager usually says: "You would have been hurt, or even killed." What if this independent three-year-old then said: "I wouldn't have been hurt! And anyway, how do you know what's going to happen to me? You don't have a crystal ball."

The teenager is forced to say: "I know because I'm older than you, and I can see the danger, even if you can't. So it's just too bad for you, because I'm in charge of taking care of you!" The teenager would probably put up with all sorts of criticism and defiant behavior from the child without changing his response. In this, he has shown responsibility. The teenager has also shown signs that his prefrontal cortex is beginning to work as it should, in this case giving him an appreciation for the meaning of time.

Whenever you see your kids acting responsibly, let them know that this is commendable behavior. You don't have to give them a car or an expensive vacation. Just let them know that you saw or heard what they did or said, and that you approve. This would be a good time for a hug or to reward them with some sought-after independence.

Once your teenager recognizes his own sense of responsibility in the babysitting situation, you can make the simple jump to his own gripes with you, with his school, or with his employer. But first, let's remember what teenagers are like: cute, but curious. They're independent and hard to control. They have to touch everything (and I do mean *everything*! Remember 13?), and they love to explore (remember 14?). Why? Neural maturation. Just like the intrepid toddler who is no longer a baby, your teens aren't children any more. Just check out *their* pelvic areas. To teenagers, there are only two types of people in the world: the ones with pelvises like that and the ones without. Since they have adult pelvises, they want to know why you're treating them as children.

But having an adult's body does not mean having an adult's mind. And many of the things teenagers do seem child-like and dangerous to their parents: skipping class, using drugs, engaging in unprotected (or even protected) sex, showing poor motivation, having a lousy work ethic—it's not necessary to go on. When you as parents see this kind of behavior, it's as if your kids are running headlong down the front path toward busy traffic. And you will do anything in order to prevent them from getting hurt, even though you must take all sorts of flak for it. You may endure verbal and even physical abuse—and you'll take it because you are in charge of your kids' safety. It's not that you're so much smarter than the kids either; it's just that you're more wrinkled, and you can see dangers that the kids cannot yet see. Just like the teenagers themselves, you aren't prepared to let *your* charges find out the hard way. Of course, teenagers are not three years old, and you can't really bring them back to the house, even if you wanted to. But by showing your kids that your "draconian" parenting style (or what seem to be unfair rules at school or work) is not a bit different from what they just finished saying *they* would do in the same situation, you impart a sense of empathy to your kids. And empathy is one of the best skills parents can give teenagers to bring into adulthood.

Personal Implications: Who Am I?

On the most personal, private level, kids wonder, "If not everybody sees the same thing the same way as everybody else, or the same way as I see it, then I guess not everybody sees *me* the same way, or the way I see myself. This means that there are many ways of seeing *myself*, and I've just learned that I could be *wrong* in my beliefs about other things, so maybe I'm also wrong in my beliefs about myself. And if I *am* wrong about me, then who is right? In other words, *who am I* anyway? And what do I do about the fact that I'm not who I always thought I was?" Another way of putting this is to say that one of the most familiar characterizations of adolescence is "the search for identity."

If a kid is having trouble fitting in, it can be very damaging to self-esteem. She simply doesn't know where she belongs or who she is. Out of desperation, she might align herself physically or ideologically with a particular peer group or a series of peer groups. Over the years, such groups have included the hippies, the punkers, the mods, the preppies, the beatniks, the goths, the jocks, the techies, and the homers. Each group has its own uniform, and by donning that uniform, kids declare themselves to be members of the group. This means instant identity. After a while, they may discover that they don't really identify with the group, and they might change to another. This moving from group to group can go on for quite a while, especially if the process doesn't produce a satisfying answer to the question "Who am I?"

CASE STUDY

Eleven-year-old Jennifer was a friendly, outgoing girl. She was interested in a wide variety of things, and she grew up in a warm, loving family. She was very sensitive to the needs of others. When she saw kids in her sixth-grade class bullying another girl, she came to the defense of that girl. But this only drew the attention of the bullies to her. She was tormented because of her refusal to pay the bullies the "respect" they demanded. She made the decision then and there to be her own person and not to conform for the sake of winning social acceptance. When she got to high school, she continued to refuse to participate in what she considered mindless social behaviors. She didn't drink alcohol or smoke cigarettes. She never tried drugs, and she didn't go to parties where those things were going on. She also didn't date or engage in even the most "adolescent" pre-sexuality (wearing sexy clothes, kissing, necking, etc.). She wanted to be accepted on her own terms. But she paid a huge price for refusing to be defined by what others thought of her.

It wasn't long before Jennifer's parents recognized that something was wrong. She didn't show the sort of defiant rebelliousness they had come, nervously, to expect: demands such as "Why can't I stay out later with my friends?" or "Why can't I have sleepovers with my friends when their parents are away?" Nor did she seem to need the sorts of hair, makeup, or clothes that typified her generation. Instead, Jennifer became sulky and morose. She closeted herself in her room and resented spending time with her parents: "How come I have to go everywhere with you?" or "Just leave me alone!"

After one particularly disturbing door-slamming incident, Jennifer's mom went quietly to her daughter's room and knocked on the door. A sound that could have been a mumble, a grunt, or a cry told her that her daughter was there but didn't want to talk about it. Instead of insisting that Jennifer tell all, her mom simply told Jennifer that she knew some-thing important was bothering her, and that when she felt more like talk-ing, she would be there to listen. Another grunt signaled the end of the conversation, but Jennifer's mom had accomplished most of what she could have accomplished at that time.

Later that day, a much calmer Jennifer approached her mom. She told her about the bullying and her decision to "be herself." She also admitted that she wasn't sure who "herself" was, and whether she liked "herself" if no one else did. She even called herself a freak who would never have friends or be normal. That was the opening her mom needed. It permit-ted the sort of dialogue that gave Jennifer some valuable choices for deal-ing with her situation. ■

It's worth remembering that teenagers often react very strongly to situ-ations that their parents don't find quite so urgent. Psychologists describe such exaggerations as "hyperbole." This is thought to be related to the teen's dependence on an emotional part of the brain (the amygdale) when making decisions, rather than a reliance on the prefrontal cortex—which is not yet finished its development. This means that the teenager's words, and sometimes their feelings, appear *extreme*, as in

■ "Oh my God! I just saw the *BEST* movie everrrrrrr!!"

■ "I'm so stupid. I'll *NEVER* get asked out again!"

■ "This is the *WORST* thing that could ever happen to me!"

So when a teenager characterizes herself as a freak who will never have friends or be normal, her parents might be tempted to dismiss the statement as typical teenage hyperbole. But if such language occurs in a context of a noticeable change for the worse in mood or behavior, parents should take it as a sign that their son or daughter is probably quite disturbed at having done something that he or she, and maybe others, considered stupid.

Regression is another sure indicator that a teenager has encountered a threatening situation and is trying to protect herself. By retreating into her childhood room and slamming the door, Jennifer was seeking sanctuary— a physical reminder of a safer, happier time.

Defense Mechanisms

Think of the most basic purpose of life: survival. If people perceive they are in psychological danger, they will naturally protect themselves. But what if they "overprotect" themselves?

Unnecessary (and possibly harmful) overreaction earns the psychological title of "defense mechanism," and psychologists have described several different sub-categories under this broad category. A person's particular defensive style is the product of a complex set of factors, including parental modeling, self-esteem, sense of humor, peer pressure, and intellectual and emotional intelligence.

Teenagers are no exception. Here are some, *but not all*, of the most common teenage overdefensive reactions:

■ **Hyperbole:** Some teens will refer to the threatening situation in catastrophic or hyperbolic terms in order to make their extreme reactions to them seem proportional. When teens do this, we say they are rationalizing, thereby giving everyone the idea that they have no choice but to act the way they do.

▌ **Avoidance:** Some teens will simply "hide out" or retreat from life, much as people do while waiting out a tornado or hurricane. They hope the storm will pass, leaving them unharmed.

▌ **Physical escape:** Some teens run away from home or willfully break the rules and get themselves kicked out of a hated school or summer camp.

▌ **Chemical escape:** Some teens may seek a temporary escape from their problems through alcohol or drug use.

▌ **Aggression:** Some teens try to distract people from recognizing that they are really insecure by acting aggressively. Some go as far as to join gangs. Psychologists call this a "reaction formation."

Regardless of which style a person adopts, defense mechanisms have to have two qualities: they must be both *effective* and *adaptive*. Effective means that the defense mechanism works. Sometimes people are described as protecting themselves by building emotional "walls." Strong walls made of stone are very effective. They keep everything that is harmful out, and we are "safe" within them. But, of course, we have no sunlight or freedom of mobility. In that situation, we couldn't thrive. Not being able to thrive is the same as dying. So while psychological wall building is a very effective defense mechanism, it is not an adaptive one and should be abandoned if at all possible.

Of course, this dual approach to defense mechanisms is much more easily talked about than achieved. People often cling to what they see as their source of protection even though that same thing is really preventing them from thriving.

Let's extend the metaphor of the stone-walled fortress. Rather than being imprisoned and immobile behind the fortress walls, we'd be better off with a good suit of psychological armor. It would allow us to leave a safe place behind and move about in a new and potentially dangerous place. With the suit, we could do this and not get too badly hurt. What's more, we can take it (or parts of it) off when we're feeling safe, as we would with friends or family.

What can parents do when they see their kids overprotecting themselves from perceived dangers? First, don't make the situation worse by trivializing your teen's reaction. Kids in these situations want to be taken seriously, and so they should. Don't tell them they're being silly or that the issue is not really as important as they think. Here is a perfect opportunity for you to show empathy. Tell them that you understand, and if you've been in a similar situation yourself (and if the opportunity is there and you think it might help), tell them the story.

Next, understand that by telling your kids to "just be themselves," you are asking them to approach a complex and abstract problem in a simplistic and concrete way. Simplistic solutions put too much pressure on newly abstract teenagers. How can a teenager be "herself" if the true nature of "herself" is suddenly so unclear?

Then look at the situation using your new understanding of your teenager's emerging abstract brain. Jennifer, for example, might not have had a problem wearing the same styles as her peers or enjoying much of their pop culture, but she might have been distinctly uncomfortable with their casual approach to sex. Still, she may have felt that in order to be accepted by her peers she had to go along with *everything* they did. And since she didn't feel comfortable doing *all* of those things, she felt forced to do *none* of them. This "all-or-none" view of things is typical of the concrete mind. But making that choice left her feeling confused and miserable. She probably knew she was being childish, but this made her confusion feel only more shameful. Knowing this, Jennifer's parents could let her know that her peers weren't necessarily saying "Be *entirely* like me, or I won't be your friend!" They could assure her that seeing the world in a more mature, but complicated (abstract) way is a normal, if painful consequence of growing up.

Finally, parents can help their teenagers take another look at who they are. They should encourage their kids to confirm that the characteristics of which they are proud (such as honesty, loyalty, and trustworthiness) are really seen that way by others. On the other hand, if a teenager is mistaken as to how he is perceived by others, he would do well to find out about it, no matter how daunting and painful the process might seem.

This self "re-examination" is kind of like looking into a mirror.

Honest Mirrors

Pretend for a moment that you're walking down the street when you suddenly feel as if everybody is laughing at you. You know they don't know you, so you wonder what they think is so funny. The first thing you'd probably do is try to find a mirror so you can see what's so funny for yourself.

When you find a mirror, you might discover that you left the house that morning without putting on any pants! Or that you've got a big "I have sex in Chevrolets" sign taped to your forehead.

How do you feel about this? Not only did you do something stupid, people *saw you do it*. Because these are silly examples, it's easy to say that most mature adults would do something to remedy the situation. Then they would likely laugh the incident off. But what if it wasn't such a silly example? What if you felt that people were shunning you because you refused to go along with actions that made you uncomfortable? It might not be so easy to shrug it off if people were reacting negatively toward you because of that.

CASE STUDY

Nick had been a really popular kid in grade school. But when he got to high school, he found it harder and harder to make friends. He wasn't invited to parties or to participate in school or sports teams. He was confused, and he found that he wasn't able to simply laugh it off. At first, he became angry at and variously blamed his parents, his teachers, and his former friends. Later, he became very angry with himself and began calling himself stupid. He also became somewhat depressed and started to believe that there was no hope.

Nick was incapable of seeing that the positive qualities he believed he had were not being perceived that way by others. He needed someone to point this out to him in a compassionate, yet forceful manner. In counseling, he learned that what he felt was his good sense of humor was being perceived by others as immaturity. When he said that he thought he was "pretty smart," others took that as evidence of conceit. And what he had believed was his natural leadership was being perceived by others as bossiness.

In a sense, his counselor was his mirror. And she was an "honest mirror." First, she encouraged him to see that other people were not reacting to him according to his own conception of who he was. Then she showed him that he had been reacting to their treatment with defense mechanisms, overprotecting himself from an uncomfortable truth. Once he began to accept a truer and more accurate self-concept, he was able to make the necessary changes so that others not only saw him accurately, but also in the way he wanted to be seen. After that, things improved dramatically for Nick.   ■

People can always break the mirror that tells them how they really look. They could simply run away. They could get drunk or try to kid themselves into believing that nobody was laughing at them after all. But that would be a lie, and lying is just one of the ways people protect themselves from the truth. That's why I use the term "honest mirror." It's an oblique reference to the "magic mirror" popularized in the children's story *Snow White*. The ugly and vicious witch employs a magical mirror that lies to her about her true characteristics. This, of course, is metaphoric for the way we often lie to ourselves. For example, we might try to convince ourselves that it's really all right to be the way we are, when it isn't. As with the wicked witch, however, this avoidance of the truth can lead only to additional troubles.

Part II: Laying the Groundwork

4 Preparing Yourself to Parent: Being Your Own Honest Mirror

You're reading this book because you're concerned about your teenager. You want to find out what makes him or her tick. You're probably looking for some support. And you want to know how you can be a better parent.

So much of the tension between parents and their teenagers stems from the struggle for independence. The kids want more. They feel their parents are treating them like children, and they resent that. As a parent, you ought to think of putting it this way to your teenager: "As long as you act like a child, you'll be treated as one. If you want to be treated like a mature adult, start acting like one."

So far, this is easy. But it gets complicated quickly. Because as parents, you might then have to add: "If you don't know what a mature adult is supposed to act like, then look at some mature adults and take your cues from them."

This, of course, implies that you are referring to *yourselves* as those mature adults. But what if you aren't?

This last point is important. Although this book is largely about teenagers, it's also about you. In order to successfully parent your teen, you need to take a good, hard look in your own honest mirror. You need to learn a few things about yourself, and then apply that knowledge to your role as a parent. Before we get into it, I want to warn you that this may be a tough chapter. I'm going to challenge you about your own beliefs and attitudes.

TOO MUCH TOO SOON

Some parents give in too early to demands for independence and give their kids all sorts of freedom before the kids have shown the requisite or proportionate responsibility. Why are they so surprised when the kids can't handle it? Just because a kid wants to ride a horse, would you start him off on the bucking bronco? Yet parents often

- allow their kids to stay at home alone when they go off for a weekend of recreation. They make the kids vow not to have any parties, but the kids often can't seem to follow through on this promise.
- give their kids access to cars in order to not have to do the driving themselves. Yet we seem always to hear of a teenage driver inexperienced in certain driving conditions making a terrible, and often fatal, mistake.
- allow their kids access to the family liquor supply based on the mistaken belief that it's better for the kids to drink at home where "it's safe" than to have them drink outside the home. The kids come to see drinking as a necessary part of socializing.

When I speak about these things to parents, there is always a lot of "tsk, tsking" and general derision in the room. You'd think none of these parents would ever permit such things. But obviously, lots of parents do just that. Why?

Guilt is one possibility. Maybe they don't spend as much time with their kids as they should, so they "treat" them to goodies to make up for it. Another possibility is peer pressure. Kids come home with stories that all their friends have this or that. It's usually not as true as the kids say, but it is true that many kids have too much for their own good. Parents feel pressured by their peers to come through or face disgrace.

Another possible contribution to the "too much too soon" trap is the "cornucopia" problem I discuss in Chapter 11. In this age of material affluence, parents can often afford to supply their kids with anything they want, especially if the parents themselves grew up in a more economically restricted time and place. This is a desirable and even laudable sentiment, but beware of the unexpected and negative impact this can have on your teenagers' motivation to fend for themselves. Rescuing helpless kids when they cannot fend for themselves is acting responsibly. Rescuing teenagers who ought to be able to fend for themselves is cruel. It robs them of the capacity to become responsible and independent.

I've already talked about what happens once the teen begins to understand that there are other points of view, but how flexible are you as a parent? How many points of view are you willing to consider? Is your attitude "My way or the highway"? Which is more important to you—to always be "right" or to have a good open relationship with your teen and see him or her grow into a responsible, creative, self-reliant adult? I think I know the answer—that's why you're reading this book. But to reach your goal, you need to do some honest soul searching.

Parenting: A Full-Time Job

Imagine that you want to be a firefighter. You've done some research and believe that this is the right career for you. You train and prepare yourself and soon you're a firefighter! You are called out with your fellow firefighter to attend some fires. But one day when the bell goes off in the fire hall and everybody is rushing to the trucks, you remain seated and relaxed. You tell your colleagues that they should go without you. "I'll stay behind to answer the phone," you say. You explain that the last time you went to a fire, it was awfully hot, and you found the whole thing quite smoky. You had to wash your clothes and hair several times to get the smell out.

How well do you think that would go over? Once your colleagues got over their shock, they might give you a bit of a talking-to. They might say that nobody forced you to be a firefighter. They might point out that not wanting to be a firefighter was fine, but that taking the job and then deciding not to do it most certainly was not. They would be well within their rights to remind you that when you took on the job of firefighter, you took on the responsibilities of being a firefighter—all of them.

The same applies to the job of "father" or "mother." It's important to think long and hard before you take on this most serious of jobs. This is not a role you want to approach in a half-assed way, or abandon altogether when it turns out to be harder than you expected.

Thousands of us do abandon our jobs. Another way to say this is that we abandon our responsibilities. If you don't understand this and apply it to your own life, you will never provide a model from which your kids can learn. They will never grasp the concept of responsibility, and they will never gain the independence that you and they want so much for them to have.

Model Parents?

Being a role model can be scary. There isn't one among us who hasn't done something they'd rather keep under wraps, especially from their teen. For some of us it might be a minor transgression, for others it could be something more serious. But most of us feel we can't let our kids know about these occasions. We ask ourselves that rhetorical question "What kind of role model would we be?" The trouble with rhetorical questions is that they don't leave room for any answers, and, as you'll see when I discuss curiosity and science, if we already believe that telling our kids about our own past misadventures would make us poor role models, then it's not a question at all.

In Chapter 6 I talk about rhetorical questions and the folly of making assumptions without any supporting (empirical) evidence. In the case of role modeling, with a rhetorical question like this it is often useful to turn it into an empirical question; use the same words, only change the inflection. In this case, change:

"What kind of role model *would we be*?" into

"*What kind of role model* would we be?" Now we're getting somewhere. Now we have room for an answer. And don't be sure that the answer is negative. Remember, that's just a belief and beliefs can be wrong.

Here's an example from the "infamous three": drugs, sex, and rock and roll. What bad thing do you imagine would happen if you admitted to your kids that you smoked marijuana when you were their age? Would you be saying that it's okay for them to do it? Or would you appear to be hypocritical by saying "Yes, I did it but you can't"? Both of these may reflect badly on you, but keep in mind that an honest reflection, while hard to take, is the best reflection possible. So don't let your fear motivate you to hide things from your teens.

Once you've opened up the discussion, you can talk about your own emotional turmoil as a teen. You can go into the sociology of the time. Were you part of the drug culture? Do you find yourself tempted to use the same excuse that scares the daylights out of you now: "Everybody was doing it!" Whatever you decide, remember that just about every generation scared its parents. What did you do that scared your parents?

I'm dating myself here, but I was of the generation of teenagers whose parents saw the highest adolescent per capita use of illicit drugs ever. We faced huge inter-generational distrust. Our parents believed that we were being brainwashed by satanic forces into becoming cultist, music-driven, anarchistic, drugged-out, antiestablishment revolutionaries. Antiwar demonstrations and occupations turned violent. Neighborhoods burned. Kids were killed at Kent State.

How is it possible that this generation of degenerates turned into parents who now decry their own kids' behavior? Can you honestly say, "But it's so much more dangerous out there for them than it was for us"? Imagine this dialogue:

Parent: "... so I'm telling you, no more dope smoking. I won't tolerate it."

Kid: "C'mon ... are saying you've never smoked dope? I've seen some of those photos of you and your friends, and you were definitely stoned."

Okay. Now what? Your child has a point, and there are several possible ways to respond. Which would you use? Which do you think is best?

▌ Option 1: Defense Mechanisms
Denial: "You're nuts. We were just tired from being up all night, studying."

Avoidance: "Can we talk about this later? I want your father/mother to be in on this."

Rationalization: "It's true, but after all, everyone was doing it./ Nobody told us it was dangerous./ The stuff we smoked was much weaker than what's out there today." (These things may all be true, and, to an extent, they explain the parents' behavior, but they don't excuse it. See below.)

■ **Option 2: Dictatorship**

"Those are my rules; I don't want to discuss it. It's my way or the highway."

■ **Option 3: Negotiation**

"Look, it's illegal. I don't want you getting into trouble. Trust me. You could get into some pretty dicey situations out there. If you must smoke dope, I want you to promise me you'll do it in our home, and no one drives away from here when they're impaired."

■ **Option 4: Honest Mirror**

"It's true. We did do some pretty dangerous things back then. [Here, some of those rationalizations—if honest—are okay.] But I know things now that I couldn't have known then. Remember when we talked about babysitting? Well, when I see you smoking dope, it's like you're that toddler, running toward traffic. I get scared. I've done my research, and I know what this drug can do. I see it happening in you. And I'm afraid. I'm sorry, but I'll never be comfortable with you smoking dope."

Discussions like these are not easy. You may feel like you're risking disaster, but if you're truly serious about your job as a mother or father, these conversations will actually be rewarding. They are one of the ways you can become closer to your teen in a respectful, affectionate, and honest relationship. Think about it. First, you've done your teen the honor of being honest, no matter how painful it was. Second, you've shown that you're available to talk about these issues openly. You're not always going to agree with your teen (more about that later), but you're also not rejecting her out of hand with a pat answer.

Commitment and Trust

Clearly, commitment is paramount when it comes to parenting. You need to commit to the job itself, to the task of providing a good role model for your child, even if that's sometimes hard to do. So if commitment is so important to how people relate to each other, why does it seem to be missing in so many relationships? Part of the problem may be due to confusion over the real meaning of the word. In fact, there are several definitions of the word "commitment" that relate to this issue. Let's look at three of them.

- **Single-minded determination:** Here, we think of being "committed" as being devoted and loyal to something or someone. We think of it as "stick-to-it-iveness," fidelity, and dedication. This seems to be what people look for in a relationship, and what appears to be missing in many relationships that fail.

- **Imprisonment:** "Commitment" is used when talking about a freedom being withdrawn. People are committed to psychiatric hospitals, for example. But there are other ways to look at this. For example, let's say your daughter joins a soccer team that plays every Saturday at 9 a.m. One Saturday, she sleeps until noon because she'd been out partying the previous night. "You can't just decide not to play," you might tell her. "You made a commitment when you joined the team. They're counting on you. Why can't you stick to something once you've started it?" Your daughter might say that she doesn't really care. "I need to be able to decide what I do for myself. You're trying to imprison me. I need more freedom!" If you try to argue her "imprisonment" point, you're not being honest. Remember: commitment does mean loss of freedom.

- **Loss of control:** When I was a kid, I used to play a game with my friends at the lake. We'd run as fast as we could down a pier and try to stop ourselves before plunging into the water. Whoever was able to stop closest to the end of the pier "won." The reason we so often plunged into the water was because we had built up such great momentum that no matter how hard we tried to stop, we went over the edge. We were, in other words, committed. Of course, this led to much plunging and lots of fun. Think about it. There were really two parts to our activity: plunging and being in the water. From past experience, we knew that both parts were enjoyable, so it was really no big deal if we "lost" the game and ended up in the water. But what if we'd never been in the water before? What if we'd only heard from someone else that being in the water was fun? What if we discovered when we got into the water that it really wasn't fun at all? Are we still trapped? Must we stay there and suffer terrible discomfort? Wouldn't we have been better off if we'd had some sense of what it was like before we made the plunge?

When it comes to being good parents, in order to avoid the painful consequences of breaking a commitment, we'd be well advised to inform our kids about the realities of marriage, jobs, and their own decisions about pregnancy and parenthood. There are some wonderful programs designed to do just that. In one of them, teenagers are required to take care of "robot" babies; in another, young men wear pillows around their bellies to simulate the discomforts of pregnancy. Finally, once committed, whether to a life partner or a friend or a job, we must accept that we are no longer in control. Moreover, I believe a major reason for the failure of many relationships is that one partner believed he or she must remain in control.

Under what conditions would anyone be willing to give up control? In what circumstances would loss of freedom be acceptable? When would it be safe to "take the plunge"? It's a question of trust, the basis of true commitment. Trust is the element that makes risk okay. I'd give up control if I were absolutely sure of not getting hurt. If I knew I'd be safe, I'd do all sorts of dangerous things.

Parents place themselves in a position of risk starting with the pregnancy and on through to the birth, the sleepless nights, the trips to the hospital, the teacher interviews, the arguments, the expenses, the drugs, and all the rest. But parents can usually handle this—they are dedicated, even though they may sometimes feel trapped. And they almost always feel like they're not in control. In other words, they are committed. But if they trust each other, and rely on each other, they'll find not only commitment, but also passion and intimacy. (I'll talk more about those later.) If they find themselves to be both untrusting and untrusted, however, if they feel threatened and at risk from within their relationship, they're lost.

The next question is this: "Is parental commitment to kids enough of a model from which kids can learn commitment themselves?" The answer, I'm afraid, is "yes." In fact, kids from families with truly committed parents do learn and practice commitment in their lives. But if kids don't pick up commitment from their parents, it's almost always because it's not really there to be picked up. I know this sounds harsh, but teenagers cannot always count on their parents to "be there." And this can cause serious problems.

When Parents Don't Commit

In situations where people don't do what we, and even they, think they ought to be doing, there are often two possible explanations: Either they aren't able to do it, or they are able to but don't. The former describes a true disability—a condition that originates in the central nervous system. There are many of these. They are subtle and complex, and they often go undiagnosed or even unnoticed.

For example, take various emotional disabilities. Since these are "of the mind," they must be "of the brain," but little is known at this time of their specific neural bases. Some believe, for example, that people raised in unloving environments have great difficulties with loving and emotional warmth later in life. Is there any science to support this hunch? In an effort to demonstrate the importance of early environmental experience for the normal development of the brain, researchers David Hubel, an American, and Torsten Weisel, a Norwegian, sewed shut the eyelids of newborn cats or monkeys (which were under general anaesthetic). The animals were raised and nourished as normally as possible, and then, some months later, their eyes were reopened. Despite having perfectly intact eyes and brains, the animals were virtually blind. The scientists went on to discover that if specific stimulation is not presented to the brain during a critical time in the animals' development, then no matter how much of that input is presented later, the animal will not be able to experience it.

Can the same be true of the human brain when it comes to things like trust or even love? This question, of course, presents extremely difficult problems for empirical investigation. Anecdotally, however, I can tell you that many of my clinical patients have what looks exactly like the emotional equivalent of blindness. Their partners seem to understand that a lack of emotional stimulation at a critical time of development might be behind why my patients don't respond "normally." These partners often say things like "Of course, he came from a very unloving family" or "Her parents never showed their emotions." But if these same people believed that their partners simply weren't trying or didn't care enough, their interpretation would be akin to chastising a paraplegic for not walking because he doesn't seem to be trying hard enough. The proper explanation to all concerned can mitigate most of the shame, guilt, and reprimand. But it is only that—an explanation; it should not be used as an excuse because it does not excuse what has happened. When trust and commitment between parents and their children have either never existed or are now lost, it is up to the parents to put them back into place. There are countless ways that parents fail to model commitment for their kids. Let's take a look at some of the "biggies."

Divorce

If a commitment is a promise, then the most solemn promise two adults can make is when they decide to become life partners. They often make this solemn vow before each other, their families, their friends, and, sometimes, their God. When adults make this type of promise, a few things are happening. First, they're taking on a title: husband or wife. Second, they're taking on a job—and it's a job that comes with a pretty clear job description. Remember those parts about "sickness and health" and "for better or for worse"? Remember those questions: "Do you take this man ...?" "Do you promise to honor this woman ...?" But here's the problem. Those questions have become rhetorical, which means that nobody thinks of them as real questions. It's as if they say, "Waddaya mean, 'Do I?' Of course I do!" But then, as too often happens, they don't. It turns out that what they meant was "For better ... For worse ... For now."

What's going on here? Didn't they hear the question properly? Did they just say "I do" in order to get the ceremony over more quickly so they could get to those cute little egg rolls faster? Were they trying to trick or deceive their partner into trusting them so they could destroy that trust later on? Or are they simply unaware of the meaning of commitment or unable to fulfill it? A person without the capacity to commit should never attempt to raise children unless they are content to see the world laden with even more commitment-challenged individuals.

Remember this: Your ability to trust depends on your personal history. If you've ever believed you can trust someone, but have then been hurt by that person, you're going to be very reluctant to trust anyone in that situation again. When people divorce, it means that something happened to break the promise made at marriage. The commitment was broken. People who have been traumatized by divorce have great difficulty trusting again. And, evidently, they transfer this caution to their kids.

Recent research has shown that when children of divorce become adults, they tend to marry other children of divorce, and that these marriages are at pretty high risk of ending in divorce themselves. It may seem innocuous, but by embracing a casual attitude toward commitment, parents appear to teach their kids the same attitude. Is it too simplistic to suggest that those kids "learn" the attitude that a commitment is something that doesn't have to be kept?

Irresponsibility

In the Foreword to this book, I wrote that most parents want their kids to turn out to be independent adults. Bringing up a child from a condition of total dependence to a position of independence is, I believe, the cornerstone of parenting. In the majority of cases, parents put all their effort into taking care of their kids until, seeing them stand on their own two feet, they can rest and enjoy the fruits of a job well done. But how is independence achieved, and more to the point, what should parents do to make sure they are correctly modeling independence for their kids? The answer lies within another equally important concept: responsibility.

The term "responsibility" has two common usages in the English language. The first might be called "post hoc" responsibility because whatever is being talked about has already occurred. Post hoc responsibility is effectively illustrated by a question: "Who is responsible for this?" This question is usually posed when something bad has happened, as in "Who

LIFE DOESN'T "HAPPEN" TO YOU: THE HOT-STOVE ANALOGY

Recently an executive came to see me as a client. His problem was that he was having difficulty staying employed. He said that he'd been fired from his last two positions. At the time of our meeting, he was working, but was again in danger of losing the job. He spoke of the downturn in the economy and recent layoffs in his industry as the cause of his distress, but added, "I want to find out why this always happens to me." Another time, a woman of 30-something came to see me. She said that she was looking for a mate and would like to settle down and raise a family. She was quite attractive and said that she had no difficulty getting a date or even a steady boyfriend. In fact, she said that she had been engaged to be married twice before, and that each time, it was she who had broken off the relationship. She spoke of men tiring of her, sexually, because she "wasn't getting any younger," but she also had the same question as the executive: "Why does this always happen to me?"

When I hear this complaint, I often use the analogy of accidentally burning your hand on a hot stove. There are really two reasons for your pain: someone else left the stove on, and you placed your hand on it. Many people can see their pain arising only out of the actions of someone or something outside themselves. They feel that these things are uncontrollable (It's not my fault! What could I have done?). This attitude creates a state of helplessness. The individuals are forced to wait for things outside their control to get better before they can expect their own lives to get better. If, however, a person accepts that they made a mistake by placing their hand onto the stove before checking it out, they will learn from that mistake and never have to burn their hand again. Now they are in control. No matter who leaves whatever stove on, they do not have to be burned. That is the definition of "independence": no longer depending on others or needing circumstances outside one's control to cooperate in order to be free of pain. In other words, by taking responsibility, you gain independence.

is responsible for this mess?" In such situations, the responsible one is often in line for something akin to blame (i.e., "Who can we blame for this mess?"). (The same holds when something good has happened, though most parents have never had to ask "Who is responsible (whom do we praise) for tidying up this room?" On the other hand, "ad hoc" responsibility is always positive—in this case, acting "responsibly" means "doing the right thing." This might refer to a past event (calling the fire department when you saw thick smoke coming out of your neighbor's home, for example, was the responsible thing to do), or it might refer to something that has not yet occurred (who is willing to be responsible for organizing this year's homecoming dance?).

How a person approaches responsibility usually provides an accurate measurement of the degree of independence they achieve in life.

As simple as this seems, a horrifying number of people—adults as well as teens—won't take responsibility for their own actions. Are you one of them? I'm well aware that there are hundreds of forces outside your control, and that those forces do affect the outcome of your efforts. But as parents, be honest with yourselves. Do you look first, and most of the time only, to excusing your own foibles and failures because of some factor or factors that were "beyond your control"?

The executive described was rationalizing that his problems stemmed from an industry slowdown. He didn't want to look into the honest mirror and see that his own aggressiveness was causing him to lose jobs. The woman rationalized that men would come to find her sexually unappealing, but didn't want to gaze into the honest mirror and come face to face with her own fears of intimacy. These examples did involve outside factors that were part of the problem, but they weren't as important as the individual's own behaviors in their difficulties.

Other such rationalizations might include "The alarm didn't go off," "The traffic was murder!", "It's just bad luck," "It's this crazy rat race," "It's city life," "It's country life," "It's my parents," "It's my kids," It's God," "It's Satan" ("The devil made me do it"), "What could I have done? The Yankees were in town!"

Responsibility and Ethics

A more insidious failure to take responsibility extends to the matter of ethics. A teenager in trouble with the law once told me that he was "no worse" than his dad. He cited several examples. This was one of them: Just after leaving an electronics store with an expensive audio system, the dad dropped the box while fumbling for his car keys. When they got home, they discovered some physical damage to the equipment, and no sound at all. They went immediately back to the store with the story that the damage was there when they opened the box and demanded another system, never mentioning the dropped box.

Sometimes we lie only to ourselves in order not to take responsibility. Sometimes we lie to others. Sometimes we lie to ourselves and to others without even knowing it. Be careful what you model for your kids. If you take responsibility, you'll never feel trapped, and you'll show your kids the truest and fastest road to independence. After all, independence isn't so much something that comes as a reward for taking responsibility; it's more that independence has a natural coexistence with responsibility, like two sides of the same coin. So although we might say that independence can be equated with the lack of responsibilities, just the opposite is true. Without responsibility, there can be no freedom.

I've been accused of being naive and simplistic when I talk about responsibility this way. One executive told me he'd really love to be home from work in time for dinner with his family, but accused me of being unaware of the pressure exerted by today's "24/7" mentality in the global workplace. He said that corporate bosses expect their executives to lead by example, and to stay till the job is done. My response was that *he* was missing the point. I do understand the realities of the corporate world. The point, however, is this: Who's responsible for your being in that job? Did you know what the pressures would be before you took the job? How well did you think through the effects of this particular career? Did you discuss the costs of this career with your wife and kids before "buying" it? Are you sure you must keep this job if it's really costing you so much? You can "buy back" your freedom by taking responsibility for the situation you're in. Don't blame external forces. All it will cost is the money you would have made in a job that simply cost too much to keep. These are the lessons we need to pass on to our teens, but it's more than just lecturing them—it's living what we believe so they can see it's possible to take responsibility and be free from the blame game.

Hypocrisy

Have you ever told your kids to be honest, and then tried to get out of your income tax responsibility by paying cash for certain goods and services? Have you told your kids it's important to volunteer for some sort of civic duty, and yet asked your family doctor to write a letter excusing you from jury duty? Answer honestly, and then think about how you would feel if your daughter lied about her age to get into an amusement park for a lower admission fee, or if your teenaged son asked his best friend's dad to write a note that would excuse him from school for a day.

Parents may claim that their own behavior is acceptable because they are older, or because "it's different when I do it." Here's another example: Your teenage son wants to get his driver's license. He's of age, so you send him to a reputable driving school, and he learns common road courtesy. Later, driving with you, he points out some obvious errors: you didn't signal a lane change, you cut off another driver, and you double-parked outside the bank. How do you respond? Do you say, "Yeah. You're right. I should have been more courteous," or "Those rules don't always apply," or "Watch me, kid. I'll show you how you can get around the rules." In the worst-case scenario, you might tell him to shut up, that it was none of his business. Unless you chose the first response, your son comes away with the lesson that just because you agree to keep certain rules, you don't always have to.

Inconsistency

All too often, parents coming to my practice with "problem kids" admit readily to their own lack of consistency. Sometimes a parent will allow one sibling to do something, but not another. If this is because of age differences or because one sibling has earned the right to do it, it's okay. But more often, there's just a lackadaisical failure on the part of the parents to remember what was agreed on when the rules were set, or what happened "last time." More insidiously, parents often play favorites without recognizing it.

Sometimes a parent will threaten punishment for bad behavior, but will let it go later on, in order to avoid a fight. Sometimes mom says there will be consequences for a certain action, but when dad hears about it, those consequences change or disappear. This generates tension between the parents. Mom wonders why she has to be the enforcer while dad gets to be the good guy. This kind of behavior supports the charge of hypocrisy from kids. And it opens the door to the kids' using the parental inconsistency as a means to divide and conquer.

In cases like these, it's not so much that the parents aren't committed to their kids; it's that they lack confidence in their approach to parenting. By not trusting your approach, you lack commitment; ironically, this lack of commitment is what the kids pick up.

The Art of Arguing: Who Started It?

Modeling commitment and responsibility isn't easy under the best of circumstances, so what are parents to do when the going gets rough? There's no question that the normal parent-teen relationship becomes even dicier than usual when conflict arises—but conflicts are bound to arise, and when they do, parents can take some solace in the fact that the rules of "proper parental conduct" remain the same. The key, as always, is to take responsibility for one's actions.

Conflict Resolution: Breaking the Cycle

When one person hurts another person, it is almost always because he feels he's been wronged in some way. And he is angry. And he wants the other person to be sorry or to be punished or both. If that doesn't happen in the normal flow of events, the person who feels hurt may take matters into his own hands and strike back. This is revenge, pure and simple, and it is among the most unfortunate and predictable of human characteristics.

Is there a person alive who, as a kid, wasn't involved in the familiar "You started it"—"No, I didn't"—"Yes, you did"—"Did not"—"Did so" refrain? I've got sad news: it doesn't go away as we grow up. It changes a bit along the way so the actual words don't seem as childish, but we can see it everywhere, including in international relations. Even countries can't get past the desire to assign blame, to seek out the one who "started it." I see it every day in the families who walk through my door, and often, they don't realize they're caught up in the tired old "who started it" dance.

As might be expected, it is usually the parents who make the appointment. It is often the parents who first express their pain, which they blame on their kids. A lot of the time, the kids don't even want to come. Some may refuse. They feel (often, correctly) that they are about to be identified as a hurtful person, a person who is, moreover, ungrateful, piggish, selfish, and generally impossible to live with. How many parents would relish being at a meeting where they were characterized that way?

Rather than beginning by assigning blame ("You are the problem"), parents would be much better off if they approached their kids with "We have a problem." They could continue by saying: "We all know things aren't very pleasant around here. It would be easy to blame you, but maybe it's more complicated than that. (Not everybody sees the same thing the same way. Maybe we were wrong in our beliefs.) Maybe we're approaching this whole thing the wrong way. We're willing to take another look at our approach, but we need you to be part of the process. After all, how can we change if we don't know what you feel needs changing. (Let us have a look at how you see things. Maybe we will change our minds.)"

One set of parents told me that their 13-year-old daughter "always had to be right," an attitude that often caused arguments in the house. If she didn't get her way, their daughter would throw a temper tantrum. The parents should have recognized these actions as evidence of a still-concrete brain that could not accept an interpretation of a situation that differed from its own. Since, to the concrete mind, any conflicting interpretation is seen as "wrong," when the parents told their daughter that she was wrong, she became frustrated and regressed to an even more child-like state. If the parents had seen that the girl's brain was not sufficiently mature to deal with such conflicts, the problem might have been avoided.

Parents generally understand that. Yet all too often, they engage in behaviors that are just as concrete as those of their children. They cling to long-standing (but often untested and often incorrect) biases, assumptions, and reactions. I speak more about this in Chapter 7.

It would be far better for them to show their kids that while they believe that they are right, they are willing to re-examine those beliefs and begin a grown-up dialogue on the matter. In this way, they model the sort of flexibility and capacity to compromise that is a hallmark of mature adult behavior.

Faced with dialogue like this, kids often feel a glimmer of hope. Maybe for once, they'll get to be heard. Maybe someone will see that they aren't being so selfish. Maybe someone will finally realize that it is the teenager who's been aggrieved, and that they would never have acted the way they did if their parents hadn't "started it" (by treating them like children and being overly strict, or by putting too much pressure on them to perform well in school, or by ridiculing their culture). When parents apply this approach, and the teenager senses the possibility of what he sees as an equitable resolution to the problem, he often comes to the appointment willingly.

Once in session, it is usually the parents who start, but both sides always express their feelings by saying something that means "Look. You hurt me. I need you to understand that, but I don't think you get it. Until you really understand the full depth of the pain you've caused me to suffer, I can never forgive you." And the response is often "Yes, it's true that I hurt you. But you deserved it. You hurt me first. You're the one who has to apologize." And we're right back on the same old merry-go-round.

What's the solution? In order to stop this disruptive and counterproductive behavior, the disputing sides must recognize that they are embroiled in a classic "who started it?" battle and realize its futility. Next, all parties need to re-embrace the principles outlined in Chapter 2:

■ "Not everybody sees things the way we do."
■ "We might be wrong in our beliefs."
■ "There probably is no completely 'right' way of seeing things."

If some inroads can be made along these lines, the process of resolution has begun. It will continue when and if both parties agree that nothing will be solved by clinging to the need to determine who started it, but that the situation will improve if we determine who is going to stop it.

Ownership

If you find yourself involved in a "who-started-it?" dispute with your teenager, don't let your actions be motivated by your own immature need for revenge. It takes incredible fortitude to overcome vengeful feelings, but if you (and your kids … but especially you) are not able to do so, you will never reach a satisfying resolution.

Instead of waiting for your kid's apology (which might never come), see if you can understand exactly how badly you hurt them. Take responsibility for your own contribution to the situation. Most of the time, you can figure this out on your own. Most of the time it's not that you don't know what you did; it's that you believe your kid deserved it because of what she did to you. So this time, why not avoid that pitfall? Instead, act as though your hurting her was the very first incident in your dispute. Act as though your actions were unprovoked. Take ownership. Say to your kid, "Look, why I did it doesn't really matter right now. If I treated you in a way I would not want to be treated myself, I acted unethically, and until I see that, we'll never get anywhere."

I know how hard this is to do, especially when your kids have been outrageous and obnoxious. It's counterintuitive. But let's face it. If you're reading this book, then what's intuitive—which is what you've been doing till now—isn't working.

As the adult responsible for equipping your kids with the skills that will make them successful, you must take the leadership role. Show the strength of character that leadership requires, and don't resort to the brute strength of dictatorship.

Unless things are settled, they will fester. At best, there will be an imposed compromise that will leave both parties feeling cheated. At worst, there will be a war, in which the stronger (not necessarily the most "correct") party will vanquish the weaker, thereby guaranteeing further enmity and the need for retaliation.

But let's be optimistic and say that, as adult parents, you are able to take responsibility for your own contribution to your kids' pain. What's the next step?

Apology

Someone must be able to say, "I don't like the idea that I hurt you. I don't get any pleasure from your pain, and I know I (may have) caused people close to you to suffer as well. I'm also sorry that I behaved in the way I did because I would never have thought I could be that sort of person. My embarrassment is another reason I'm sorry."

This is the apology. And it must be sincere. It must reflect a true comprehension of the depth of the pain that was inflicted. If there's even a shred of insincerity or the slightest evidence that true comprehension did not occur, the apology will be empty. It will sound like "You want me to say 'I'm sorry'? Okay, I'm sorry! Happy? Now can you get over it?"

The man who leaves his wife and teenage kids for another woman may have no idea how deeply he hurt all three members of his family. He wonders why his kids won't speak to him, and he often blames his ex-wife for turning the kids against him. Everyone says to him, "You just don't get it, do you?" Instead of becoming defensive or angry, he should say, "No, I guess I don't. But I see that I've got to 'get it' before we can move on. So, I promise I'll work on it. Maybe I'll get some counseling." In the meantime, instead of apologizing, it's better for him to say, "I know I owe you an apology." Then, when he can give them what they really need, it will allow the healing to begin.

Atonement

Once a sincere apology has been offered, the next step in the process is atonement. Atonement is a promise, a commitment, whether spoken or not, that you will learn something about yourself from the fact that you hurt your child, and that you will behave better next time. It's not that you won't make other mistakes. But at least you can dedicate yourself to not making that mistake again. Let's see how the monologue in the case of the man who left his family might continue into the atonement stage:

"Finally, I see how deeply I hurt you. I failed in my commitment to fatherhood by leaving you without any warning. I've discovered that I was blaming your mother and my marriage in general for the emptiness in my life. Now I see that my emptiness had more to do with my own issues than with anything or anyone else. It may be too late to save that marriage, but at least I can dedicate myself to being more responsible in my future relationships, including the one that I share with you. I'm aware that I haven't been so good at keeping commitments in the past, but I really need to do better if I'm ever to become the kind of parent that both you and I can be proud of."

Forgiveness

Now that you have apologized and promised to atone, the ball goes back into your kids' court. Remember that both parties are going to feel injured. You each want the other to really understand the full extent of the pain they have caused. Moreover, you each want the other to apologize and atone for their actions. If all that occurs, then it is possible, and, in my opinion, essential for both sides to let go of their anger, to stop holding the need for revenge inside, to purge the venom that prevents them from trusting. Now, finally, you can jettison all that extra baggage. You can become free to get on with your lives.

Trust me, you can break the "who-started-it?" cycle. But you must take responsibility for your own contribution to whatever disputes you find yourself in with your kids. This removes their anger and need for revenge. You'll probably find that your kids will take your lead and begin accepting responsibility themselves. This is what you wanted in the first place. But you can't force it on them. You have to show them how it's done.

Your apology gives your kids a chance to forgive, or "give over," their pain. This too seems counterintuitive. Many people think that when a person apologizes to another and asks for forgiveness, he or she is asking for something that he or she needs: some sort of pardon. But I don't see it that way. The way I see it, by apologizing and atoning, the injuring party will have achieved the highest level of human possibility and need not receive any additional reward for it. In fact, forgiveness is the gift the forgiver gives to him- or herself.

Holding on to Pain

I realize that this sounds very formulaic. "Sure," you might say, "that's all very nice on paper, but there are situations when things don't run so smoothly. What happens then?"

I often see injured parties who appear to need to hold onto their pain, even though a sincere apology has been given. It's as if they need to continue suffering in order to make the one who hurt them keep on suffering. Yet, as I have said, it is they, not the injuring party, who carry the pain.

Often a mom or dad behaves in a punitive way toward their children long after the initial pain was inflicted. So hurt were they by their children's actions they cannot let their pain go. This is no good for anyone. Sometimes I see this type of painful behavior acted out between a former husband and wife. For example, a custodial ex-wife whose non-custodial ex-husband hurt her deeply during their marriage carries that pain and prolongs it by keeping their children from seeing and even loving their father. The father may, perhaps with the help of counseling, "get it" with respect to how much he hurt his ex-wife. He might apologize; he might atone. Still, the ex-wife continues to punish him by turning the kids against him. The father's situation is tragic, to be sure, but it's not the worst tragedy, because he has done what he could do. This is a good time to emphasize that the "goodness" of a person is defined not by the effects of his or her behavior on others, or how others see him or her, but solely on whether they have done what a good person should do. This relates to ethics, which is discussed at length in Chapter 6. The greater tragedy in the case we are discussing is that of the ex-wife, who must carry her anger and poison wherever she goes, and it is the tragedy of the kids, who may come to believe that a boy can one day turn into a husband and a father who is not to be trusted. What chance do such kids have of developing healthy relationships themselves?

Distinguishing the "Explanation" from the "Excuse"

What happens, though, when the injuring party is not apologetic? This is a very tough question, and my answer might seem like a slick way of avoiding it altogether. But in all truth, that answer lies in the importance of living our lives ethically. In other words, parents must find a way to forgive their kids, and kids must find a way to forgive their parents. That is the goal. And kids and parents must pursue this goal with courage and vigor. If we fail to do this, we will be forced to suffer doubly, first at the hands of the "oppressor" and second, by carrying our pain and anger with us for the rest of our lives.

The most common usage of the word "forgiveness" is synonymous with excusing someone for what they did. But, as we've seen, this is simply not possible or even necessary all the time. On the other hand, if we can explain the "inexcusable" behavior, we can invoke the principles of empathy and ethics to help us through the pain.

CASE STUDY

Ted, 43 years old, was having marital difficulties with his second wife. In fact, she had threatened to leave him if he didn't seek some sort of psychological help. Not wanting another failed marriage on his hands, Ted sought counseling.

In taking Ted's life history, I learned that his father had been physically and emotionally abusive to him and to his mother when he was a child. He saw his father abusing his mother. He was forced to suffer tirades and explosions. He wanted it all to stop. He wanted his father to love him and notice him. Yet when he begged his father to stop the beatings, the situation got only worse. His father would beat him as well as his mother. Ted eventually learned that the only way to gain his father's attention and approval was to be just like him. That's when Ted himself began to abuse his mother. He was doing only what he knew his dad would do in the same situation.

Perversely, and to his great shame and amazement, he took on his father's misogynist characteristics because it bought him peace and hope (at least in the short term). In the long term, of course, he was doomed to re-experience his own childhood pain when he became emotionally involved with women. Moreover, he lived in constant fear that he would one day repeat his father's abusiveness. To avoid that, he remained subconsciously distant and aloof from his wife. His emotional unavailability led to problems with intimacy, and to her ultimatum.

In Ted's case, it was quite easy to explain how his father's misogyny and abusiveness was transmitted to Ted himself. Still, all the explanations in the world would not excuse the lousy behavior of both the father and the son. As a clinician, my job was to release Ted from his self-imposed isolation and bring him to a place where he could save his marriage. This meant that he had to let go of his pain. In other words, even though Ted believed that his father was clearly the one who had "started it" he still needed to forgive him.

Now, Ted's father might have been long gone, dead, or disappeared. No such luck. He was alive and absolutely unrepentant. There would certainly be neither apology nor atonement. Was Ted able to *forgive*? Here is another of those times when the rhetorical question should be asked empirically. Was he able to forgive? The answer is this: He had to. Not in the conventional sense that he pardoned his father, but in his ability to overcome the impact his father had on him. For this, he needed my help and guidance. In therapy, he forgave himself by dedicating himself more openly to his marriage, and by refusing to be defined by his father's behavior toward him, his mother, and women in general. He learned to use his powers of empathy, and he applied his principles of ethics in order to let go of his pain. He learned more about intimacy, trust, respect, honesty, and commitment, and he used this new understanding to improve his family relationships. In other words, he applied himself assiduously to the task of doing what a good husband and father ought to do. As I have said, that, and not the impact of that, is what made him a good husband and father. His self-esteem and his confidence rose dramatically. Because he saw no choice but to forgive, he did. And he was by far a happier man because of it. Slowly but surely, trust was built among family members, and with it came a new, sincere commitment to the marriage. The cycle of abuse and divorce can be broken. ■

Being a parent does require hard work. Parents need to take a good, hard look at their own habits and be willing to see them through the eyes of their teenagers. That requires a lot of self-reflection and the ability to compromise. At the same time, while self-examination is a good and utterly necessary thing, parenting does not take place in a vacuum. To effectively navigate the difficulties of adolescence, the practices of the family unit itself also need some attention. Read on.

5 Preparing Your Family: Democracy Rules

In an earlier chapter (Chapter 3), I defined a society as a thing that is formed whenever two or more humans decide that it would be to their mutual benefit to do something together. Clearly, then, a family is a society—and a family that includes a teen is a society rife with its own particular challenges. How do societies (of all shapes and sizes) deal with challenges and conflicts? You may remember that I also argued that, whatever its underlying purpose, no society has ever existed without ground rules. Families are no different.

But how are the rules of a society determined? Usually, the process begins with a very strict philosophical statement about how that society will go about setting its day-to-day rules. This philosophical statement is called a constitution, and it is usually the society's most cherished document. Here are just a few of the constitutional styles the world has experienced. Which one best describes your family's approach to rule setting?

- **Dictatorship:** In a dictatorship, one person decides arbitrarily on the rules. Force is often used to silence any possible opposition to such declarations.
- **Monarchy:** A monarchy can, of course be dictatorial or not, depending on the monarch. In any monarchy, however, the vast majority of the governed people have no say in who becomes their leader.
- **Socialism:** In socialist societies, power is theoretically shared among all members of the society. In order to ensure that this is done fairly,

the state becomes more important than the individual, whose freedoms can become severely curtailed.

▌ **Democracy:** In a true democracy, power is extended to all adult members of the society, often through freely and openly elected representatives. Rules are set by legislative votes but only following public debate. Dissent is permitted through freedom of speech, freedom of assembly, and freedom of the press.

Democracy is certainly my first choice for a system of rule making—whether we're talking about a country or a family. I believe in democracy because of the valuable psychological impact it has on the individual, provided it is implemented correctly. I am well aware that many societies claim the title of democracy without any apparent awareness of what that means. This contradiction crops up—catastrophically—in many families as well. Here's how it should work.

Democracy: It's Not a Free Country

The word "liberty" is often used in association with democracy. In fact, many people complain about government restrictions to individual liberty. Their common cry is "It's a free country!" (by which they seem to mean "I can do whatever I please"). The members of a democratic society want "individual freedom." If they're being honest, though, they also realize that in order for a democratic society to exist, some restrictions must be placed on that freedom. The simplest example is that individuals must stop at red traffic lights, even when there are no cars or pedestrians around. Society does not grant the individual the freedom to decide when or whether a law can be broken. In democracies, as in all societies, a law is a law.

Once a law is passed, it must be adhered to, regardless of whether we voted for it or not, or whether we're inconvenienced by it. If we're not happy with the laws that a particular government is implementing, we must wait until the next election and vote for a party that's more compatible with our views. While we wait, we are welcome to lobby for changes to the rules in any number of ways: we can write freely in the press; we can speak openly in the media; we can appear before committees. But we cannot take it upon ourselves to break the law or encourage others to do so, either overtly or by example.

Empowerment and Representation

Most experts on the topic agree that psychological well-being is rooted in a person's sense of empowerment. But what does this mean? Empowerment is a feeling that comes from a belief—the belief that, if you put forth some effort, that effort will have a good chance of improving a situation. Put more simply, the disempowered person rhetorically asks, "Why *bother*?", by which he means "It won't do any good anyway"; the empowered individual empirically asks, "*Why* bother?", to which the inherent answer is "Because if I bother, I can change things." Like it or not, empowerment is at the very center of all conversations about rule setting, whether in a community or in a family.

Far too often, when rules are at the root of family troubles, teenagers feel as if their parents are being arbitrary, dictatorial tyrants. For their part, parents feel that their teenagers are selfish anarchists who blatantly disregard rules. Dialogue and understanding rarely characterize such families. Parents will say, "You can't talk to these kids! They won't listen to reason." Teenagers will often respond, "What good is talking? No matter what I say, my parents don't listen. I have no choice! If I try to speak up, I'm called rebellious, and I get punished." Such families are labelled "dysfunctional," because both the parents and the kids feel victimized and disempowered. Even worse, each side blames the other for its pain. In doing so, both parents and teens miss the opportunity to take responsibility for their situation and thus lose out on the independence that would be generated. This is a real shame, and a costly one for the family in particular and for the larger society in general.

What's the solution? Let's take a quick look at the democratic process in government for some ideas. Western democracies feature central or federal governments. These governments put out general calls for people all over the land to voice their concerns. In this way, the governments can make rules to deal with those problems. But if everybody in the nation sent in their problems and demanded action, there could be millions of submissions! That's way too many. So the government says, "Let's break the country up into regions (states, provinces, counties, etc.). Each region can send a representative to a central place—the nation's capital—where he or she can summarize all the problems of that region for the government." Someone volunteers to represent the people of each region. If more than one person volunteers in any given region, the people vote on whom they want to represent them. The winner usually promises to represent all the people of the region, whether they voted for her or not.

So the people of the region hold meetings to identify all the problems they'll want dealt with in the central government. As it turns out, people from one part of the country, where there are lots of forests, want the government to deal with the forestry industry; people from the agricultural regions want rules to make things better for farmers; and people from coastal regions, where fishing has been a way of life for centuries, want a better deal for the fisheries. Those in the technical, industrial, and commercial regions want things to improve for industry and commerce. A pretty self-centered approach, no doubt, but it's universal. The same thing happens in countries all over the world, so why are parents surprised when their teenagers lobby for family rules that benefit them? It's always been this way, and it's good in terms of empowerment. And yet teens are often criticized for thinking only of themselves.

So now we have the representatives gathered in the nation's capital. Their job is to make rules that represent everyone—rules that everyone can live with and that everyone must obey. They add the list of problems from their region to those from all the other regions, and from this list, the government must decide which matters are most urgent to society as a whole.

Empiricism in Government

The next step is to try to come up with a rule to diminish the problem. But how? How does a guy who sells shoes for a living in a small town in one region of the nation help make up a rule that will make it easier for people to make a living in another, very different region? As you might expect, many plausible answers are presented—different people see the same issue in different ways—and it is by no means certain which one is the best. That's why some research is needed. Research will provide valid, reliable empirical evidence to support one answer over the others. For any government, this means speaking to people who have experience in this area, who care the most about the issue, and who have studied the matter in a formal, scientific way. Once its research is complete, the government is presented with the best available idea for a rule that could address the problem in question. In turn, the government presents the idea to the country's democratically elected representatives.

Opposition and Debate

In order to make sure that power never gets monopolized by special interest groups, Western democracies include in their constitutions a system of checks and balances. This allows everybody to know what the proposed rule is and gives all the interested parties a chance to speak up if they believe it contains omissions and flaws. In other words, everyone has a chance to be involved in designing the rule before the proposal becomes a law. The politicians responsible for this process are often called the opposition.

I'm always fascinated by people's reactions to opposition politicians. It is common to hear someone denounce a politician whose party stops being the opposition and becomes the government. "What a hypocrite!" their detractors say. "When you were in opposition, you were against this legislation. Now that you're in power, you're in favor of it!" That's a misguided view. It's the job, indeed the responsibility, of the opposition to oppose. That's what the people who are not in favor of a certain rule expect and require them to do. We want them to oppose and debate. We want them to tell us what's been left out, or why the government is being unfair or short sighted. In that way, the government can hone or amend the suggested rule before it becomes law. This is the only way to guarantee that all the voices in a society can be heard.

But even the opposition must follow some rules. Their demands need to be made in a respectful way. If an opposition member is rude, she is not being helpful to the process. In some cases, the constitution requires that she be asked to leave the room. In other words, while oppositional people don't have to be loyal to the specific government, they do have to be loyal to the process, as defined in the constitution.

Families as Societies

While a society is often thought of in terms of nations, a society can just as legitimately have as few as two members. It can be a football league, or a school, or a church, or a family. Up to now, I have been talking about this process at the level of nation. But since this book is primarily about teenagers, let's apply this idea of governmental democracy to a family with adolescent kids.

Parents as Leaders

Since it was the decision of the parents to become parents, it is assumed that they are prepared to do the job. An integral part of that job is to take on a leadership role, and that job description includes initiating and administering the process of rule making. Parents are, and should be, the de facto government in any family. But remember, they should not have taken on the job if they weren't really prepared to do it. And leadership is not easy.

If the parents are the leaders, the kids make up the rest of the people in that society. And in democracies, the people demand and deserve representation. Just as in any society, a family has many areas that need rules: allowance; curfew; homework; TV use; Internet access; dating; sleepovers; clothes and makeup; "free" time; tidiness of rooms; household responsibilities; etc. Democratic governments rarely set up arbitrary rules (despite what people opposed to those rules might think!). They need to base their rules on the valid and reliable information that is provided by empirical research. But parents often do set up arbitrary rules, an action that has to do with their own agendas, which in turn are based on their experiences as kids. Here's an example of a parent's agenda at work.

CASE STUDY

George, a father now himself, remembers his parents forcing him to take violin lessons after school. Despite his protestations, he eventually came to appreciate the violin and music in general. As an adult, George often says how grateful he is that his parents didn't let him stop taking lessons when he wanted to. He now uses this experience as a rationale for forcing his own son, George Jr., to persevere with his piano lessons. Because it "worked" for him, George Sr. sees nothing wrong in imposing this arbitrary rule on his son. However, George Jr. resented this imposition and lost respect for his dad, which saddened both men in the end. ■

Here are two ways that stories like George's can play out:

▮ **Scenario 1:** George Jr. really liked music. The music that was always playing in the house made that almost predictable. But he particularly loved the music of his generation and wanted to play the instruments of his generation. When that music was ridiculed by his father, he gave up on music altogether. This is a real shame, because music could and should have been a wonderful part of his life.

▮ **Scenario 2:** George Jr. really *didn't* like music. He found it tedious and had trouble reading the notes. He would rather have played outside on his skateboard. In fact, he spent hours on that board, practicing tricks.

In my opinion, George Sr. blew it. While he has every right to make a case for music lessons by relating his own story, he shouldn't use his experience alone to justify the creation of a family rule. If he were to open the topic up for discussion and debate, allowing George Jr. a chance to state his own case, he might find that his son is willing to compromise. But even more importantly, George Sr. will have demonstrated his respect for George Jr. and his willingness to discuss contentious issues. The "leader" should have left his door open. How?

■ **Scenario 1:** George Sr. should have encouraged his son to take up any instrument he wanted, and shown that while he didn't really like listening to his son's music, it was still music and deserved his respect.

■ **Scenario 2:** George Sr. should have seen that whether it was music or skateboarding, his son was learning the same valuable life lessons: the importance of practice, perseverance, self-discipline, eye-hand coordination, spatial intelligence, pride in accomplishment, emotional ease in performance. He should have encouraged George Jr.'s interest.

Parental agendas aren't the only problem facing family government. Here's a truth that few of us ever really consider: No one belongs to just one society. The fact is that we live in many societies, simultaneously. Moreover, each society has its own rules. Most of our problems begin when we find ourselves obeying the rules of one of those societies at a time when we're expected to obey opposing rules set by another society at the same time. For example, a father says to his daughter, "No daughter of mine is going out dressed like that!" The father is setting rules for his daughter based on the morality of his generation. If she obeys, she'll have to break the rules of her own generation and peer group. She is not being rebellious. She is genuinely in a bind. (We'll talk more about these types of conflict in Chapter 7. In order for a democracy to thrive, it's imperative that the governing body avoid proposing rules based either on uneducated, uninformed hunches or on the self-serving fulfillment of its own psychodynamic agendas or moralities. Yet this is exactly what most parents do most of the time. Instead of consulting the experts or seeing what works in other families, they create arbitrary and wholly unworkable rules. These are governments in trouble.

Empiricism in the Family

Even if the parents agree that there has to be a rule about a particular issue, how on earth would they know where to start looking for ideas for a reasonable rule? Would they simply guess, based on a hunch that this rule or that would be best? Would a government decide on a rule for the coastal fisheries based on a mid-western shoe salesman's hunch of what might work?

Hunches are simply beliefs that don't have a basis in empirical support. When I talked about abstract thought in Chapter 3, I discussed the dangers of acting on the basis of beliefs that turn out to be false. Where do these hunches come from? Sometimes they are passed down from generation to generation. Often, these "truths" (or "old wives' tales," in less flattering terminology!) turn out to be rooted in superstition or based on the realities of another time or place. On other occasions, hunches come from what appears to intuitively make sense.

CASE STUDY

Marge and Bill decided on a rule for their teenage daughter, Sandy: She had to be home before midnight. Sandy objected, saying that all her friends were allowed to stay out until 1 a.m. on Saturdays. She challenged her parents to give her a good (empirical) reason for the curfew. Marge replied that they didn't want Sandy coming home from the party by subway after midnight. She and Bill believed that the subway was more dangerous after midnight than before.

In fact, Marge's belief was really a hunch, or a theory. And while it made sense intuitively, Bill was a bit uncertain. Was Marge's belief valid? How could they find out? After some discussion, Bill and Marge decided to call the public transportation commission and the local police to inquire about the relative safety of the subway at various times. They were told that the highest crime rate on the subway—things such as assaults— occurred between 9:00 and 11:00 p.m. After midnight, crime rates actually went down! Under the weight of empirical evidence, Bill and Marge were forced to change their minds. Armed with facts, they had to approach the problem of Sandy's curfew differently. They still needed to feel that Sandy would be safe—and crimes were still committed on the subway after midnight. But by abandoning their previously unsupportable argument, they made Sandy more receptive to making her parents feel better about her safety. Now that the facts were in, Sandy and her parents could negotiate based on those facts. The family compromised. Sandy agreed not to be alone on the subway at night, if at all possible. She carried a cellular phone and stayed in well-lit areas. Her parents agreed to give her rides home, if they could. ■

Just as governments must base their rules on empirical facts rather than on intuitive hunches, so should a family that wants to respect all members of its small society. If you aren't sure what is likely to make an effective rule (that is, one that will make a problem better), do some research. Then discuss your finds with your kids. Together, you should be able to come up with a workable solution. What's the alternative, laying down the law? No! That's dictatorship.

Opposition and Debate in the Family

How many of you remember thinking how absurd some of your parents' rules were, only to find yourselves now setting down those same rules for your own kids? As I said earlier, if parents are the democratic administrators of the family's rule-setting process, the kids represent the rest of the society. And within that society, there may well be those who do not agree with the policies and rules that the government is proposing.

This should not be a big surprise: Sometimes teenagers don't like the proposed rules. At those times, think of your kids as the opposition. Remember, it's their nature to question and to demand answers. Remember, too, that it is the responsibility of the opposition to oppose. That's what democracies expect from the people who are not in favor of a certain rule. This is healthy.

It's also in the opposition's nature to point out the weaknesses they see in the system. This is also healthy, and it's a process that will serve your teens well. It would be a huge mistake to discourage or squelch this type of opposition with punishment. American author John Steinbeck said it well in his book *America and Americans*: "In the face of inequity, dishonesty in government, or downright plundering the word is 'Go fight City Hall!' The implication is, of course, that you can't win. And yet in other times we did fight City Hall and often we won."

Parents often haul out the old complaint: "Those kids want to rule the roost!" But it's really not true. What teenagers truly want is to be *part* of the ruling of the roost. By doing this, they are actively working to help devise your family's rules. They see, almost intuitively, that their best chance at this is to take on the role of the opposition. If they accept this responsibility, they gain independence, control over their own lives, and a sense of empowerment. What's more, because they participated in making the rule, it becomes their rule. And that ownership goes a long way toward ensuring their compliance and mitigating their defiance. In other words, if the kids don't like what they hear, they can make the parents an offer to change things in such a way that will suit the kids better, but it has to be an offer that everyone can live with.

As in government, parental leaders have the right to expect that a teenager's opposition is respectful. Here, the parent may assume the dual roles of government leader and speaker of the house (who is responsible for seeing that the rules of the constitution are obeyed as the laws are being hammered out). If you find yourself in a debate that is becoming increasingly unpleasant, remind your kids of the rules: "You can point out my weaknesses, but don't call me a liar. Don't use profane language. And don't raise your voice or storm out in protest."

Ready, Set, Go?

Just as in society, once a rule is made in the family, it must be followed. This is true regardless of whether certain family members approve of it or not, or whether they are inconvenienced by it. Once a rule is agreed to, all family members must stick with it.

Before even attempting to put this whole thing into practice, parents should have a good idea of whether they are dealing with a teenager who is able to be part of the democratic process. (That's why I've spent so much time making sure that you understand what's going on in your kids' brains. If the teenager is not developmentally ready, asking them to participate is like asking a physically disabled person to perform in ways his disability prevents.) The same applies to parents. Parents must take an honest look at themselves and be sure that they too are able to be part of a democratic process. Things fall apart when one or more of the following three necessary developmental antecedents to democratic participation are not in place:

■ **The ability to grasp abstract meaning:** Do you and your kids realize what a compromise is? Do you and they know that, in societies, we must all live together? That means that we must make everybody as comfortable with the rules as possible. Can you all accept that not everybody can get everything they want out of the rules? Do you and they know what we mean by "the greatest good for the largest number of people"? Or are you and they still too "concrete"? Do you—or they—keep insisting that it all must be your—or their—way?

■ **The ability to take responsibility:** Do you and your kids know that participation in a society (a family, in this case) means that they have a responsibility to contribute? Do you and they contribute spontaneously, or do you and they have to be told each time what to do? When you or they have caused some sort of problem (started a fight or left a mess in the hallway), do you or they accept responsibility, or do you or they insist on blaming someone or something else?

■ **The ability to make a commitment:** Do you or your kids promise to be somewhere but fail to show up? Do you or your kids promise to finish a project and then fail to keep that promise?

Expectations of participation from teenagers who are not ready will lead only to disappointment. Expectations of participation from parents who are not prepared have the same effect. If this is the case, the family will fall back into the same cycle of blame, shame, guilt, dashed hopes, accusations, and punishments.

CASE STUDY

Megan was 16. Her grades were quite good but not good enough for her father, a twice-divorced man who wanted her to go to the same prestigious university that he had attended. Megan needed her high-pressure father to quit bugging her about her study habits.

After some debate, the family decided to let Megan apply her own study plan. If her grades did not slip below 90% of the class average, her plan would be seen as successful, and her father would remain silent. If her grades did slip below that mark, the consequences would be the natural fallout from poorer grades (i.e., she might not get into the prestigious university) and the deployment of Plan B. (Plan B was more in line with what her father had been doing all along: bugging her to study more, get off the phone, etc.)

At first, Megan's father did back off considerably, and Megan's grades stayed well within the agreed-on acceptable range. But her father could not maintain his part of the bargain. He was not confident enough to let her succeed or fail on her own. He returned to his old behavior of bugging her until she could not stand it any longer. She finally decided to leave her school, which she had really liked, and move to the city where her mother lived. She studied at her own pace and was accepted at the university her father had attended.   ■

Did Megan's case end in a positive way? Maybe; but maybe not. Yes, she was accepted into the school her father had wanted her to attend, but at what cost? She'd been forced to leave a school and a community that she'd loved, and she'd had to face the fact that her father didn't trust her to succeed on her own. Although Megan and her father eventually repaired their relationship, the tension and stress could have been avoided under different circumstances.

Setting the Criteria for Evaluating Rules

Once the family has had the debate and any amendments to the proposed rules have been offered by the "kids-as-opposition-members," is the law ready to pass? No! This would be folly. Before the proposed rule is passed into law, it's important that everyone possess the prerequisite cognitive capacity to understand and agree on the desired result and how it will be measured.

Consider the following questions:

■ "What exactly is supposed to change—for the better—as a result of this rule?"
■ "How will we know if the desired change occurred?"
■ "What will we do if the desired change did not occur?"

These are imperative questions. Yet, in most families, they are never asked, let alone answered.

If family life were a scientific experiment, the proposed rule would be called the "independent variable," since you are at liberty to change it. The observed effect of the rule on family life would be called the "dependent variable," since it occurs as a direct result of the rule itself. This dependent variable should, if possible, be objectively measurable. That way, there can be no arguments about whether the desired outcome occurred. Here's how this can work:

CASE STUDY

Throughout her tenth grade, 16-year-old Emma hadn't been doing her homework and her year-end grades were disastrous. Before the new school year started, her parents, Debbie and Chris, wanted to institute a rule about how many hours of homework Emma should do per day. They knew they shouldn't set the number arbitrarily, so they did some research. They contacted some teachers at Emma's school and asked what an appropriate number of hours might be, and they read some books from the educational psychology section of the library. Based on this research, Debbie and Chris proposed that Emma complete two hours of homework a night. They were comfortable with this, because Emma's compliance with the rule could be verified objectively. In other words, there was neither the opportunity nor the need for disagreement as to whether the hours were actually spent with the books. Of course, they realized that Emma might spend her two hours staring at a page or doodling or day-dreaming or she might spend them on a single math question. But all in all, it seemed like a good start.

In scientific terms, the study plan would be the independent variable. The dependent variable(s) would be the outcome, or what happened when the hours were or were not spent studying. This too should be indisputable and quantifiable. The best candidate? Grades. But again, grades are not the only criteria upon which to measure the outcome of the study plan. Teachers' comments on effort or attitude might be equally telling, and Debbie and Chris decided to take these into account as well.

Debbie and Chris presented the plan to Emma, explaining how they'd arrived at their proposed two hours. Emma reacted to this emotionally. She complained that Debbie and Chris were nagging her and argued that she needed to study at her own pace. Debbie and Chris simply couldn't go along with this. In their view, Emma's "studying at her own pace" wasn't working. Why would they allow it to continue? They suggested to Emma that they negotiate and reach a compromise. It's important to note that both parents and teens should unequivocally agree—from the outset—as to what will happen if the negotiated rule is not followed or does not have the desired effect. In this case, it was decided that Debbie and Chris would keep their distance and not nag. Emma would do at least one hour of homework per day (verifiable). And she would reach and maintain at least a B+ average (also verifiable). Furthermore, consistent with the plan, they would monitor its efficacy by measuring other dependent variables, including grades and teachers' comments.

In a boxing match, the referee will stop the fight if one of the pugilists is being so badly injured as to be unable to defend him- or herself. With that in mind, Debbie and Chris suggested a time frame for their plan. With the school year beginning in early September, they proposed to evaluate the plan at the end of October. If that date arrived and Emma's grades and/or other variables were falling below the agreed-on levels, they would abort the plan so that she would not find herself in an academic position from which she would not be able to recover. If this happened, Debbie and Chris suggested a contingency plan: Their original two-hour-a-night plan would be put into effect. Emma agreed. To everyone's delight, however, Emma was able to raise her grades with the one-hour plan. She once again felt proud of her academic achievements, and she was equally pleased about having compromised with her parents in a way that worked for her.   ■

A Law Is Still a Law: Avoiding Anarchy

As I've said, once all eligible family members show that they are able to grasp the concepts behind the democratic process, that process will flourish. Now everyone has a voice. And once a rule is set and agreed to by the majority, as in Emma's case (above), no one will be able to complain about not having been heard.

But what if someone seems to have met the cognitive requirements for participation in the democratic process but continues to oppose the rule? Unlike democratic national politics, a teenager can't simply wait for the next election and vote the government out of power. So what are his options? He could wait until he's old enough to leave home; he could spend as little time as possible with the family (including running away in extreme cases); or he could simply treat the family government as if it were illegitimate. This unilateral declaration of independence usually results in what parents describe as anarchy. If this is happening in your home, and if you can honestly say that you've adhered to the rules of a democratic society, it may be necessary to seek help from a counselor.

The Advantages and Benefits of Democracy

Parents often complain that their kids have taken over the household and are holding it at ransom. They say that the kids are happy only when they get their way, that they have no concern for the needs of others. Parents often see this self-centered solipsism is a hallmark of adolescence. I disagree. As I've said, I believe that kids neither need nor want to run things. But they do want to be part of the decision-making process. The benefits of such participation to the teenager are immense:

1. Adolescents are introduced to the experience of shared responsibility. In a democratic family, they become a key player in setting the guidelines that will influence their own lives. Because of this, they take ownership of those rules and are far more likely to comply with them.
2. They come to value debate and compromise—as opposed to confrontation and ultimatums—as mechanisms for resolving disputes.
3. They take responsibility for their own behavior. This means they change the things they can change. It also means that they don't depend on circumstances outside their control to change in order for things to improve. Responsibility means taking control of your own life, and this sets people free.

4. They see that, by adhering to democratic principals, they do have the power to "fight City Hall." This empowerment has long been recognized as armor against all sorts of adolescent troubles. This was discussed in Chapter 5.

When faced with this compelling evidence for the benefits of democracy, parents sometimes think I'm suggesting that kids should be able to amend any proposed rule. I'm not. Here are a few things that go along with my suggestion for a democratic approach to rule setting.

The Majority Can't Always Rule

Let's face it. A family can't work exactly like a democratic government, if that means that all members of the family get equal voting powers. After all, if the three kids vote to go on vacation in a too far-off, too expensive, or too dangerous place, the parents have the right and obligation to veto that majority. It could be likened to what the British and Canadians call a majority government: No combination of opposition (kids') votes can overrule the votes of the government (parents).

The Myth of the United Front

When a national governing party proposes legislation, it usually presents as a united front. It would be political suicide to allow for a rift in party solidarity. The opposition would see this as an inherent weakness, and they would use it in an effort to overthrow the government. Parents also feel that if their teenagers sense that they aren't really in agreement with each other over proposed family rules, the kids will use the old "divide and conquer" technique to get their way.

While these two situations seem to be the same, there's a very big difference. In the case of the government, the party in power is dedicated to keeping that power. If the governing party got its way, the opposition would never have the chance to govern. But in a family, it's the "governing" parents' responsibility to model fair and effective governance as they train their kids to become independent "governors" themselves. In other words, if parents don't invite their kids into the process of governing, the kids will not learn responsible government. They will feel disenfranchised and opt out of the process altogether. They will simply break whatever rules they feel like breaking; they will become anarchists.

That's why I believe that parental disagreement is healthy—provided it is based on the principles of open and honest communication, respect, and trust.

CASE STUDY

Brenda feels strongly that her kids should finish all their homework before they turn on the computer or pick up the phone to call friends. Warren doesn't see why the kids can't have a bit of relaxation time before finishing their homework, as long as they manage to finish it and get to bed on time. The first thing Brenda and Warren should do is determine whether either position is based on an unfounded hunch. Since there is no empirical data to support either side, Brenda and Warren are left with opposing points of view.

They decide to sit down with their kids and tell them that there are two ways the rule can be set. They explain both Brenda's idea and Warren's. They suggest that the family decide to use mom's idea first, for a specific period of time, and see how that feels. If people are comfortable with that format, and the grades aren't affected adversely, the family could keep that rule. If things deteriorate, then dad's rule could be put into place. The family could even alternate between both rules, if that will satisfy everybody. ■

Brenda and Warren's approach perfectly illustrates how to handle dissension in the ranks. Although the pair started with different ideas, a workable compromise has been reached. Meanwhile, their kids have learned that not all solutions come from unanimous governments. In fact, most solutions are arrived at by compromise. When parents model such an approach, they give their kids valuable life skills.

Health and Safety Issues: Pick Your Battles

If a parent knows that something is threatening to their kids' health and/or safety, they will never be comfortable permitting it. A mother once asked me what to do about her son smoking cigarettes. Her son had come to her and said, "Mom, I don't want to have to sneak behind your back. I want to be honest with you, so I'm telling you straight out. I smoke." The mother told him she didn't like it but was stymied as to what else she might do. In the end, she made a rule that he could never smoke in the house. Her son left with the impression that his mother was "cool" with the idea of his smoking, as long as he didn't do it at home. I asked the mother if she really was cool about it, and of course, she said no. So I told her to be clearer with her son. You can adapt the following for many similar situations.

I suggested the mother who didn't like her son smoking tell him, "Look. I appreciate your honesty. That was good. But I hate that you smoke. I'll always hate it. But I can't follow you around, checking up on your behavior. So whenever you place a cigarette in your mouth, you have to know that you're doing something that angers me, and scares me, and disappoints me, and lowers my respect for you. I won't make it easy for you. You have to deal with that."

In this way, the mother correctly places responsibility for her son's actions directly onto him. What's more, the consequences of his behavior go way beyond future health consequences, which he may or may not be in a position to fully grasp. I'm talking about the much more immediate, but still painful, family and social consequences; they present the teenager with a valuable opportunity for learning and growing.

What happens if you only suspect that something is unhealthy or dangerous? This isn't so easy, because many questions don't have empirical answers. And, in many cases, there are strong emotional components to them, making the whole issue very complicated. Still, the answer lies in the area of communication. Those questions that don't have empirical or universally accepted answers are still worth asking and still worth discussing and debating. This provides for the allowance of and respect for other points of view.

Also, clearly defining the areas in which you must be inflexible may encourage you to become more flexible in other, less crucial, areas. You may not like your teenager's clothes or music, but these are not inherently dangerous. And by showing acceptance and even approval for much of the cultural and behavioral content of their lives, you can exert more credible influence in the areas that you truly find scary.

6 A Crash Course in Parenting (or Parenting 101): The Do's and Don'ts of Parenting a Teen

By now, you should know that I believe the single most important cognitive event for adolescents occurs when the neurological maturation process takes them from concrete to abstract thought. That's when teens realize that things don't have to be the way they are. Not the world. Not their families. Not themselves. Their innate curiosity spurs them to ask abstract questions about the inequities they see. If parents ignore these questions, or trivialize them, or offer inappropriately concrete answers, the kids become more demanding. This can lead to power struggles, which can lead to battles and even wars.

The question of how parents can avoid this downward spiral is an important one. In other words, how do you cope? What follows is a general look at some important do's and don'ts.

Don't Ignore Your Teens

Because teenagers are the age they are, their parents are usually around 40 years old. And that can be deadly, because 40 is a notorious age for callous self-absorption. Most of us would be pretty content if we lived to be 80. So 40 means that we're "halfway there." And believe me, the second half doesn't promise to be nearly as much fun as the first! Look at all the exciting "firsts" that happened between zero and forty: you got your education; learned to drive; fell in love; "did it"; left home; got married; "did it" again; had your kids; found out what you were going to be; maybe bought a house; and much more.

None of these firsts can happen again. So 40-ish parents can become depressed, even desperate. We try, in vain, to replicate our youths. Sometimes, we do positive things like quit our unfulfilling jobs and start anew, or we go back to school or finally begin writing that book. These are good things to do. Other times our efforts take us down very negative roads. We become devoted to physical perfection. We have love affairs or impulsively leave our families for "newer model" partners who seem more attractive. These negative choices almost always turn out to be dead-ends. Regardless of whether your reactions are positive or negative, they are likely to distract you from the task of raising your kids.

As if that weren't enough, all this is happening as our bodies begin to betray us. That temple of power, that sleek machine, starts to sputter. All of a sudden, things like the gall bladder or pancreas—organs that used to be just words—become enemies that torment us. What's more, gravity becomes an issue. Parts that used to be over here are now, expressly against your will and despite your interventions, over there. And there's often much more of many parts than there used to be (and more than you really need!).

And that's not all! If you're the age you are, that means your parents are the age they are. And that usually means they're facing crises of their own. They're getting old. They're getting sick. They're dying. They're becoming become much more dependent on you, and this can drain you emotionally and financially.

So when your teenagers come home from school and say, "Hey mom, dad, guess what's going on in my life," it's no surprise that many of them sense that you aren't paying attention. It would be pretty easy for them to misinterpret your lack of attention as lack of concern. This can lead to at least two possible further misinterpretations on their part: either that their concerns are not very important, leaving them feeling trivialized; or that you are too busy for them, which leads to resentment. So be careful. When you ask the kids "What's new?" don't treat it as a rhetorical question and then turn away. Make it a real question, with the two most important features of a real question: be curious, and listen to the answer. When they tell you the answer, make eye contact, and empathize with their concerns.

Do Give Your Kids the Gift of Ethics

Earlier, I discussed the problem of raising kids in a society where limits are like endangered species More than ever, parents need a boundary they can set for their kids—a boundary that is fixed and unchangeable. To my mind, the best example of such a limit is ethics. Ethics are easy to understand. There's really no need to take a whole university course on ethics because it all comes down to one rule: "Don't treat people in a way that you wouldn't want to be treated."

Ethics tops the hierarchy of rules because it never changes. It remains constant from generation to generation and from culture to culture. Moreover, you can always know if you're acting ethically or not, simply by being honest with yourself. No need for any wise sages to interpret your actions. Parents ought to understand that their kids may challenge this pillar. Let them. By crashing into it and discovering that it hasn't budged, kids will come to trust in the stability and reliability of ethics, and they will count on ethics to get them through some of life's toughest situations.

CASE STUDY

Eric was 17 years old. He was a good kid, but a bit shy. As a result, he ended up feeling left out a lot. There was a girl at school he was interested in. One day, Eric finally got up the courage to ask her out for the following Saturday. To his amazement, she accepted! Later that same day, he was approached by a guy he had been wanting to get to know better. The guy said that a few of his friends were going up to his parents' cottage on the weekend. Did Eric want to come along?

Eric was thrilled with the invitation. It looked like he was finally being accepted into the group! Instead of taking some time and using better judgment, he accepted the invitation right away. He knew he'd have to do something about the date, but he didn't want to seem uninterested in the cottage invitation. So he avoided the conflict by pretending, temporarily, that it didn't exist.

When Eric got home, he sought his parents' help. He told them honestly about his dilemma and suggested a possible solution. What if he told the girl that he couldn't go with her next Saturday because his parents wanted him to be at a family event?

Naturally, his parents were disappointed with Eric's behavior. He had disregarded the commitment he'd made to the girl—something he would not have liked, had it been done to him. He had been willing to shift the apparent responsibility for his misjudgment to his parents. And he hadn't seen the unethical nature of the proposed lie.

Being good parents, they first expressed empathy. They showed Eric that his actions weren't so monstrous, but rather quite human. They told him that they had found themselves in similar situations in the past. They showed him that he had acted with good intentions, but poor judgment.

They suggested that he should explain what had happened, honestly, to the guys. They recognized that this was more easily said than done. They did not trivialize his situation. They acknowledged that from his point of view, the fact that he had in effect lied to them about the date with

MORALITY VERSUS ETHICS

Like ethics, morality speaks to the issue of what is right and wrong; but morality changes across religions, culture, and time. A few of the recently changed moral rules in contemporary Western religious communities are the acceptance of women into leadership roles in various churches and synagogues; the ordination of gay or lesbian clergy in some churches; abortion; and the performance of marriages in same-sex couples in some churches and synagogues. Once, each of these practices was thought of as wrong. Now, they have been declared right.

This is what makes for arguments and wars between cultures, nations, religions, and even between generations who were raised in cultures of differing morality. Parents who worry that their kids are doomed for their moral degradation have always done so to the great puzzlement of their kids. In the kids' eyes, their behavior and morals are not only perfectly fine, but they conform to the rules of their society. To break them carries negative social consequences the kids may not be prepared to endure.

By obeying the laws of the society in which they must live their lives, they accept the negative consequences of breaking the rules of a previous generation, one in which they will not live. Some call this "growing up."

the girl in order to gain their friendship might be taken as a sign of his unreliability. As honest mirrors, they told him that this was a chance he would have to take, having gotten himself into the bind in the first place. But they also pointed out that his actions might be seen in a positive light as well. Regardless, Eric would have to wait for another chance to gain their friendship.

His parents also suggested a Plan B. Eric could approach the girl with the truth. The boys' offer had been for a specific weekend; his date with her had been spontaneous and could be rescheduled. Though honest and ethical, this was not the optimal plan. After all, he'd made his plans with the girl first, and she might be offended by his willingness to postpone their date. Either way, however, he'd be establishing and relying on honesty as the solid basis of whatever relationship was to develop.

Eric opted for Plan A. The other guys said it was no big deal and assured him there would be other chances to get away to the cottage. In fact, such an opportunity did come up a few weeks later, and Eric went on to become close friends with the group. His date with the girl was also a success. He and she found that they had a lot in common, and when he felt comfortable enough to do so, he told her of his dilemma prior to their first date. This honesty deepened the intimacy of their relationship and they dated for another year. Acceptances to different universities ended their romance, but they remained close friends well into their young adulthoods. ■

In the case study above, Eric's parents needed to demonstrate to him the impact of his actions. In order to do this, they needed to first respect his dilemma and treat it with the seriousness that it deserved. It wasn't easy, but they got their point across, and as a result, Eric learned a valuable lesson about commitment, responsibility, honesty, and intimacy. Above all, he acted ethically.

Do Be an "Honest Mirror"

As parents, you may be required to take on the role of honest mirror. In other words, it may be up to you to show your children how their actions and behaviors appear to the rest of the world. In some cases, this might seem difficult, or even cruel, but it's not. Remember Jennifer, from Chapter 3? She's the girl who refused to go along with many of her peers' behaviors, something that left her socially isolated and sad. Let's visit her again.

CASE STUDY

Jennifer's parents knew of her torment. She was isolating herself, missing out on what was supposed to be the best time of her life. They decided to give her a chance to talk about it. They set the stage for a dialogue and allowed her to release her emotions. It also allowed them to empathize. Then they told her that they admired her morality, her maturity, her courage, and her wisdom for opting to do what she (and they) considered to be the right thing. But they also reminded her that those same actions could be seen by a group of peers as snobbish and conceited. By refusing to obey the rules of her peers' society, Jennifer was implying that these rules—and the people who made them—were stupid.

Jennifer didn't like hearing this. But since it came from honest, supportive, and loving parents, she saw the truth in it. She recognized that she was responsible for many of her own problems. She realized that her peers had isolated her not because she wouldn't do what they were doing. It was because she had insulted them and made them feel stupid for doing what they were doing. This realization allowed her to change her point of view. Rather than helplessly blaming her peers, she began to take some positive steps to change her image without abandoning her determination to be her own person.

With her parents' encouragement, she approached the one peer whom she felt might be the most receptive to a "peace offering"—a girl she had always liked before things went sour. The two began an honest dialogue about what had happened. Jennifer expressed her distaste for things like the formation of exclusive cliques and the shaming or bullying of others. She also explained that she hadn't liked feeling out of control when she tried alcohol, so she decided it wasn't worth trying it again. Finally, she took responsibility for what she realized must have been an insult to the others, and she apologized for that. This triggered a strongly empathetic response in the other girl. She said that she had been feeling most of the same uneasiness as Jennifer. She went on to admit that she lacked the parental support and guidance as well as the self-confidence to give voice to her discomfort. Jennifer's small gesture resulted in a solid friendship that lasted for many years. ■

Believe me, if you are supportive and loving in your efforts, your kids will benefit enormously from the honest mirror approach. It shows your kids that you mean it when you praise them. That way, they don't have to worry that your comments come from a lack of love or a failure to appreciate their positive attributes. It also shows them the benefits of accepting constructive criticism. Anyone—the artist, the politician, the educator, the athlete, the educator, the student—might disagree with their critics, but they know that the criticism is offered in order to help them see how others see their work. Such criticism is also a source of ideas for improvement.

Do Teach Your Kids to Think Critically

Earlier I wrote about how humans are overwhelmed by a tidal wave of information. I pointed out that much of this information is not professionally scrutinized, and it is often not identified as being opinion rather than fact.

If what we believe to be true is critical to our survival, we had better learn how to avoid accepting invalid and unreliable information as the basis for our belief systems. This is true both for you, as a parent, and for your teen. To help us decide what to believe, we really should use the most powerful approach available to us. In my opinion, this is empirical science. And it is based on curiosity.

Curiosity, Philosophy, and Science

Humans are motivated by the same survival needs that motivate all animals: to nourish ourselves and to avoid being destroyed. Both of these are goals are presumably dedicated to giving us the opportunity to reproduce, so that not only we, but the entire species will survive.

In the case of humans, our very complicated brains help us survive. Put most simply: the more we know, the better. The more we can remember about what's "out there"—both what's good for us and what's bad for us—the better. The more we can use our powers of judgment, delay impulsive behavior, and delay gratification (if necessary), the better.

We call this need to know curiosity. We simply have to know … everything! Teenagers are especially endowed with this motivator. Remember, the all-important question that is spawned by the uncertainties of growing up is "why?"

Here's how it usually works. Teenagers wonder about lots of things. To wonder is, as I've said, terribly human and the need to know terribly urgent. And until we are sure we have good answers to our questions, our brains usually kick in and provide some plausible alternatives. Consider these examples from your teen's world:

▌ Why can't I stay out later than midnight?
>   Because my parents are overprotective.
>   Because my parents want to control me.
>   Because my parents don't want me to get into trouble.
▌ Why do I have to clean my room now?
>   Because my parents are jerks.
>   Because it's the only way I'll get out to see my friends.
>   Because my girlfriend is coming over, and she'll be grossed out if I don't.
▌ Why doesn't anybody like me?
>   Because I'm a loser.
>   Because they are all losers.
>   Because they don't really know me.
>   Because they do really know me.

Each of these answers seems plausible, but without any evidence to support them, each must also be considered a hunch. To ask questions and then delineate the most plausible answers to those questions is what humans call philosophy. But to accept any of these answers without the support of credible evidence is folly. We can avoid folly by endeavoring to go beyond the level of the hunch, and bring valid, reliable evidence to support our hunches.

The very moment I actually set out to prove or disprove my hunches, I switch from being a philosopher to being a scientist. In order to celebrate this evolution, I dignify my lowly hunch by calling it a theory, or thesis (although Greek or no Greek, it's still a hunch). By extension, since I am recognizing that I don't yet have a trustworthy answer to my question, my question is best described as a theoretical question.

The next step in the proving/disproving process is crucial. I need to base all my efforts on a certain assumption. But I need to pay particular attention to two specific and essential words: "if" and "then." Here's the assumption: If my theory is correct, then certain things must be true. These certain things are the conditions that will either lend support to or cause me to reject my theory. Because they subtend (or underlay) the theory, they are called "hypotheses" ("hypo" is Greek for "beneath").

The Lamp Analogy

Here's an example. Let's say you're sitting across from me in my office, and I ask you to name the object on the table. "It's a lamp," you say. I say, "Okay, so you believe it's a lamp. But are you absolutely sure, or is it just a hunch?" How would you apply the scientific method to support your belief? You'd use a bunch of "if/then" hypotheses. For example, if it's a lamp, then it would have a base, a cord, a switch, a plug, a shade, etc. In answering these empirical questions we determine that, so far, this object has all the features we'd need it to have before believing that it is a lamp.

I must insert one final caution about science. In order for scientists to be able to keep an open mind, they must never stop looking for evidence. I know this is silly, but what if I asked you, "Did you check for a pulse?" You'd think I was crazy. You'd say, "No way it'll have a pulse!" To that, I simply say, "Fine, so why are you so afraid to check for one?" So you go over and check. And *wow*! It has a pulse! And lamps don't have pulses! So no matter how many ways this thing conformed to the definition of "lamp," it's not a lamp, and you have to come up with another theory about what it is, because in order to be accepted, a theory must be supported by all the observed data. Encourage your kids to be philosophers by thinking about all the possible explanations for the things they wonder about. Teach them to seek out valid and reliable evidence to support their hunches before accepting things as true. This is critical thinking.

Just think about this for a minute. What allows a human to enslave another human, or abuse another human, or torture or ridicule or even kill another person? Usually, these despicable acts stem from a belief about those other humans—a belief that the other human is not really as human as they are. What did the Nazi believe about the Jew? What did the Roman believe about the Christian? What did the Ku Klux Klansman believe about the black man? What can any person who participates in hatred and genocide possibly believe is true of the ones they torment? Those beliefs almost never have any basis in fact, and that makes them the basest of all beliefs. Such beliefs are otherwise called intolerance, hatred, racism, bigotry, biases, or prejudices. Parents can and *must* do their bit to eradicate such things. But to do so requires that they take a look in that honest mirror and gaze on their own unfounded and unquestioned biases.

Remember, the vast majority of scholars, including scientists, in the world hold the degree Doctor of Philosophy (Ph.D.). Did you think this was because they studied Socrates and Kierkegaard? No. It's because they wondered, and they divined solutions by researching possible explanations. That's what makes a scientist, not a white coat and an electron microscope!

Finally, fill your kids with the zeal to seek out valid and reliable empirical evidence that will either support or reject their beliefs. Show them how to apply this at all levels: global, social, and personal. Teach them by example to have an open mind and to recognize and respect the observations and perceptions of others as essential in optimizing their own beliefs. They may never become professional scientists, but they will refrain from the close-minded cynicism that generates intolerance of all stripes. By incorporating the principles of empiricism into their world view, you give them one of the most powerful skills they can bring into their adult lives.

Do Foster Self-Esteem

Who are you? This seems like a pretty straightforward question, and yet, when most people are asked it, they seem to be stuck for an answer. Interestingly, when I ask moms this question, the first thing they say is "I'm a mom." When dads are asked the same question, the first thing they say often relates to their occupation: "I'm a lawyer/salesman/bus driver." Some people think of themselves in terms of their relationships to other people, while others think of themselves in terms of a career or other occupation. Still others respond with a statement that reflects their belief system: "I'm a Christian/socialist/liberal." What would you say first?

Here's an exercise you can do to think about who you are. Consider the following graph:

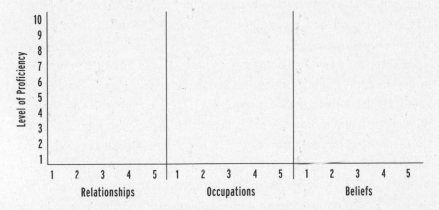

Each of the three "sections" on the horizontal line represents one of the overall ways we define ourselves: relationships, occupations, and beliefs. Each of these three sections is further divided into a series of numbered categories that can be labeled according to common definitions within that section (in relationships, for example, you might have father, son, brother, friend, colleague).

Let's start with the relationship category. If you're a woman, you must be a daughter. Identify this as, say, number 1 in the relationships section. But don't stop there. You're really two daughters, right? After all, how you relate to your mother and how you relate to your father are bound to be different. So maybe you should have two places for the "daughter" category: mother's daughter and father's daughter. You are also four granddaughters, sixteen great-granddaughters, etc. (If you don't really know these people or relate to them in a specific way, don't include them here.) Are you a sister, aunt, cousin, niece, wife, daughter-in-law, sister-in-law, friend, neighbor? Include it! In the case of neighbors, you might relate more closely to the people geographically closest to you. As this proximity becomes more remote, you still relate: you're a New Yorker or a Vancouverite.

Although we never think of ourselves as all these things all at once, they still make up who we are. So each of these aspects of our identity is placed along the horizontal line.

Similarly, you might place all things you do to occupy your time on the occupations segment of the horizontal line. Obviously, your job will go here. But what about all the other things you do? What about your interests, hobbies, volunteer work, household jobs, schooling? These are certainly occupations as well.

Beliefs are a bit trickier. You now know that many of us don't even know what most of our beliefs are. So here are a few questions to get you going: Do you believe in God? If so, do you believe in the God of a specific religion, or is it a more personal concept that defies description? Is yours the sort of God that is omnipotent and omniscient? Does your God have a specific plan for your life?

What if you don't believe in God, or can't make up your mind on the subject? Do you still sense some sort of force or creative power in the cosmos? Are we all going in the same direction? What about fate and free will? What about the concepts of spirit and soul? What about afterlife, reincarnation, karma, and all that?

Now that you have all the points along the horizontal line, you need to ask yourself how good you are at these various things. Your answers will be represented by the elevations you give yourself for each of the points on the graph. Think about those numbered categories as if they were bank accounts. The better you feel about yourself in each of those spots, the more you have in that particular account, and the higher the vertical elevation.

Have a good look at your chart now. How evenly your marks are scattered across the three columns is a good indicator of how diversified a person you are. How high up on the vertical line is a good indicator of how well you think of yourself, i.e., your self-esteem.

WELL-BALANCED INDIVIDUAL (MODERATE SELF-ESTEEM)

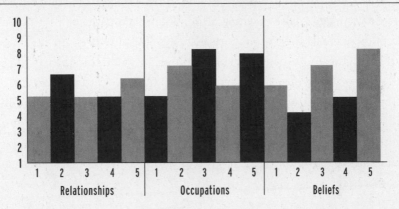

You've probably heard about the advantages of financial diversification. This harkens back to that old saying I used to illustrate the concept of concrete thought: "Don't put all your eggs in one basket." The same principle holds true for the investments we make in ourselves.

I can't tell you how many troubled people (and I must say that men make up a greater proportion of these) have the following said about them: "He's always working," "We never get to eat together," "He really has no close friends," "He has no interests or hobbies," "I wish he had a better relationship with his siblings." What makes a person well-rounded and well-integrated?

POORLY BALANCED INDIVIDUAL (LOW SELF-ESTEEM)

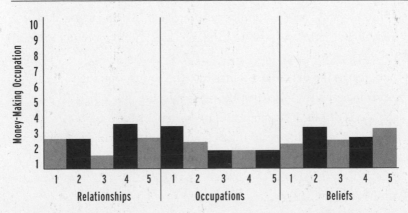

When you "invest" in a balanced way across all aspects of yourself, you derive a very stable sense of who you are. There are other benefits, too. The first of these is that the various parts of yourself tend to become integrated with each other. Your comfort with relationships and ethics has a beneficial effect on your business practices. Your interest in reading or art or history gives you a perspective on such things as values and family. In this way, stability is enhanced by a sense of self-integration—the coming together of your parts to make a better whole. In other words, by virtue of your efforts to integrate your parts, you develop integrity—one of life's glittering prizes.

The Loss of Interest

The relationship between self-investment and clinical depression is quite significant. The American Psychiatric Association's *Diagnostic and Statistical Manual of Mental Disorders* (Fourth Edition, 1994, known briefly as the DSM-IV) includes in its definition of a major depressive episode the following: "At least one of the symptoms is either (1) depressed mood or (2) loss of interest or pleasure." (p. 327). In Chapter 12, we'll look at clinical depression in more detail. For now, let's look at one aspect of it: the loss of interest.

What is interest? And if you haven't got any, can you get it? If you do get it, will it prevent or diminish depression? The word "interest" itself seems to have at least three usages in our language. The first two can be illustrated by asking a judge if she's interested in the case she's about to hear. Let's say she says, "Yes! I'm very interested. I've spent the past few days reading up on the law surrounding the case, and I'm looking forward to it."

Then, just as the defendant comes into the courtroom, the judge stops the proceedings and says she can't hear this case after all. When asked why, she says, "Because I have an interest in it!" When asked to explain, she says that she just realized she knows the defendant and has had some personal or business dealings with him. In other words, she cannot be impartial or "disinterested" in the case because there's a chance that she cares how the case will be resolved.

For the third usage of the word "interest," let's look once again to the bar graph, and the benefit of self-investment. In the financial analogy, any deposits into a savings account earn interest, which is essentially your gift for having made the deposits in the first place. It's no coincidence that the gift you get for having invested in yourself will be self-interest. And, if you have this "vested" self-interest, it means that you care about yourself.

Parents of teenagers often worry about their kids' morose, depressed appearance and noncommunicative demeanor. Their fears of the worst are fueled by media reports of teenage suicide and by depressive fashions. What parent in the 1980s and 1990s wasn't alarmed by kids dressing in black, with pale-white-made-up faces and purple lips, listening to song lyrics telling them to end it all?

Depressed people, including adolescents, will tell you that they don't care what happens to them. This is often because they haven't got anything invested in themselves—and, by extension, they don't care about themselves. These kids can't be counted on to do anything to protect or defend themselves. Some end up on the street or worse, simply because they don't care enough about themselves to prevent it happening.

Sadly, the one behavioral thing that stands a chance of reversing their lack of self-interest—self-investment—is the very thing the depressed teenager feels least like doing. Getting depressed kids to begin making investments in themselves is one of the most difficult challenges in clinical psychology.

What Can Parents Do About Low Self-Esteem?

If a teenager with low self-esteem is convinced that she is worthless, and she feels helpless and hopeless, she will not be able to invest in herself. When faced with this challenge, it's worth remembering that teenagers are just beginning to realize that not everybody sees the same things the same way. Parents can build on this by shaking the teen's confidence in her self-deprecating belief system. Why not try the setting sun exercise from Chapter 2? If she works through it honestly, she will have to admit that the negative beliefs she holds about herself may not be held by others. Moreover, she will be forced to admit that she might just be wrong about herself.

This provides the crucial starting point for the process of self-investment. And once your teen buys into that process, you can help her construct her own bar graph—a personal chart that lets her see who she is and helps her to believe again in the possibility of liking herself.

I cannot give you a specific age when self-esteem issues become particularly relevant, nor can I point to any specific warning signs. For the first time in this book, I have to tell you that you are on your own here. You need to rely on both your wisdom and your judgment. Trust in these, and you'll do well.

If, however, you want to bolster your teen's self-esteem by helping her acquire and enjoy the benefits of integrity, there are a few specific things you can do.

Relationships

Here are some ways to invest in your own relationships. By making these second nature in the family, you convey their importance to your kids. This is where modeling, as opposed to coercing, is the way to go:

- Make family and friends come first for your kids. Make sure they know about family birthdays, graduations, moves, career changes. Get them involved in their relatives' lives.
- Encourage them to keep in touch with friends.
- Encourage them to get involved with community issues. Have them reach out to new neighbors or classmates. Encourage them to vote during school elections and to volunteer their time and talents to community projects. Show them not only to display empathy when a family or community you know suffers tragedy, but also to roll up their sleeves and help out with the recovery process.
- Have them come along when you visit people you know who are ill or in the hospital. Show them how to empathize with individuals you hear or read about in the news. Just think of the thousands of cards, letters, flowers, and toy dolls or teddy bears that are left by strangers at the home of someone who has suffered a very public tragedy. This may seem trivial, but it is a move in the direction away

from the rhetorical question "What can *I* do?" (i.e., "nothing") to the empirical question "What *can* I do?" (i.e., "something"). The difference is huge.

Occupations

Couch potatoes breed couch potatoes. If you want your children to be active, with a wide variety of interests, here are some ideas.

▌ Get your kids involved in hobbies, clubs, and societies. Make sure they follow through on things that interest or fascinate them. Encourage them to ask questions. My daughter once mentioned that we ought to have a rope fire-escape ladder on the third floor of our house. I agreed but asked her to look into getting one. She said she wouldn't know how to begin. I encouraged her to examine the three key words in the object she was seeking: "fire-escape," "home," and "ladder." I then suggested she go to the people who would know about these three things for advice: the fire department, a home-supplies store, and a ladder manufacturer. She could find all three in the local phone book. By doing this research, she not only found what she was looking for, but also was introduced to people and places she would never have known existed. Most important, by taking responsibility for getting what she wanted, she fortified her sense of empowerment and self-esteem.

▌ Show them how to find more than one thing that they can do to earn some money, and encourage them to volunteer their time. You can do this by bringing them with you on food drives or to soup kitchens.

▌ Bring them to your workplace and introduce them to your workmates and colleagues. You can't imagine how many teenagers I see in my practice who have no idea—beyond perhaps a job title—how their parents actually spend their time in the workplace.

Beliefs

By now, you've got the point: Don't just tell them, show them. By doing so yourselves, you teach your kids to accept and embrace the fact that other intelligent, good, kind, concerned people see the same thing differently. Keeping an open mind is not only the key to advanced knowledge and improved interpersonal relations, it is also the prescription for neurological well-being. It keeps the brain active and challenged, and that, in my opinion, prevents loss of mental capacity at all stages of life.

■ Talk to your kids about your own beliefs, including the ones that you might question, such as the meaning of life or the existence of God.

■ Talk ethics and morality with them. Find out where they stand on accepting society's rules.

All parents hope to see their kids living up to their potential and enjoying all that life has to offer. Too often, however, parents seem to think this will happen by itself. Never believe that. Don't leave it up to the school or the church or the summer camp or the sports team. Take responsibility for raising your kids yourselves. Life can be a dangerous journey. Giving them the tools they will need along the way is the best gift you can bestow. Those tools are responsibility, forgiveness, commitment, self-esteem, curiosity, empowerment, ethics, etc. With skill and experience, these tools will serve your kids well throughout their lives. Let's take a look at some of the myriad ways they'll get a chance to put them to good use.

Part III:
Putting Theory
into Practice

7 Teens in Their World: Testing the Boundaries

If you've read this far, you are now well aware of the skills you'll need to successfully parent a teen. Now it's time to put the theory into practice. In the next few chapters, I'll look at some of the things that influence your kids—things that frighten and alarm many parents. But by remembering how the democratic family works, you can help keep the lines of communication open and lessen everyone's fears and concerns.

A Society Unto Itself

A lawyer came to my practice for a consultation and complained that he didn't have a good relationship with his son. He admitted that his career didn't permit him to be home every evening for family dinners, or to take a very active involvement in his son's life. He said, "I just can't leave my job at 5 p.m. I'd get fired!" I knew he wasn't lying. I asked if he'd had any idea, when he decided to become a lawyer, of the time his career would require. He said he did. I then asked if he had given any thought, when he chose to be a father, to the time demands of *that* job. He said he hadn't. It was pretty easy to see that the combined time that these jobs required were beyond what this man could afford to give. The term "afford" is appropriate, because that's exactly how I believe this matter should be treated. The money and prestige that this man derived from his career came at a price. The question, of course, is which of this man's two jobs is more important to him? Though he might be loathe to admit it, this man valued the prestige and money that came from his career more than he did the "pay-offs" that came from being a good father. Was his choice partially made under the influence of peer pressure? Probably.

Just as we are influenced by the values and opinions of our society, so our children are influenced by the values and opinions of *their* society. In the case described above, the father's values had led to an estrangement with his son (though, to give him credit, he recognized it and seemed to want to do something about it). In the case of our kids, the values of their world and their search for independence often seem to threaten even the tightest family. This is hardly surprising. The whole purpose of adolescence is to shift the primary focus of emotional attachment from parents to peers. After all, it is within the society of their *peers*, not that of their parents, that kids will have to live and prosper.

In addition, if conforming to peer rules means that your kids are faced with the necessity of breaking family rules, chances are pretty good that they will. Indeed, in many ways, they must do just that. Don't take this as an insult. Your kids are not being oppositional to hurt you. They are testing their newly abstract realities, questioning their old ways of doing things, and feeling the empowerment that you gave them when you decided to run your family as a democracy. By negotiating limits with your kids, you generate in them a sense of ownership and involvement. Of course, some things are not suitable for compromise—things like health, safety, and ethics. But by being open to their input in other areas of rule setting, your inflexibility with these three will seem much less onerous. In other words, pick your fights. Here are some key areas where you can afford to be flexible.

Fashion Rules: Making a Statement

I remember going into a deli in Montreal when I was about 15. My friend Joey had let his hair grow longer—over his ears!—in the fashion of the early Beatles. The deli owner took one look and made us leave. He didn't want any "riffraff" in the place. Joey had been obeying the rules of *his* peer society; so had the owner. When the rules conflicted, the owner prevailed.

A few years later, this same owner had grown *his* hair—over his shoulders! When *his* peer society made long hair the fashion again, he conformed.

Fashion is like the weather. If you don't like it, just wait a while. By definition, fashion changes. Still, fashion, as always, is used to make a statement. That statement is usually one of conformity to the uniform required by a group to which one wishes to belong. It is a declaration of affiliation and loyalty directed to the group, and it is a public declaration to those outside the group: "I'm with them."

But this is not the only interpretation, and the intended statement might not always be easy to discern.

■ CASE STUDY

Russ was 14 years old. He had long blond hair and a real "baby face"; in fact, he was quite pretty. When he was younger, he'd been picked on relentlessly by some of his peers because of his appearance. But now, as a teen, Russ wore clothes that were the "uniform" of some of the more dangerous teenagers in town—even though he was not that tough. He was using a uniform as a costume, the purpose of which was camouflage.

When asked why he dressed that way, he said, "If I sit down on a subway, people move away. I look dangerous, so they give me lots of room. That way, I'm safe." In other words, he was making the public statement "Stay away from me, or I'll hurt you!" What he was really saying was "Stay away from me, *or you'll hurt me!*" ■

See if you can decipher the fashion code by watching how your kids (and their friends) dress. Who chooses their clothes? Are your kids still content to let you do it, or do they insist on making their own choices? (Notice that I didn't ask who *buys* their clothes. Being the purchaser does not entitle you to dictate what they wear.) If their choices frighten you because you feel the styles are too provocative or revealing, by all means confront them, but do so respectfully. There's a huge difference between "Oh, no you don't. No kid of mine is going to dress like that! It's way too aggressive!" and "Yikes! That's pretty scary. It reminds me of what I see being worn by street gangs. Should I be worried?"

Dressed for Sex-cess?

It's worth remembering that there's generally nothing dangerous about clothing or hair or makeup. The attraction of the current rage may be lost on you, but does that mean the rage is harmful? Absolutely not.

When I was writing this book, there was a distinct fashion trend in which girls as young as 10 or 11 were wearing clothing and makeup that seemed (to their parents) unduly revealing and sexually provocative. That trend might still be underway and is upsetting to many parents, to be sure. Though it might be of little consolation, remember that fashion is always changing: trends come and go like the weather, and this trend will likely change over time. Perhaps it will put things into perspective if we remind ourselves that many of today's moms wore very short miniskirts when they were young girls.

The point? Your teens are not much different than you were as a teen, and if you were a normal teen, you were acutely aware of your nascent sexuality. And it didn't really matter much what girls were wearing as the fashion of the day, boys were turned on by them. Can you just imagine the impact of those ankles on the guys of the 1900s? Talk about sexy!

I attended a public school in the early 1960s. The school had a dress code. The girls had to wear white blouses under dark blue tunics. The tunics came in two styles. One had a pleated skirt and a squared-off front, which came pretty high up on the girl's chest. In those days, this was clearly the more old-fashioned looking of the two. Girls who wore this style usually complained that they'd been forced to do so by "uncool" parents. The other tunic had no pleats in the skirt, which was more in line with the sexier fashions of that day. The front featured a V-neck that, although the girl was wearing the white blouse underneath, exposed more of the blouse than the square-necked style. Of course, the first thing the girls did, regardless of the style, was to raise the tunics' hemlines as high as they could. The idea was to expose and display as much of their bodies as possible.

When the school board slammed a length restriction on the tunics (three inches below the knee, or you were sent home), the girls responded by finding loopholes. For example, until the "clothes cops" shut them down, they took great advantage of the fact that they were not required to keep all the buttons of their white blouses done up. And believe me, they knew exactly how many undone buttons they could get away with! What's more, they knew among themselves what each number of undone buttons signified: attractive, sexy, or promiscuous.

Once the "apparel narcs" clued in to this game, button rules were put in place as well. Not to be outdone, the girls then went for the jutting breast option. Two kinds of belt were permitted for these tunics. The square-necked tunic came with a clunky-looking belt that was closed at the front with buttons. The buttons rarely permitted the belt to be closed very tightly. Besides, it was flat and decidedly old-fashioned-looking. The V-neck tunic came with a similar belt, but it was almost always discarded by the girls in favor of a black sash that tied in a knot. The girls would slide the sash forward from behind through the two side loops at their waist. Instead of continuing to pull the sash forward to be tied in front, however, the girls doubled it backward and tied it in the back. This had two immediate effects: it left the front of their tunics free of any belt (which again was more in the style of the day), but more importantly, it made their breasts appear to be thrusting forward. This was no accident. As a boy, I can tell you that it worked very well.

My point is that girls are always sexy to guys. And their fashions have always scandalized their parents. That's part of the fun. If you find yourselves scandalized by their attire, just remember that you were probably doing the very same thing.

So what can you do? Try applying the democratic model we discussed earlier. First, *identify the problem*: You're worried that your daughter's attire is too sexy and provocative for her age. Then, *think about the problem more specifically*. What, precisely, are you worried about?

- That she's sexually (and possibly unsafely) active?
- That she might attract unwanted (even criminal) sexual advances?
- That she is too immature to grasp the moral and ethical complexities related to intimacy, commitment, and trust?
- That she'll develop a reputation for being sexually easy and that people will make fun of her or treat her as trash?

■ That she's attracted, in a rebellious and dangerous way, to the Wrong Crowd?

Next, *do some research*. Find out from experts (authors, psychologists, a family doctor, school administrators or guidance counselors, or the parents of her friends) what the norm seems to be for her age. Find out if anything negative is going on at school (if so, this could be where you begin your talk). Then, when the atmosphere is friendly and communicative, *tell your daughter in explicit terms what worries you*. If she's truly mature about her sexuality, she won't balk at this. She'll agree that your concerns are reasonable, and then she'll calm you down by assuring you that she is both physically and emotionally safe. If she is embarrassed or angry, it's a sign that she's not ready for the responsibility of mature sexuality. Tell her that you understand that this is what everybody is wearing, but ask if she is aware of the sexual impact of her exposed body parts on males. You can then present some rules that will act as limits to guide her. I'll discuss specific rules later, but as you can imagine, they relate to curfew, disclosure about where she is and with whom, etc.

Although the age at which girls are being "sexy" does seem to be decreasing, I'm not worried. This behavior does not reflect deteriorating morals on the part of the girls; it reflects the kids' conformity to adult-driven fashion. We should be more worried about the deteriorating rates of marital success and commitment to relationships. We should also worry about the accelerating rates of sexual irresponsibility on the part of the adults who run the fashion and media industries. The argument that the fashion industry is just giving kids what they are demanding is irresponsible drivel, in my view. Since when is it responsible for adults to simply give kids what they demand? This is a case of kids doing what some adults (those who work in the fashion industry) have deemed profitable and, hence, desirable. And when the kids do what those adults want them to do, other adults (the parents) freak out.

I've told you what to watch for and what to do about it if you're worried about this. No one can predict where this will all lead. Some people joke that you should start to really worry when you're at the supermarket buying disposable diapers for your baby, and your baby insists on getting the "thong" style "'cause everybody's wearing them"! Seriously, though, remember that every generation wants to be different from the generation that preceded it. They want individuality for their generation, but not for themselves *within* that generation. Instead, they all want to be different in exactly the same way, by wearing the same clothes and having the same hair.

Hair Today, Gone Tomorrow?

Just like the deli owner who couldn't accept my friend's Beatles hairstyle, you may intensely dislike your teen's hair—spiked, braided in corn rows, colored fluorescent red or purple, dreadlocks, or even shaved off totally—but it's not actually hurting anyone and it *will* grow out! What's more important than the color, length, or shape of the hair is the message it conveys. Russ, the 14-year-old, was sending a message (mixed though it may have been) with his clothes. Hair is a harmless part of that fashion statement. Don't sweat it.

Body Piercing and Tattoos

And don't sweat body piercing or tattoos either. Neither piercing nor tattoos are inherently psychologically dangerous. By that, I mean that they do not signify membership in today's antisocial groups. On the contrary, piercings and tattoos are so common now that, like all other fashions, they soon will be rejected by the coolest of the generation, who are tired of being copied by every geek in the world.

Once piercing and tattoos come to be declared by the fashion leaders to be uncool (and they certainly will), and more importantly, when those same leaders declare the new cool fashion, piercing and tattoos will be forgotten.

This is not to say that piercing and tattoos are always physically safe. For example, there may be cases where infections occur. Does this really sound so foreign to earring wearers? Just remember, piercing is not permanent, and even tattoos can be removed, if so desired (ask your friendly dermatologist more about this).

CASE STUDY

John, the father of 18-year-old Ryan, was freaked out when his son announced he was getting a tattoo. John rationalized to Ryan, an aspiring actor, that he was concerned with the tattoo's potentially harmful occupational consequences. Specifically, John worried that it might eliminate Ryan from consideration for certain roles in a world where competition is already very tight. Of course, had Ryan really wanted to argue, he could have pointed to the widespread appearance of tattoos on all sorts of anatomical parts on all sorts of movie screens. In this case, however, Ryan saw his father's point and didn't get the tattoo. ■

Entertainment and the Media

Because fashion reflects culture, youth fashion must reflect youth culture. How our teenagers entertain themselves is no exception. The need to belong is central to the human psyche, and there is nothing quite as heartbreaking as a teenager who feels left out. Just as societies have always striven to establish and maintain their unique identities, young people have—and always will—strive to find music, movies, and video games that set them apart from other cultures and lend to their generation a lifelong identity. More to the point, consuming this culture grants them membership in that generation.

Our kids often listen to what we consider mind-numbing, soul-destroying music; watch violent, stereotyping TV and movies, and play video games that we fear will turn them into serial killers. Many, if not most modern parents generated the same type of fear in *their* parents. When I was studying psychology at graduate school in the early 1970s, I was aware of rampant drug use, free love (a.k.a. sex), and student rebellion among my own generation. This even led to violence and death. I saw a generation gap that seemed unbridgeable. And I wondered, "What will our kids be able to come up with that will scare the living daylights out of us?" Well, they managed to find things!

Music

Adults have never liked the music of their kids' generation. This is because, as with any fashion, it is determinedly different from that of their own generation. When I was a teenager, bands like the Rolling Stones and the Animals came on the scene to the horror of our parents, who described them as rough, vulgar, and obscene. This, of course, is what we loved about them. They were dangerous, and they were ours.

Some years later, I was in Minneapolis to give a talk at a major scientific convention. On my way down to the hotel lobby on the morning of my talk, I noticed a familiar tune oozing like syrup from the elevator speakers. It was an "easy listening" version of "Louie, Louie." This juxtaposition of predigested elevator music with what I'd come to love as hardcore rock and roll was too much for me. I took it personally. I think I cried. When had I become respectable?

If you don't like the music your kids like, don't panic. Talk to them about it. Let them tell you what they like and why. Listen to it. I remember trying to get my father to like the music of the 1960s. My dad loved opera. When he listened to it, he would sing along in whatever language was being used. I'm sure he had no idea what the words meant, but he would belt it out in Italian or German or whatever. Imagine trying to get a guy like this to appreciate the Stones. To his credit, though, he sat and listened. Afterward, he told me he didn't like it. But by listening, he had legitimized *my* love of the music. Instead of making me feel stupid for liking something so "radical," we'd communicated and shown each other some respect. In the end, this is far more important than trying to get your kids to share your taste or trying desperately to share theirs.

If you're worried about misogynist, racist, or suicidal lyrics, listen to the music with your kids and talk to them about your concerns. You'll probably find that they don't share the views presented in the lyrics. Like you, your kids may even think that the lyrics are stupid and potentially dangerous.

CASE STUDY

Steve felt the musical lyrics his 16-year-old son Adam was listening to were too violent. He feared they might lead his son to violence. Steve knew that if he ridiculed his son's music, he would be ridiculing his son. He knew this would elicit an angry or noncommunicative response. It would also deny him the opportunity to learn whether there might be a real problem. Instead, he decided to tell Adam plainly that he was afraid.

He then sat with Adam and they listened to the lyrics together. Steve pointed out the most troublesome words. While he was at it, he took the opportunity to check out his son's attitudes about other lyrical content, such as racism, misogyny, and homophobia. He acknowledged that the problem with the lyrics was his. This put Adam at ease. It gave Adam a chance to tell his dad that he needn't worry because he (Adam) was also aware of the content of the lyrics and would never allow violent or otherwise socially inappropriate art to incite violence or bigotry on his part. It also allowed Adam and Steve to disagree as to musical taste while maintaining respect for and communication with each other. ■

So remember, unless you're certain that an ethical, health, or safety matter is at stake, cultural fashions can provide you with the grist for meaningful and respectful discussion, including disagreement. Allowing a certain amount of leeway in these areas will also give your kids a sense of legitimacy and ownership, and it encourages them to participate in the ruling of the roost. When you talk to your kids about their music, video games, and fashion, don't ridicule these things but express your concerns and try to see the attraction they have for a different generation. Finally, try to remember that every generation has produced its geniuses. That we cannot identify them yet is no reason to condemn their art.

Violence on TV, Film, and Video Games: Monkey See, Monkey Do?

Violence certainly isn't restricted to music lyrics. It shows up on your television screen, in movie theaters, and in video games. It is often gratuitous and ugly. I personally don't like it. But again, for kids that's the whole point.

As with lyrics, I believe you don't need to sweat this issue as long as you have an open relationship with your kids. Have you actually taken the time to examine these games? If not, do so. Sit down and play a few. Do it with your kids. You'll probably start to understand the attraction and may even feel the games' addictive powers. If so, you'll be able to identify with your kids when you discuss your concerns about violence and sexism and other issues featured in these games. Calling the games stupid is the same as calling your kids stupid for liking them. They will take this insult personally and will wait to get back at you for hurting them. If you object to the games without giving them a try, your kids will simply roll their eyes or give you that look they reserve for those who don't get it.

There is no shortage of studies *correlating* media violence with real violent behavior. But remember that *correlation is not causation*. It simply means that two things are seen to occur and to vary together. There is a danger in interpreting this as a causal relationship. Consider the following:

- **True:** Adults, not teenagers, create and administer society's laws.
- **True:** Society's laws include the condemnation of violence.
- **True:** Adults, not teenagers, create and publicize the media.
- **True:** There is a lot of violence in the media.
- **True:** Violent content is popular.
- **True:** Violent media content *correlates with* violent behavior.
- **True:** Popular violent content is economically lucrative for the adult-run media.
- **Commonly believed**, but not empirically proven: The media create and deliver violence to consumers in order to make money.
- **Commonly believed**, but not empirically proven: Media violence causes teenager violence.
- **True:** Society does not condemn the media or punish them for contributing to societal violence.

What does this all boil down to? One really interesting question: If we are *so sure* that media violence is the cause of real-life violence—something we find so disturbing—why don't we outlaw media violence? There can only be two reasons, and they are not mutually exclusive:

- We don't really want to outlaw media violence because it's too lucrative to certain powerful adult members of our society, and, as a result, the required laws might not pass.
- We recognize that media violence is not the true cause of real-life violence, and that eliminating media violence would not change things.

Violent acts are usually committed by angry people. We'd be much better off in our fight against social violence if we asked ourselves the question "Why are so many of us so angry?"

Try not to focus on the violence—unless you truly believe your child is being affected by it in some way. If you've noticed a change in behavior or attitude, it could be the video games, but it could be any number of other things. Certainly, any observed violent behavior must be dealt with—simply banning video games is not the answer. I'll talk more about teen violence later.

ANTISOCIAL BEHAVIOR

Kids are often oppositional and defiant. Remember the value of opposition to the democratic process (see Chapter 5), and don't try to squelch it Defiance is another thing. It may or may not reflect a serious underlying problem. When the behavior turns into what clinicians call "antisocial," it borders on and often crosses the line into what most lay people call "criminal." In its milder versions, we apply the term "conduct disorder"; in its more severe forms, we use the term "antisocial personality disorder." In either of these cases, professional intervention is highly recommended. Here are some "red flags" that clinicians watch for:

- bullying
- initiation of physical fights
- carrying a weapon
- physical cruelty to people or animals
- stealing while confronting a victim
- forcing someone into sexual activity
- setting fires deliberately
- destruction of others' property
- breaking into someone's home or car
- robbery, burglary
- frequent lying to get out of trouble or get someone else into trouble
- frequent breaking of rules
- frequent truancy from school
- running away from home

See video games for what they are, not what they aren't. Remind yourself that a lot of good can come out of games. For example, in playing these games, your kids are acquiring and perfecting skills that will allow them to do the work that their generation will demand: the knowledge of digital thinking; rapid keyboard operation; logic; etc. When you do object to a game—whether a video game or a more physical game or activity—know *why* you're objecting. Examine what it is that bothers you. Look at the issue in several ways, which is how you want your kids to look at things.

Here's an example of what I mean. When I moved onto the street where I live, there were two teenage brothers who spent what seemed like every waking moment on their "trick" bicycles. These were the bikes that went forward and backward, and were so balanced that you could do back or front wheelies and many other neat tricks. And believe me, these kids were good! Now, their parents might have preferred them to be spending all that time on music lessons or their homework. But trust me, what they got on those bikes was just as good. They developed perseverance, discipline, courage to try new things and to stretch their potential, brotherly bonding, and more.

Violence and Retrogression

"Retrogression" is a term that is sometimes used when economists discuss fiscal policy. Put most simply, retrogression occurs when something harmful (like taxes) exerts its *most* harmful effects on that portion of the population (low-income earners, for example) that can least withstand it. That's why many societies insist that their wealthier members pay a higher percentage of their income as taxes than their less affluent members. But the term finds its uses in the practice of clinical psychology, too. People who can least afford the impact of society's many negative influences are the very ones who usually succumb most to those influences.

Those negative influences include (but are by no means restricted to) the need to become sexually active at a very early age; the lure of drugs; and the possibility of being influenced to become aggressive, depressive, or obsessive in response to all sorts of environmental stimulation, including violent video games. In all of these, the least resilient of us are the hardest hit.

Sir William Osler, a famous medical educator, once answered a student's question about how a patient is likely to do after being diagnosed with a certain disease this way: "It is more important to know what patient has a disease than what disease the patient has." The same holds true for teens and media influences. "It is more important to know what kids are listening to the music, ... or playing the video games ... or watching violent TV or movies than the music, games, TV shows or movies the kids are listening to, or playing, or watching." We can't simply say that violent song lyrics or video games will produce violence in their consumers. The fact of the matter is that people who act violently are pathologically angry over real or imagined wrongs. The lyrics and the games did not make them angry. If you, as parents, have given your children the gifts of self-esteem, family support, and ethical and moral role models, you need not worry.

Friends and Peer Pressure

It is healthy for our kids to identify strongly with the culture of their peers. After all, as I have said earlier, that is the culture, with all its rules and expectations, in which they must live their lives, find their friends, discover their mates, and set out on their careers. We as parents must become comfortable with the fact that morality changes from generation to generation (just as music and fashion do). In order for our kids to gain acceptance within their own peer culture, they *must* conform strictly to the rules of a society other than that of their parents and family. I can't tell you how many times I've given talks to teenagers about this shift in morality and had many of them say to me afterward, "Can you please come home with me and tell this to my parents?" These are good kids for the most part. They realize that, in rejecting the standards of a past generation, they may hurt people they really love. They don't do this as easily or as heartlessly as you might think.

The "Wrong Crowd"

Parents often fall into the trap of identifying their kids' acceptance of a morality other than their own as a mark of open rebellion. At the first sign of trouble, they fear their kids are being led down the road to ruin by unscrupulous and immoral peers. Not many parents who have troubled kids complain about how *wonderful* their kids' friends are, unless it is to compare their own kids bitterly to them ("Why can't you be more like Marvin?"). Indeed, the lament I hear most often from parents is that their kids are "getting in with the "Wrong Crowd"." Exactly where do they think kids find this "Wrong Crowd"? Do you imagine them looking around for activities on the first day of school and signing up on a list with the heading "Wrong Crowd—Tuesdays and Thursdays, 4:00–5:30"?

Let's state the obvious. What's the "Wrong Crowd" to you is, by virtue of the fact that he's in it, the *right* crowd to your kid. This is how the "Wrong Crowd" thing often works. A kid feels pressured to do better—in school, at home, on the playing field. But for many reasons, most having to do with motivation, he *doesn't* do better. That's when he becomes attractive to other kids who aren't doing so well. Those kids need to recruit as many people as possible to the ranks of those who support and even glorify doing poorly. Attitudes develop, and things get worse.

For example, many kids start smoking because they like how smoking makes them look to others. The same thing happens if they feel pressured into going along with what the leaders of their peer group want to do. They may even go along against their own moral and ethical better judgment. The activity might involve something relatively minor like teasing someone or acting up in class. But it gets uglier when it takes on the form of bullying or, even worse, gang attacks, including those that are driven by racism or misogyny. Let's have a look at what you can do in situations where parental involvement is warranted.

Encourage Involvement with Multiple Peer Groups

One way to combat the wrong group syndrome is to encourage your kids from the earliest age to become involved with a *multiplicity* of peer groups—the neighborhood kids, the school kids (these days, these may be two different groups), the kids on the soccer team, the kids in the Saturday morning drama or dance group, a garage band, a 4-H club, or computer club. By doing this, you protect them from feeling forced to participate in *all* the activities of a lone peer group. But remember, one of the best ways to encourage this sort of involvement is to have them grow up in a home where the parents also belong to multiple groups and model the benefits to their kids. Be honest. Are you trapped into doing only what your peer group does, like drinking heavily at dinner parties or engaging in gossip? Even if you are a good model, your teen may be reluctant to get involved (just the fact a parent is suggesting it can be the kiss of death!), but recall how the democratic family works. Negotiate with your teen and see what kind of compromises you can work out to widen your teen's horizons. Keep in mind that if your teen has only one group of friends, and the friends want to try dope or skip class, it gives your kid little maneuvering room if that behavior makes him uncomfortable. By having alternative groups, your kid can opt out of selective, uncomfortable behaviors without feeling socially threatened. He hasn't put all his eggs in one basket.

Get to Know Your Kids' Friends

Even if you think your teen's friends belong to the "Wrong Crowd," invite them for dinners or along on family trips or vacations or out to a show. If your kids don't want to have their friends meet you or if your kids' friends don't want to meet you, you can bet there's trouble somewhere. Talk to your kids about it. Here's the sort of conversation that can come up:

Mom: How come Jason never comes into the house?

Teen: He does, just not when you're here.

Mom: Why's that? Doesn't he want to meet me?

Teen: Come on, Mom. It's because you're so embarrassing with my friends! It's like you're always giving them the third degree.

Mom: I'm only trying to get to know him better. That's what polite people do.

Teen: Yeah, well, he doesn't like all those personal questions. It makes him think you're judging him or something.

Mom: Is that how you feel when your friends' parents want to talk to you?

Teen: I'm not as sensitive as he is, I guess.

Mom: Okay, but it sounds as if he's not used to what regular families talk about. Maybe he's having a tough time at home. It's none of my business, but you can see why I'm a bit concerned.

By making her teenager compare his own family experience with that of his friend, the mom was able to explain her concern while avoiding blaming or otherwise denigrating Jason. By humanizing your kids' friends, they will come to humanize you. And once humanized, it's tough to revert to demonizing.

Learn to Resolve Moral Dilemmas

If your kids obey the moral rules established by their peer group, they must, at times, break the moral rules established by their family. As I have said, they don't always do this easily or thoughtlessly. But they must do it, and so they face a moral dilemma. The resulting discrepancy and distance from the family can be resolved only by communication. Parents and teenagers must come face to face with the difference in morals and handle it in a mature way.

Often, the way out of a moral dilemma is via ethics; this never changes. Your teen owes you an acknowledgment of what is happening and an apology for being the cause of your discomfort.

A 16-year-old came to my office with his parents, who were desperate about his constant and nonapologetic use of marijuana. When they said that they were ashamed of him, he said, "Yeah, well, that's because you're a couple of a_____s." His parents gave me that "See what I mean? He's hopeless" look.

I don't think he really wanted to hurt anyone, but he was doing so anyhow, and it wasn't responsible for him to blame his parents for being hurt by what he had said. I told him that by using profanity, he only made himself look more like a child than an adult, which is what he was trying to avoid. By giving him the backhanded compliment that he was too big for that now, he was forced to take a more mature approach.

Similarly, if your son or daughter suggests that this is *your* problem and *not theirs*, you can agree. You can then tell them that in responding to your problem, they are demonstrating the mature and responsible way to approach problems in general. You can express your honest feelings about their peers, including the good stuff as well as the things that frighten you. You may remind them that you would see it as a sign of maturity on their part if they showed some empathy; it would be nice if they understood how you feel. But if they don't, that is only a sign that they aren't ready to handle the more mature responsibilities of being an adult. Don't push it, because they obviously don't possess the cognitive capacity to get it, and you'll only invite anger and frustration all around.

As always, let them know you love them in spite of this difference. It may not seem to pay off at the moment, but over the long term, it will. Your teen will recognize the respect with which you treat his or her opinions, even when you don't agree with them.

Oppositional Behavior

Sometimes kids don't behave at home but seem to do well at school or in their friends' homes. They are probably allowing themselves to express their frustration in the presence of the people they feel most comfortable with— their family. Their friends or school officials might abandon them, but their parents never will. They feel they can be at their worst with them. This is small comfort to parents who feel constantly under attack, but if you know this behavior is confined to home, learn to look on it as a good thing! They trust you to listen, not to judge harshly, and to forgive them their outbursts.

You'll be glad to know that as the adolescent makes his or her way through the teen years, and especially if the teen has stayed in school, the peer pressure changes and your kids experience *positive* peer pressure. Toward the end of high school, they look around them and see their friends buckling down for final exams. That's because by the age of 18 or so, the meaning of time becomes more real. And as it does, the impact of today's behavior on future events in their lives also becomes real. And when the true leaders of the school are drug free or don't cut classes, your kids will, as always, do the same, in order to identify with and be accepted by those same leaders. And it is partially through this positive pressure from their peers that kids grow up.

Risk Taking

How many times have you said, or heard another adult say, "Teenagers! Don't even try telling them how dangerous it is to do what they're doing. They think it'll never happen to them. They think they're immortal!" Adolescents do seem to engage in riskier behavior than adults. Traditional (and intuitive) thinking on this is that teens lack both the experience and the awareness of the future that would normally make them wary of the potential dangers involved. This undoubtedly relates to their neurologically immature sense of time. In order for teenagers to gain the requisite insight into the social and other consequences of their behaviors, their prefrontal cortex must reach its full state of development. Until the prefrontal cortex becomes fully involved, teenagers use a much more emotional part of their brain—the amygdale—to make decisions about what is going on around them. Because of this, teen behavior seems to be less "intelligence and experience-based" and more "impulsive and emotionally-based."

Everybody knows that risky behavior is potentially harmful and that teenagers engage in proportionately more risky behavior than adults. But that does not make it abnormal. In her recent book, *The Priamal Teen*, Barbara Strauch (a journalist, not a scientist) suggested that extreme teenage risk taking is not only undesirable, but also ought to be eliminated "in certain teenagers" if possible. She wrote: "By understanding how a normal brain works, scientists hope they can eventually find ways to protect certain teenagers from their own, extremely risky behavior and destructiveness."

The clear implication is that "extremely" risky behavior is the product of abnormal brains in "certain" teenagers. This whole line of research raises some serious issues:

■ Even though we may be able to identify the neural basis of risk taking and thrill seeking in the normal brain, we would have to be absolutely certain that the brains of "certain teenagers" *are* abnormal—and in exactly what way they are abnormal—before taking any steps to protect those individuals from their own potential destructiveness.

For example, many teenagers are killed by trains each year as a result of walking along the tracks. Though such behavior is certainly extremely risky, it would be hard to argue that there is anything abnormal about the brains behind it.

▌ What kind of steps are we talking about? Medication? Surgery?

Don't get me wrong. Clinicians should try to intervene in and prevent extremely harmful behaviors, but unless brain pathology is clearly identified in such cases, I believe that such intervention is best left to psychotherapy and counseling. But most teenagers have normal brains. And the risky behavior associated with normal brains is what concerns most parents.

I subscribe to the belief that nothing happens in the brain without a good reason. Therefore, we must consider the additional (and counterintuitive) notion that risk-taking behavior, while inherently dangerous and certainly undesirable, is not only the product of a *normal* brain, but also developmentally beneficial. If that were the case, then every time a teenager engaged in such risk taking and sensation seeking, he would be rewarded for it because it is actually developmentally healthy for him to do so.

I realize that this contradicts my premise that the brain evolved out of the organism's fundamental need to approach what is good for it and withdraw from what is bad. We'd have to make a pretty strong case for any exceptions to this rule. See how this sounds to you.

Teenagers must learn that they are no longer children. Independence is what they seek, but this also means that they cannot rely on adults to come to their rescue when their behavior results in painful consequences. This is their introduction to the process of accepting responsibility for their own contribution to those consequences. Risk taking enhances the potential for painful consequences; as such, the argument might well be made that it provides kids with repeated and necessary opportunities for the very sort of learning that must occur during this phase of their lives.

Every parent wants to protect his or her kids from harm. But they know that there are strong social forces drawing kids close to dangerous things—alcohol, other drugs, immature and/or unsafe sex, etc. Even if they could, parents will *never* be able to protect their kids by keeping what they see as destructive forces in nature or society away from them. Nor will they succeed in keeping their kids away from those forces. The best parents can do—and they really must do this if they are to fulfill the job requirements of parenthood—is to prepare their kids for those forces.

We've already discussed many of the important strengths that parents can give their kids to shield them from potentially negative forces: a strong sense of ethics; a strong sense of empowerment; a strong sense of involvement, membership, and ownership in society; good insight into one's own beliefs; powerful self-esteem; and so forth. We've seen that you do this by modeling this kind of behavior yourself, talking to your kids, and engaging them in discussions about issues that might appeal to them.

In the next few chapters, we'll look at the strongest attractions out there for kids. Ironically, if our kids are not properly equipped to confront these attractions, they risk experiencing the worst of the preventable tragedies that can befall teenagers.

8 The Big Three, Part I: Alcohol

Let's say you accept the futility of trying to keep all dangerous people and things away from your kids, or of trying to keep your kids from being drawn toward those dangers. Naturally, you can't be with them at all times—and even if you could, they wouldn't want you to be! Given that, you must occasionally send them out into that danger. There's simply no choice.

As you get to The Big Three on the checklist of parental concerns—alcohol, drugs, and sex—you're going to find yourself thinking about your own experiences with each of them. How well did you handle these issues when you were a teen? How well do you handle them now? Indeed, it is your current attitudes and behaviors that may cause you the most discomfort as you talk to your teen. This is why many parents shy away from discussions about these things, preferring to simply lay down the law in an effort to fulfill their parental duty. I'm afraid it's not that easy. If you're sending them into danger, you can at least equip them for the journey.

The Appeal of Experimenting: Inquiring Minds Want to Know

Throughout this book, I have emphasized that curiosity—the need to know—is an essential and adaptive animal trait. This is as true of the human as it is of the single-celled amoeba I described in Chapter 1. Like those simple creatures, the more we know about our surroundings, the more accurate our beliefs are likely to be, and the greater our chances of survival. No wonder curiosity is so powerful.

For the concrete preteen brain, beliefs tend to be hard wired. This means that children tend to believe—and hold rigidly to believing in— what they are told. However, once they achieve the capacity for more abstract thinking, they realize that not everybody sees the same thing the same way. They realize, moreover, that what they have come to believe may not necessarily be true. They begin an odyssey of discovery that leads them to question everything, including their parents' infallibility. I discussed the implications of this transition in Chapter 6, when I labeled the questions "why?" and its more adolescent cousin "why not?" as the veritable mantras of the curious and inquisitive teenager. In Chapter 10, I'll discuss the importance of curiosity in the context of sensuality and passion. It is a major motivator for all human behavior.

No one need be surprised, then, by the teenager's curiosity when it comes to alcohol, drugs, and sex. They may have heard all sorts of conflicting things, but they are in a time and place when questioning what they are told is second nature. So, while they understand—to the extent that their developing brains permit—that there may be dangers, those dangers seem quite remote. In addition, the teenager's curiosity is often more powerful than her fear.

If parents and other adults trivialize this powerful force when talking to their kids about The Big Three, they are sending a clear-cut message of isolation and alienation, and kids are likely to respond with an equally clear-cut "You just don't understand!" Let your kids know that you *do* understand their need to know. Tell them this, in what you consider to be an age-appropriate manner. Tell them about your own experimental or even more serious involvement. Don't be afraid of this. Honesty is the best policy. We'll revisit this concept shortly, but first let's spend a little time on the appeal of alcohol and other drugs.

Changing How You Feel

A good definition of a drug (including alcohol, which is very much a drug) is a chemical that changes the physiological function of the cells, tissues, or organs of the body. If those cells and tissues are part of the brain, then a drug that changes their workings is said to affect the mind. The word we use for such drugs is "psychoactive." Clearly this change of function could happen in two different scenarios:

■ The body's cells, tissues, or organs *are not working properly* due to a genetic disease, or a disease caused by a toxin, virus, or bacterium, or due to some sort of injury. This results in the person experiencing sickness, which is often signaled and accompanied by pain. In such a case, pain would be considered a symptom of the illness. The purpose of the drug would be to restore normal function, which usually results in relief from the pain of illness. When the illness is mental or psychological, the malfunction is associated with the brain and the pain associated with it is emotional in nature. Chemicals used to treat mental illness strive to restore normal brain function and to relieve emotional pain. We call this sort of chemical a *medication*.

But what if a medication does nothing to restore normal function of the affected organ and merely blocks the pain associated with the disease? This would certainly be beneficial to the person. But it might also prevent them from either knowing that something more serious is wrong, or worse, doing something about it when they know something is seriously wrong.

■ The body's cells, tissues, or organs *are working properly*, and the person does not feel sick. However, they have learned that if they take a certain chemical, even though it would induce some sort of *abnormal function*, that abnormal functioning makes them feel better than they normally do. This is due to the chemical causing the individual to experience the world in a way that is different from reality. In ways that I will describe later, experiencing things different from reality is often inherently pleasurable. Using the chemical to achieve pleasure is often labeled substance abuse; we call this sort of chemical a *recreational drug*.

Things soon get complicated. Let's say that an individual's reality is full of psychological or emotional pain. Maybe that person wakes up in a world where reality means poverty or racism, war or an unwanted pregnancy. No one would question that for those people, anything that allowed them to experience the world in a way that is different from their reality would be very attractive. To understand the demand for psychoactive drugs by our teenagers, it is worthwhile to take yet another look at the role of pain in our lives.

In Chapter 2 I pointed out that while nobody really likes pain, we realize that it is both normal and necessary. It's is our first line of defense. It tells us that something is wrong and warns us: "Whatever you were doing when the pain started, *stop doing it, and if you're ever in the same situation, don't do it again!*"

That "don't do it again!" part is crucial, because if you actually *don't* do it again, you will have learned from your mistake. You will have taken responsibility for your pain, and gained greater independence in your life. That's why it's so important for teenagers to be able to experience the pain of growing up.

Painkillers

Pain is an inextricable risk factor for drug use and abuse. Though it's certainly not the only possible reason for using drugs, many people who drink alcohol or who ingest other mind-altering substances do so in an effort to escape from pain. If they are honest with themselves, many parents must admit that they've "been there and done that." When many of us experience physical or emotional discomfort, we turn to our doctors and ask if there is anything we can take for it. We are so accustomed to seeking a seemingly innocent chemical fix—everything from aspirin to anti-inflammatory drugs to antidepressants—that we fail to recognize how this attitude gets transmitted to our kids.

It should not be so surprising that the emotional stresses associated with becoming a teenager are often emotionally painful. As I said in Chapter 2, parents may not get the chance to say to their kids: "Look. Something is about to happen to you. You're going to feel a sort of pain that won't feel exactly like any pain you've ever felt before. ... It means that you are *healthy*. I can't take away the pain of growing up, but I can try to prevent your fear."

But what if nobody warns the teenager or prepares him for the pain? Teenagers may conclude, erroneously, that something is very wrong with them. And this *normal* pain can lead young people to seek relief in the way they have always sought it and seen their parents seek it: with medication. The problem is that the medications prescribed by physicians or those available over the counter have been screened rigorously to rule out harmful consequences. Drugs taken without the benefit of such screening cannot be said to be as safe, and hence, they remain illegal.

Since pain is such an essential part of human experience, why do we go to the greatest lengths to avoid or escape it? The answer, of course, is "Because we *can!*"

A Different Reality

Not everybody who uses drugs is treating an illness or escaping from physical or emotional pain. As I said earlier, some people use drugs recreationally, in order to extend their experience beyond the reality provided by the normal working of the brain. Because the chemically induced brain change is not normal, it is common to refer to this as drug or substance *abuse*.

Drugs that have what scientists call a recreational "abuse potential" fall into three families: depressants, stimulants, and hallucinogenics. For each family, the subjective sensation to the user is one of pleasure. But the brain mechanisms underlying each family's capacity to induce pleasure are very different.

Parents who are baffled by their teenagers' attraction to recreational drugs need to understand these mechanisms. This is because the answer to the parental question "What do kids get out of using psychoactive drugs?" is found in the specific brain change associated with the teenager's drug of choice. If your kid is a user, it is because she likes and/or needs the feeling that using a particular drug creates. Let's look at alcohol first.

Alcohol

If there was ever a substance suffering from an identity crisis, it's alcohol:

Identity 1: Here is a substance we despise. It's a drug—an addictive drug—and the ability to become addicted to it is transmitted genetically from generation to generation. Over time, it causes brain damage and kills the liver. It impairs driving and the operation of machines and equipment in general; as such, it is responsible for hundreds of thousands of accidental deaths and injuries each year. It is a common risk factor in acts of violence against women and children. It is also a major factor in the breakdown of families and the loss of employment. If such a substance were invented today and brought to governmental review for the purpose of potential commercial availability, it would be rejected immediately.

Identity 2: Here is a substance we glorify and crave. It's a "beverage"—the very first thing offered to us at restaurants and social gatherings. It is a necessary and traditional part of the concept of celebration: "This calls for a drink!" "I propose a toast!" "I'll drink to that!" It has become synonymous with having a good time: "happy hour." And it is seen as a common way of coping with stress: "You look like you could use a drink." I recently discussed dating with two unmarried women in their early thirties. They told me that on a first date, alcohol is a necessity in order to make what might otherwise be difficult communication easier.

Is it any wonder, then, that we're conflicted and confused as to our feelings about alcohol? We'd love to get rid of the destructive consequences of alcohol use and abuse—and we have the means at our disposal to do just that. It is not for lack of knowledge or resources that we are burdened by the damage caused by alcohol. No. We are stuck with the damage because we lack the confidence and the will to do what is necessary. Why do we do this? The answer lies in the neurology of alcohol's impact on the brain. Here's how it works.

How Alcohol Affects the Brain

Alcohol is part of a family of drugs called central nervous system depressants. The word "depressant," as used here, does not mean something that makes you depressed. Instead, it refers to a drug that depresses or slows down the metabolic physiology of cells in the brain and spinal cord. Different parts of the brain, controlling different functions, get slowed down at different times when you drink alcohol. The first part of the brain to be affected is the prefrontal cortex. You'll remember that this is the executive part of the brain, responsible for good judgment. It reminds you of the potential consequences of your behavior *before* you act, giving you time to decide whether the consequences are worth it. Remember that the prefrontal cortex is just coming into its full potential in the teen brain. Until it reaches that potential, less "intelligent" and more "emotional" parts of the brain are behind behavior that is consequently more risky. This is all relative. The prefrontal cortex is there and working, just not fully. The brain is in a state of flux, but teens are still capable of rational decisions, to some extent. If you decide not to go ahead with a certain course of action, we say that you inhibit that action. If the prefrontal cortex is not working to its maximum capacity, we can say that the person becomes disinhibited. And this is the single most desired effect of alcohol. As such, people should learn what dose of the drug alcohol is effective in achieving disinhibition.

Of course, with drinking, the question of when to stop is bound to come up. Let's say a person is disinhibited and having a good time. He knows he is having a good time because he has consumed the drug alcohol. He'd like to keep on having a good time, and he believes that if he continues to drink, he'll have an even better time. Normally, his prefrontal cortex would step in and remind him that if he keeps on drinking, he'll overshoot the desired effect of disinhibition. But his prefrontal cortex isn't working well, so he might blow it by continuing to drink. This brings about successive depressions of successive brain parts dealing with wakefulness and ultimately with what we call vegetative or life support functions, like breathing.

Generally speaking, the course of alcohol effects looks something like this:

NORMAL → DISINHIBITION → DROWSINESS → SLEEP →
ANESTHETIC SLEEP → COMA → DEATH (RESPIRATORY ARREST)

It's easy to see that, apart from disinhibition, none of these effects is socially or biologically desirable. So let's look at disinhibition more closely.

Disinhibition

We all have things we want to do, like skip work, or tell our boss exactly what we think of her, or tell that new guy in accounts receivable how hot we think he is. Of course, we don't always do those things, because we predict that they might have negative outcomes. In those cases, it's good that we inhibited ourselves. But then, we also often inhibit ourselves from doing things that we probably should do—like apply for a promotion, or ask that new guy in accounts receivable out for lunch. We stop ourselves for exactly the same reason—we predict possible or even probable failure. We are inhibited.

In depressing the prefrontal cortex, alcohol acts as a disinhibiter. Negative outcomes go unpredicted. And that is why alcohol can be such an indispensable social lubricant. To use the analogy I gave in Chapter 2, putting the executive prefrontal cortex to sleep would eliminate the importance of time from our awareness. We would not be reminded of all the lousy things that could happen (in the future) if we were to do something we really want to do. It is, after all, the fear of a bad outcome such as rejection or failure that leads to the behavioral appearance of shyness and lack of self-confidence.

CASE STUDY

Fifteen-year-old Julio never had fun at parties because he was very shy and lacked self-confidence. At one party, his friend saw him looking over at a girl. The friend knew that Julio was interested. "Why not ask her to dance?" the friend said. "She'd never dance with me," replied Julio. He felt that the girl found the other guys more attractive. The friend said, "Why not take a chance? What have you got to lose? If she turns you down, it's only because she's so superficial as to not give you a chance. You'd be better off without her in that case!" Julio wasn't convinced.

The next week, before going to another party, his friend convinced Julio to have a few beers. By the time they arrived at the party, Julio was in a state of disinhibition. He asked the same girl to dance. She accepted, and the two found that they had a lot in common—so much so that Julio asked if he could see her the following week. She agreed.

But Julio knew that his "success" had been the result of the alcohol he had consumed. And when the following week's date came around, he showed up at her home having had a few beers. His behavior was erratic. His speech was slurred, and she could smell the booze on his breath. It was all over before it began.

Julio's mistake was in believing that the only way he could be attractive to her was if he were under the influence of the alcohol. He depended on the alcohol, and he knew well before the date that he would consume alcohol before it started.   ∎

The irony here is that the alcohol didn't give Julio any special qualities. It simply overcame his shyness. Alcohol is attractive to people who lack self-confidence. For those with confidence, alcohol offers nothing. The attraction of alcohol, then, must derive from its physiology, specifically, its ability to render helpless the part of your brain that predicts probable future negative consequences. This is why it seems to be such a necessary social lubricant. It's why we, as a society, can never get too far from alcohol. Put most simply, we are hopelessly dependent on it.

What Parents Can Do

What do you do if you suspect that your son or daughter is experimenting with or abusing alcohol? As much as I'd like to give you a five-step program to solve the problem, I'm afraid it's not that simple. On the other hand, it's not terribly complicated either. It involves adhering to the principles that we've been discussing in the preceding pages, and it all starts with taking a look in your own honest mirror.

Know Thyself

When you go to a friend's house for dinner, almost the first thing you hear after you're greeted at the door is something like "What can I get you to drink?" If you say, "Thanks. I'll have some mineral water with a slice of lime" the response *used to be* "Oh, come on, have a *real* drink." The same thing happens in restaurants: "Hi! I'm Chad. I'll be your server tonight. Can I get you anything from the bar?"

What would happen if you decided to do without alcohol? Could you get through a New Year's celebration without champagne? Could you watch the Super Bowl without pouring beer all over yourself (and showing your kids that alcohol is a necessary part of any celebration)? Is "happy hour" happy only because of alcohol? Finally, ask yourself if you know anyone who simply won't put themselves into a social situation with other people unless there's an alcoholic drink nearby. Have you ever used the term "alcohol dependent" (another word for "addicted") to describe him or her?

Why do we resist saying "This calls for a drug!" or "You look like you could use a drug?" Alcohol *is* a drug, an addictive drug. Why are we so surprised that so many of us are dependent on it? When you start talking to your children about alcohol, be sure you've been sending them the right message in your own actions and behaviors.

I know how hard it can be to change social habits, but it can be done. For ten years, I served as consulting psychologist at a private boarding school. I'd visit regularly, giving lectures to students and staff, as well as holding clinical sessions with whoever needed them. One of my regular duties was to address the parents on the Saturday morning of Parents' Weekend. The preceding Friday night, the headmaster held a reception for the same parents at which alcoholic beverages were traditionally served (by just-underage students of the school, by the way!). One year, I suggested to the headmaster that we make a statement to students and parents alike: hold the reception *without* alcoholic beverages. After a great deal of debate, we decided to try it. The purpose of the exercise was to introduce one of the school's drug awareness strategies—a strategy based on a common cry from parents: "I don't want you going to that party! There's going to be alcohol there, and I don't want you to be there! Can't you have fun without alcohol?" We wanted to show the students that we could have fun without alcohol.

Since it had been my idea, I was *very* nervous. I did get some strange glances, which I took as the disappointed reactions of people learning whose bright idea the "no alcohol" rule had been. But I also got some very positive feedback. If you find in your family that alcohol is served at every festive occasion—and especially if that festive occasion degenerates into family quarrels—make it a goal to try some birthdays or anniversaries or Thanksgivings without alcohol. Show your kids it's possible to have fun without it.

Some parents believe that if they give kids alcohol at home, it will make them less likely to drink outside the home. I'm afraid it's much more complicated than that. As you might guess, it depends on how alcohol is used in the family. If it is used occasionally and moderately, it will come to be used that way by the kids when they grow up. Likewise if alcohol used immoderately and often.

Banning alcohol outright is not the best route, either. That would turn it into the proverbial forbidden fruit. So here's what you should do. Monitor your own attitude toward drinking alcohol. If you have a drink every day after work, break the pattern. Show that alcohol is not the only way to relax and wipe away the stresses of the day. Barring pathological drinking, your kids will adopt your style.

Every chance you get to drink, at home or away, ask yourself this: Am I able to say, "I can take it or leave it"? If you always *say* you could take it or leave it, but each time you say that, you *take* it, then you probably can't *leave* it. And you are probably dependent on alcohol. Tough words, I know, but you must know they're true. What's worse, this is exactly the drinking pattern you teach your kids.

Get Talking

Talk to the kids about alcohol—both its positive and negative sides. Together, come up with a list of those different sides. Your list might look something like this:

POSITIVE	NEGATIVE
"happy hour"	alcoholism
"this calls for a drink!"	"I need a drink!"
"partying"	drinking and driving
celebration	loss of job, family, or income
"feeling no pain"	family violence
"fine wine" with dinner	fetal alcohol syndrome

We seem to like the positive things, but we hate the negative ones. Get your kids talking about how we can keep the positive attributes of alcohol without succumbing to the negative. People often seek the answer in moderation. But this doesn't appear to be working too well. We also assume that prohibition is not successful and leads to a sort of forbidden fruit attraction. But real, governmental prohibition—such as happened in the United States between 1919 and 1933—actually resulted in a significant reduction of alcohol consumption as well as a corresponding reduction in many public health and safety problems related to alcohol consumption, including arrests for public drunkenness, admission to mental hospitals for alcohol psychosis, alcohol overdose deaths, and the rate of mortality due to liver cirrhosis (*Alcohol and Public Policy: Beyond the Shadow of Prohibition, Panel on Alternative Policies Affecting the Prevention of Alcohol Abuse and Alcoholism*, M.H. Moore and D.R. Gerstein, eds.), Committee on Substance Abuse and Habitual Behavior Assembly of Behavioral and Social Sciences, National Research Council, National Academy Press, 1981). Nevertheless, prohibition is a supply-side approach. In my opinion, people drink not because alcohol is placed in front of them, but because they demand that it be placed in front of them. In other words, they need it to be there. A more effective approach would be a "demand-side" approach that forces people to take an honest look at their own dependency. Here's an exercise you can adapt for your kids. Start with a discussion of one of the public health or safety risks related to alcohol consumption—say, drinking and driving. Mention that you've seen definite changes for the better as a result of public service warnings and the "designated driver" concept. Follow that up by suggesting that there's still far too much drinking and driving. Here's a potential way to change things. Say there's a city that has a major league baseball team. The team is owned by a brewing company, and the company also owns the stadium in which the team plays. Not surprisingly, the company sells its product (beer) in that stadium during the games. Let's say the stadium holds 50,000 people. Understanding that this is not a scientific study, but just a rough poll of what people think is happening, ask your kids what percentage of the fans at the game *they believe*

- drank beer of any amount
- were intoxicated when the game ended
- drove a car from the game while intoxicated

If only one in five people were drinking beer, that's still 10,000 people drinking. If only one in ten of the beer consumers were drunk when the game ended, and only one in each group of those ten drove a car while drunk, that's still 100 drunk drivers leaving every ball game. If a major league team plays 80 home games, that makes 8,000 incidents of drunk driving, and it's entirely likely that accidents, injuries, and even death could result from such a number.

It's important to note that these incidents are entirely preventable, but at a cost. Ask your kids who they think is responsible for putting those 8,000 drunk drivers on the roads. Ask your kids who would be responsible for paying the cost to prevent this: Would it be the fans? The brewing company? Then ask them whether the responsible people ought to do something about it, and if so, what: ban the consumption of alcohol at sporting events? This sort of discussion opens our teenagers' eyes so that they can challenge our own beliefs and become empowered to do something about society's problems.

Make Sure Your Kids Know the Risk Factors

Nobody who is an alcoholic is glad they are an alcoholic. They often ask me, "Why didn't someone warn me?" If we were better informed about alcohol and its effects, we wouldn't need someone else to warn us. Here are three issues you can explore on your own and discuss with your teens.

Genetic Predisposition

Maybe your uncle Fred tells you he'll come over right after his Alcoholics Anonymous meeting. Or maybe your mom tells you she once had a serious drinking problem, but that even though she overcame it years ago, she still thinks of herself as an alcoholic. Maybe no one admits to being an alcoholic, but you notice things that make you suspicious. Your cousin always seems to have alcohol on her breath, even in the morning. Your brother goes straight to the fridge and grabs a beer before just about anything else whenever he comes over. If you suspect you have alcoholism in your biological family, please ask. People who have close relatives with alcohol dependency problems have a three-to-four times greater risk of developing such problems themselves. Parents have a responsibility to tell their kids about their family history. Just be open about it; it's easier than you think. Don't let your kids find out the hard way. You wouldn't keep some other genetic disease predisposition like diabetes or cancer from your kids, would you?

It's also a parent's responsibility to inform his or her kids about the risks one takes when one decides to drink. Because drinking is so common in our society, it won't be hard to broach the topic. Newscasts frequently include a horrific car crash related to teenage drinking, or tell of a young person found dead at a party due to alcohol poisoning. Like most tragedies, no one thinks this sort of thing will ever happen to them. But it can, and it's a parent's job to make that clear.

A Taste for Alcohol

Most people don't like the taste of alcohol at first exposure. When I finally sipped my first beer (I must have been around 13 or so), I was shocked. It tasted so bad! I was also embarrassed, because I was pretty sure that this was a bad or rotten beer. This could not possibly be what that gorgeously golden liquid I'd seen on TV could taste like. But it did! I almost betrayed my naiveté and ignorance, but I managed to keep quiet. Be honest about your own consumption patterns. If you didn't like alcohol when you first tasted it, you aren't alone. Almost nobody actually likes alcohol's taste when they are first exposed to it. Moreover, it's almost impossible to get nonhuman animals in research settings to drink the stuff unless you make it the only way they'll get anything liquid in their diet. But if you didn't like the taste, yet went back for more, you owe it to yourself and to your kids to ask yourselves why. The only answers that make sense are these:

- You liked "being part of" the group that was drinking.
- You liked how the alcohol made you feel.

Assure your kids that they don't have to drink alcohol if they don't like the taste or how the alcohol makes them feel. Tell them, moreover, that it's likely that most of their friends don't like the taste or the "feel" either. Ask them what they thinks this means. Underline the fact that people who drink if they don't like the taste are after the drug effect, and that it's really no different from smoking a joint or taking a pill.

High Tolerance

One of the saddest teenage spectacles is the celebration of immoderate drinking. Indeed, among many teens, the words "partying" and "drinking" are used interchangeably. Included in partying is the well-known drinking contest, in which the individual who can drink the most the fastest wins. He is praised for his accomplishment and made to feel proud of his drinking prowess. But his success is generally due to his genetically based tolerance to the intoxicating effects of alcohol. This places him at greater risk for developing alcohol dependence. In other words, the winner of the drinking contest is almost always an alcoholic. We should never make an alcoholic feel proud of drinking. It's actually quite cruel.

TRY THIS You can use the concepts of friendship and compassion as a way to talk about alcohol with your teen. Bring the topic up with your kids, and ask if they'd intentionally be cruel to one of their friends. Chances are good that they'll say no. One standard psychological test asks people to complete partial sentences with the first thing that comes into their heads. One of these sentences begins "A real friend. ..." In my experience, the two most frequently used completions to this sentence are "accepts you for who you are" and "is always there for you." Now, ask your son what a real friend would do if he saw someone he cared about drinking too much.

Ask your son to consider the following dilemma: He's becoming uncomfortable with a friend who always seems to need to drink. This friend never shows up at parties or concerts or football games without drinking beforehand, or doesn't come unless he's sure that alcohol will be available at the event. Your son decides to mention it to his friend, but the friend responds badly. He says, "Hey come on, man! You think I have a problem? I can stop whenever I want. It's not like I need it or anything. And anyway, you're supposed to be my friend! You're supposed to accept me for who I am!"

Ask your son what he thinks would happen if he said, "I am your friend, man. That's why I can't stand by and let you ruin your life. A friend wouldn't do that. And anyway, real friendship is based on respect. And I can't respect what you're doing to yourself. Then, when I try to help you, you don't respect my concern. So if there's no respect, where's the friendship?"

Once you've worked through this exercise, you can point out to your son that when you get "on his case" about drinking, not only are you being a parent, but also you're playing the role of a real friend. He may not like what he's hearing, but if he's being honest with himself, he'll have to respect your concerns.

9 The Big Three, Part II: Marijuana, Hallucinogenic Drugs, and Stimulants

I can't tell you how many times I've heard the following sentence: "I don't use the hard stuff. I only take 'soft drugs' like pot." Let me make this as clear as I can: *There is no such thing as a soft drug.*

I often wonder where the term even came from. I imagine it's used as an analogy to the more understandable "soft drink," which refers to a drink that does not contain alcohol. And let's not get bogged down in the possible added confusion associated with the term "hard liquor"—which refers to products like vodka, gin, and whisky. Products like beer and wine obviously also contain alcohol, so they cannot be called "soft drinks." The problem, I believe, derives from the relative concentrations of alcohol (by volume) in the various products. So-called hard liquor contains approximately 40% alcohol, wine contains approximately 14% alcohol, and beer contains approximately 4% alcohol. Regardless of the concentration, however, the amount of alcohol entering the brain is what determines the effect. Since much higher volumes of beer are consumed than volumes of, say, whisky, the impact of these two products on the consumer is usually identical.

Getting back to the concept of "soft drugs," I've heard many people rationalize their use of marijuana by saying "I do smoke weed (marijuana), but I won't touch chemicals." This nonsense is both ill informed and irresponsible. I often respond to this by asking the person using it exactly *what they think marijuana is* if it is not a chemical.

Here are some other informal criteria that seem to be used to define a "soft drug":

1. It's from nature; it's a plant: it's "organic"; (it's not a "chemical").
2. It may be "psychologically" addictive, but it's not "physically" addictive.
3. It doesn't impair performance in school, the family, social life, athletics, etc.
4. It doesn't pose any personal or public health risks.
5. It's safe. No one dies from using it
6. It doesn't present any personal or public safety risks.
7. Doctors prescribe it in the treatment of their patients.

Later on in this chapter, we'll take a closer look at how marijuana bears up under these criteria. But first, we need a better understanding of why marijuana, and other drugs like it, hold such appeal for teens.

The Appeal of Hallucinogenic Drugs

In the previous chapter, we learned that people take certain drugs recreationally in order to get the inherently pleasurable feeling that comes with experiencing things different from reality. Since hallucinations are defined as experiences that differ from reality, substances that generate them are called hallucinogenic drugs.

Marijuana is often discussed and classified separately from other hallucinogenic drugs like LSD, peyote (mescaline), and psilocybin ("magic" mushrooms). However, because it derives its pleasurable qualities largely by altering the user's perception of reality, marijuana fits the hallucinogenic category well.

To identify with the pleasurable experience of altered reality, think of going to an amusement park that features a hall of mirrors. The reason those curvy mirrors are so amusing is that when you peer into them, you get an image of yourself that is different from reality. And that's funny. For most of us, there's nothing particularly amusing about seeing ourselves as we really are.

Hallucinations, Illusions, and the Perception of Reality

Whether you're a kid or an adult, you can't help but be fascinated by magic shows. Think of any magic trick—say, an illusionist pulling golf balls out of the ears of someone he's invited up to the stage. You *know* that person doesn't have golf balls in his head, but right before your eyes, the illusionist is pulling golf balls out of his ears! So what do you believe? If you believe your brain, you realize it's an illusion, and even though you're not quite sure how it works, you can sit back, relax, and enjoy the show. You've paid money to have your brain fooled momentarily into believing something is true when you really know it isn't. You're experiencing things in a way that's different from reality.

Experiences like this reinforce our belief that seeing things in a way that's different from reality is inherently amusing. As I said earlier, people looking for that inherent amusement are abusing the drug involved, not to self-medicate, but in order to entertain themselves. And, while this can be amusing, it is also intrinsically dangerous.

This danger is illustrated by the individual who is *not aware* that what he is seeing is an illusion. That person can—depending on his age, intelligence, and the nature of the illusion itself—react in a way that differs completely from the intended amusement. For example, a child who is still very concrete may believe her eyes. She'd *believe* that the person really had golf balls in his head. She'd attribute it to real magic, and she'd likely be amused. But what if the same child witnessed a lady being sawed in half? She might be terrified and even traumatized. The explanation that it is an illusion doesn't do anything for her.

Seeing that the woman was really not harmed might soothe her. But she would likely believe that the injuries to those people had been real, and were *reversed* only by magic; or else that the injuries had never occurred and that her mind had been fooled by magic. Either way, she might still be frightened by a belief in very powerful and harmful forces that are unexplained. If she also believes that those forces were in the hands of someone who would want to harm her, she might become terrified and display very unusual self-protective behavior. Trying to convince her of the truth could be as difficult as convincing a psychotic person that the voices he hears are not real, or like convincing a person who is experiencing a bad acid trip that the terror he is experiencing is also not real. Both are the result of abnormal brain chemistry that results in experiencing things different from reality. In the former case, the mental illness is unavoidable; in the case of the acid trip, the hallucinogenic terror was chosen and initiated by the user. That user might not have made that choice if he understood the intrinsic danger involved.

Everybody knows Lewis Carroll's story *Alice in Wonderland*. Ask your kids to take another look at it and to regard it from a more abstract point of view. Alice enters a strange place populated by some very amusing characters. One character—the caterpillar—sits on a mushroom smoking "something" from a water pipe. None of these characters is particularly helpful to Alice. In many cases, they suggest that she eat some sort of mushroom, which will change her relationship to the world around her. But her main goal, which is to find the white rabbit and get out of there, is essentially thwarted. Things get "curiouser and curiouser," and (in the Disney version) she finds herself in a maze, pursued by a deck of crazed playing cards wielding battle axes and the Red Queen crying "Off with her head!"

Alice in Wonderland is a perfect replication of a bad acid or psilocybin mushroom trip. This exercise is a great way to initiate a discussion with your kids about how these drugs aren't always so much fun and can often be downright terrifying.

Broken Telephone: How Hallucinogenic Drugs Affect the Brain

The brain allows us to experience things as they really are in order for us to be able to make safe decisions as to how to act. It does so by receiving information from the environment via our senses: vision, hearing, touch, taste, and smell.

Our sense organs send this information into the brain, using nerve cells (neurons). Unlike wires, which can carry an electrical impulse the entire distance from the source to the destination, neurons conduct the information for only a very short distance before they must transmit it to another neuron in the chain. This is much the same as when a baton is passed from runner to runner in a relay race.

In the nervous system, the information is passed from one neuron to another in the form of a "chemical messenger" (sometimes called a neurotransmitter). This messenger is released by the sending neuron and is recognized by the receiving neuron. If the chemical message remains unchanged as it travels from cell to cell, the individual will experience the world as it really is.

But what happens if the receiving neuron doesn't recognize the message? Imagine a pitcher (the sending neuron) throwing a baseball (the chemical neurotransmitter) to a catcher (the receiving neuron). The catcher has a special glove designed to recognize and receive the baseball. The catcher's glove cannot receive any object that is significantly different from a baseball. It would immediately reject a basketball or a medicine ball. But what if the pitcher were to throw a lacrosse ball or a cricket ball or even a tennis ball? These objects have the right shape and size, but the wrong weight and texture. Still, if the imposter object were similar enough to the real thing, the catcher might be fooled into accepting it.

Sometimes, quite by coincidence, the chemical shape of a drug that enters the brain resembles the chemical shape of the brain's natural neurotransmitter. This confuses the receiving neuron, which mistakenly accepts the drug as part of the message being sent to it from the neuron ahead of it in the chain. Of course, this changes drastically the nature of the original message itself. This is how drugs of this sort cause individuals to experience things in a way that is different from reality.

Interfering with the way synaptic neurotransmission works is not unlike the results of the children's game "Broken Telephone." In this game, someone whispers a message into the ear of the first person in line: "The brown cow wore red shoes to work." The message is whispered from person to person, until the last person reveals what he or she believes the message to be. In this case, it might be "Green roses are always asleep." There's great laughter and amusement among the kids, which was the object of playing the game in the first place. This game is fun because it creates an illusion (an experience that differs from reality) and exploits the fact that experiencing things in a way that's different from reality is inherently amusing.

THE APPEAL OF A DIFFERENT REALITY

Knowing that drugs cause people to experience things in a way that is different from reality, we cannot overlook or trivialize the fact that for all too many people, reality is decidedly unpleasant. For those who wake up each day to a reality that includes poverty, depression, abuse, war, sexual harassment, or bullying, taking a drug that alters that reality can seem appealing. But these people are, in essence, medicating themselves. Professional help is warranted.

But imagine that someone needs to get an urgent message to you: "You have to go home right away! Your family is trapped in the house, and there's a gas leak. Only you can get in to save them! Please hurry!" But the person with the message can't find you, so he gives the message to someone else, who promises to give you the message right away. The first person's job is done—he's passed the baton. But what if the second person gives it to another person and that person gives to someone else, and it takes a dozen transmissions to finally get the message to you? And what if there's been a "broken telephone"? What if there's been a misunderstanding or interference? The message that reaches you is "Your family called. The gas company is sending an inspector later this evening and wanted to make sure you'd be there when he arrives."

There'd be no way you could ever know this was *not* the original message. This is what happens when a person is under the influence of LSD, magic mushrooms, or any other hallucinogenic drug. It's a virtual guarantee that the message *will* be distorted. In the case of the emergency message, your response to what you think is reality might prove disastrous in the real world. Remember:

1. Experiencing things different from reality is the single most common goal of the user of hallucinogenic drugs.
2. Experiencing things different from reality is how we define an illusion, and illusions are inherently pleasurable to the human brain.
3. Experiencing things different from reality inherently places the individual in a state of danger.

Marijuana: The Myth of the "Soft Drug" Debunked

Earlier, I listed some informal criteria that people use to identify (and rationalize) their use of what they believe is a "soft drug." That some people choose not to see marijuana as a chemical simply betrays ignorance. Like all drugs, marijuana is a chemical. The psychoactive *chemical* ingredient in marijuana is δ-9-tetrahydrocannabinol (THC). Let's revisit our list of "soft drug" criteria. *Remember, the following headings are what someone arguing that marijuana is safe might say:*

Myth: Marijuana Is Natural

If the person I'm debating still wants to impress me with his idiocy, he will usually say: "Yeah, well, okay. It's a chemical, but what I mean is it's a *natural* chemical, from *nature*." When I hear this, I usually reply, "From nature? You mean like cobra venom? Or arsenic? Or the paralyzing (plant) agent *curare*?" All those things are organic and from nature. No added artificial ingredients. And *naturally*, each will kill you.

Myth: Marijuana Is Not Psychologically Addictive

People often find comfort by trying to convince themselves that addiction to marijuana is not as serious as addiction to other drugs. They apply the term "psychological" in an effort to make it appear that the addicted person will not suffer any damage. One of my most important messages in this book is that the mind is nothing more than the subjective awareness of the working brain. Because of this, if a drug is psychologically addictive, it must, by definition, also be physically addictive. Marijuana use, like the use of many other drugs, does not always lead to addiction. And I do not believe that marijuana use necessarily leads to the use of other drugs. But two universally held criteria for addiction apply to marijuana: the development of tolerance, wherein the user needs more and more to get the same high; and the appearance of withdrawal symptom upon cessation of use.

As a clinician, I have had numerous clients present themselves for treatment of what they've acknowledged was an addiction to marijuana. They had tried to stop and assumed that they could whenever they wanted, but their efforts often resulted in relapse. Anyone who lives with a marijuana addict will readily tell you that the drug is addictive. The following words are from a 19-year-old. She was interviewed in *Maclean's* magazine for a 2004 article dealing with teenage problems:

> I was into marijuana really heavy until about a year and a half ago— It was really bad. … I couldn't go one day without having it. … I realized everything was going downhill for me and it wasn't going to get better—and I didn't want to be like that. So I stopped hanging around with that group of people and began going around with people who weren't doing it. I stayed at home a lot and barred myself in my room. It was very hard coming down. I couldn't sleep, and I'd get the shakes and crave it.

Myth: Marijuana Doesn't Impair Performance

One of the leading proponents for the legalization of marijuana in Canada has been reported to have said that it is "one of the most benign substances on this planet." He was then quoted as saying, "If you spend five minutes with a marijuana smoker, you know they'd never be able to rob banks. They can't get it together."

I believe he was trying to be funny. But the fact is that marijuana smokers really *can't* "get it together": they have difficulty sustaining attention to complex tasks and generally lack the motivation to carry them out. Since this is the case, should we really be comfortable depending on marijuana users to attend school, do their jobs, drive cars, operate industrial machinery, be good parents?

The following remarks were taken from the 1999 comprehensive review *The Health Effects of Cannabis* (Center for Addiction and Mental Health [Ontario] and the World Health Organization).

> With an increase in the prevalence of cannabis use among adolescents and young adults, there has been a growing concern about its possible impact on the psychological development of young people. This is important because of the possibly deleterious effects of such a psychoactive substance upon psychosocial adaptation and matu-

ration during their formative years, and the effects on cognition, learning and scholastic achievement. ... Users [of cannabis] were most impaired in their ability to learn from experience, their capacity for compromise, elaboration of adequate judgments and situational adaptation, and organizational, verbal and communication skills. Many of these abilities are thought to be under the control of the [pre-] frontal lobes.

In other words, it's official. Marijuana users really can't "get it together." The next time your kids tell you that marijuana doesn't affect them, ask them why the World Health Organization (WHO) would say that it does. Is the WHO just making these findings up? Let the WHO be your experts and ask your kids who their experts are. After all, we've seen that beliefs are often held without the benefit of any empirical evidence to support them. When empirical evidence supports a different or opposing belief, an intelligent, mature person will drop the erroneous belief and adopt the one supported by the evidence—at least until new evidence is presented to the contrary.

Another thing to consider when talking about marijuana's effects on performance is that it stays in the body a lot longer than you might think. You don't feel "high" for more than a few hours after a typical dose, but three or four days later, the drug that remains might still be affecting your short-term memory.

CASE STUDY

Teddy was 16. He smoked weed on the weekends. He was a reasonably good student. He had a girlfriend and a decent family life. He played basketball for the school team. His family and his girlfriend didn't really like that he smoked dope so regularly, but he felt it was harmless, and they couldn't convince him since they weren't aware that it was affecting him in subtle ways:

• He studied for his math exam on Wednesday evening. He thought he knew the material, but he couldn't remember it on Thursday and did quite badly in the exam.

- He forgot that he'd promised his mother that he'd meet his little sister at her piano class after school on Tuesday. His mother and sister were upset with him. His mom told him she couldn't trust him.

- His girlfriend was upset because he'd agreed to take her to a movie for her birthday, but when the birthday came, he'd invited some friends over to help celebrate. His girlfriend wondered whether he respected her wishes after he'd promised one thing and then forgotten it.

- His girlfriend was upset with him when she brought her parents to see him play in a basketball game. He ended up on the bench because he couldn't remember the play sequences, and the coach felt he couldn't count on him.

When his girlfriend tried to talk to him about all this, he wasn't interested because she insisted that this might be related to how much marijuana he smoked. She might not have known the exact physiological basis for it, but she was quite correct. His weakened short-term memory was affecting his schooling, his social life, and his family life. After a while, his girlfriend told him that since he was so good at forgetting things, he might as well forget about being her boyfriend, too. She couldn't count on him, and trust is essential for family and friendship ties.   ■

Myth: Marijuana Doesn't Present Any Personal or Public Health Risks

Here's what Dr. Donald Tashkin wrote in *The Health Effects of Cannabis*:

Cannabis yields many of the same smoke contents as tobacco, including respiratory tract irritants and carcinogens.

The tar phase of the smoke of marijuana has about 50% more of some of the carcinogens than a comparable quantity of unfiltered tobacco.

… marijuana smoking, particularly if continued over several years, has a significant deleterious effect on chronic respiratory symptoms and ventilatory function that is at least as great [as], or greater in magnitude than, the effect of regular cigarette smoking.

... habitual smoking of marijuana may be an important risk factor for the development of respiratory tract malignancy.

Malignancy means cancer. People die from cancer. Yet we often hear that marijuana is safe because you can't die from using it. No wonder our kids, parents, and politicians are confused! What's going on? The answer lies in what scientists call the "safety margin" of a drug. This compares the amount of a drug a person takes to feel a "desired effect," such as getting high to the amount of that same drug they would have to take in order to kill themselves by overdose. Obviously, if that "lethal" dose were much higher than the "effective dose," the drug would be deemed "overdose safe." Here's what I mean. Say a kid needs to smoke half a joint to get high. Once high, he'll stop smoking, and, if he wants to continue the experience, he'll start again only when he feels the desired effect begin to wear off. If he'd have to smoke 30 joints to die by overdose, it's highly unlikely he'll do that, so marijuana can be considered "overdose safe."

This is complicated by two important factors:

■ The potency of marijuana has risen significantly in the decades since the 1960s. So the user might not be aware that he surpasses the "desired" dosage before it's too late and the drug exerts a much more toxic effect than the user anticipated.
■ The user can never be certain whether non active and potentially harmful chemicals have been added to the product he's consuming.

But even if the product were pure marijuana, and even if it were "overdose safe," it is still not proper to refer to marijuana, per se, as safe. After all, have you ever heard of anyone dying of a tobacco cigarette overdose? No, because you'd have to smoke several packs of cigarettes all at once in order to die that way. And no one does. But how would you feel if someone told your kids that cigarettes are really safe, and that no one has ever died from tobacco smoking? I can't decide which would be the worst part of such "misinformation," the ignorance or the deceit.

The health risks of marijuana are not in dispute. It is for political reasons (the fact that so many people, including people of influence, smoke and enjoy marijuana) that there is a systematic ignorance of its harmfulness. Why are we shocked to hear this and averse to accepting it?

Myth: Marijuana Doesn't Present Any Personal or Public Safety Risks

In a recent conversation with a dedicated marijuana user, I asked if she thought that the substance impaired timing and memory. She said, "Of course it does." I then asked if she thought marijuana impaired driving. She said, "Of course it does." I asked her if she drove while under the influence of marijuana and she said that she did. I was dumbfounded. She explained that the impairment caused by marijuana made her, if anything, a safer driver because she drove more slowly and was less aggressive.

Dr. Alison Smiley admits that slower speeds and less aggressive driving do tend to occur when one is under marijuana's influence. She wrote the following in *The Health Effects of Cannabis* (1999):

> … in terms of car control measures, marijuana appears to induce more conservative behavior, that is lower speeds, in order to offset the effects of feeling impaired. In contrast, alcohol appeared to induce higher speeds, that is, more risky behavior.

So my dope-smoking friend was right! Or was she? Dr. Smiley went on to write that this more conservative behavior behind the wheel was seen only in certain, more predictable driving situations. She said that because the user knows she is impaired, she is usually able to compensate when she knows a response will be required. Dr. Smiley went on to say that "such compensation is not possible, however, where events are unexpected or where continuous attention is required." (p. 188)

Let's see if I've got this straight. Marijuana smokers are dangerous only when they are required to be able to respond to *unexpected situations* or when they are required to pay *continuous attention* to their driving! I'm sorry, but I don't find this comforting at all. In my experience, driving *always* demands being ready for unexpected situations and driving *always* requires continuous attention. Even the most vocal advocates for the legalization of marijuana (The National Organization for the Reform of Marijuana Laws—NORML) say publicly that "the responsible cannabis consumer does not operate a motor vehicle or other dangerous machinery while impaired by cannabis. ..."

Too bad this message doesn't seem to be getting through.

Myth: Doctors Prescribe Marijuana

The medical communities of several countries, including Canada, are currently looking into marijuana's possible medical benefits for people suffering from cancer, AIDS, and other disorders. Specifically, marijuana is considered helpful in many instances for its antinausea and other properties, which can bring relief *to people suffering and dying from terrible diseases*. We know that most of the drugs doctors give sick people would never be considered safe or desirable in healthy, young individuals; marijuana is no different.

In summary, marijuana does not meet our criteria for a "soft drug." Parents must bring this reality to their arguments when discussing their concerns with their teenagers.

Here are some other arguments presented by the defenders of the "soft drug" identity of marijuana. The Netherlands decriminalized, *but did not legalize*, the possession of small amounts of marijuana for personal use more than a quarter of a century ago, and Canada has proposed to do the same thing in 2005. This does not mean that marijuana is harmless. Speeding in your car is not considered a criminal act, but it is both dangerous and illegal. If you speed and are caught, you will be fined and possibly given demerit points that will apply to future violations. If you are an unrepentant and repetitive speeder, you may have your license removed or you may even be sent to jail.

The movement to decriminalize marijuana may be interpreted by those who are ignorant as a sign that the drug is relatively harmless. Instead, it is an effort to deal more efficiently and fairly with those who might otherwise unfairly suffer the life-long consequences of a criminal record. Marijuana is still illegal because it is toxic and addictive. It cannot be considered a safe substance.

Marijuana and Retrogression

Remember our discussion of retrogression in Chapter 7? It can apply to drug use as well.

CASE STUDY

Two friends got summer jobs in the same company. Rob was a nice guy, but his intellectual potential (his IQ was average) was lower than his friend Jennifer's (whose IQ was well above average). One night, they shared a (marijuana) joint. The next day at work, their boss asked each of them to complete a complex set of duties:

- She asked Rob to go to the receiving department, pick up a package for the print department, deliver it there, and pick up a set of copies for her. On the way back to her office, Rob was to stop at the cafeteria and get her a coffee with one cream and one sugar.
- She also asked Jennifer to go to the receiving department and pick up a package. This one was for the Human Resources office. She was to drop off the package and pick up some application forms for her to inspect. On the way back to her office, Jennifer was to get the boss a prune Danish.

Jennifer completed her task perfectly, but Rob forgot some of the details and didn't complete his assignment. Unfortunately, this was not the first time this had happened. Rob lost his job.   ■

Rob was the victim of retrogression. The short-term memory impairment induced by the marijuana the two had smoked the night before had a more serious impact on Rob, who was the less intelligent of the two. With his lower IQ, he really needed to keep his job. Jennifer was going to go on to university and the job was just a way to earn extra money.

Retrogression, in this case, meant that the person who was in the weaker position to withstand the effects of marijuana was the one most seriously hurt by it. This is a crucial concept, because from watching very successful people who appear to use marijuana with impunity, many young people get the idea that marijuana is harmless. They cite cases of rock stars and movie stars and star athletes or top-level business and social leaders who smoke marijuana. They believe that if those people can smoke dope and still succeed, they can too. The trouble is that those people are the strongest and most able to withstand the impact of the dope on their brains. That's why they rise to the top and are so visible. But the vastly more numerous weaker segments of the population are not so fortunate. They are weakened by marijuana and, of course, because they are less visible, their failures go unnoticed.

The same is true for so many other socially harmful things: gambling, divorce, mental illness, peer pressure, etc. People who are in the weakest position to withstand negative social pressures, and can least afford their impact, are the very ones who usually succumb most to those pressures.

Central Nervous System Stimulants

The ability to experience pleasure seems to depend on the biochemical balance in certain brain systems. These systems were identified by Canadian scientists in 1954. Using rats as subjects, they inserted tiny metal electrodes into their brains. Through these electrodes, the scientists were able to deliver tiny electrical currents directly to the rats' brains. When the rats recovered from the surgery and resumed their "normal" activities, they gave every appearance of absolutely loving the feeling whenever the scientists stimulated their brains. In fact, when given the opportunity to do so (by turning on a switch in their cages), the rats learned to deliver the current to themselves; they delivered this stimulation to their own brains repeatedly for hours.

The reward they evidently experienced from this stimulation was so powerful that the rats devoted all their attention to delivering it. During such episodes, they might even ignore food and become so thin and weak that unless the scientists stopped the experiment (which they did), the rats would have died of starvation! This showed how powerful the activation of the brain's reward mechanism is. This has three very significant implications for humans:

1. **Depression:** The experiment may have identified areas that allowed people to experience pleasure. If people could not experience pleasure

(one of the important concomitants of depression), maybe it was because this area of the brain was not functioning correctly.

2. **Learning:** The experiment may have identified areas of the brain that are active and reinforce desired behaviors when people learn. If people have problems with learning, maybe it was because this area of the brain was broken or missing.

3. **Addiction:** It may have identified areas of the brain that were activated by certain drugs of abuse.

Drugs like cocaine, amphetamines, and ecstasy induce the brain's reward systems to unnaturally heightened levels of activity. As with laboratory rats that ignore food and become moribund if given the chance to deliver electrical current to these parts of their brains, people will regularly sacrifice health and even life itself in order to maintain their use of cocaine or other stimulants. While the nicotine in tobacco products does not elicit the same euphoria as those other drugs, it is still classed as a stimulant, and tobacco smokers are perfect examples of people who knowingly risk and lose their lives because of their need to deliver nicotine to their brains.

Many people think that the only danger of smoking comes from the tar and its effects on the lungs. However, there are many poisons in tobacco smoke, and these affect others organs too, including the heart.

Another major danger of smoking is the nicotine itself. This is a psychoactive, highly addictive drug. As with other stimulants, when nicotine enters the brain, it initiates a process related to what psychologists call "arousal."

The Allure of Arousal

Arousal is what we feel when something important is either happening or about to happen. The arousing situation might be a good or pleasant thing, such as the anticipation of playing in a championship game, or getting ready to start university, or having sex with a much desired partner. It could also be bad such as being lost in a dangerous neighborhood, or having to confess to a crime, or not feeling capable of meeting an obligation.

Regardless of the good or bad quality of the situation, psychologists refer to this as "stress," and within the brain, stress causes the body to respond in what has come to be known as the "fight or flight" mode. Changes to our blood pressure, heart rate, vigilance, and glandular secretions such as perspiration are all geared to allowing us to respond best to the situation.

Here is where personality and temperament play big roles. Some individuals are optimists. They have strong characters, and they react to stress as though it were a challenge to be overcome. In an arousing situation, they get "psyched up," and this heightened level of arousal usually results in optimal performance.

Other people are pessimists. They react to stress as though it were a threat, and they become fearful. When they become aroused, they get "psyched out," and the heightened level of arousal results in lowered performance. Of course, different people will see the same thing in different ways. Even optimists might become fearful and get "psyched out" when they see that the arousing situation was much more threatening than they had originally believed.

Nicotine, caffeine, cocaine, and amphetamines all create bodily conditions that are similar to those seen when arousal occurs (hence the term "stimulant"). As I have said, at low doses, especially in individuals who like to be in arousing situations, this might be very pleasant, and even beneficial to their performance. But these drugs are all highly addictive; regardless of their initially pleasant effects, they tend be used in increasing dosages and frequency. This changes the initially pleasant aspects of arousal into the more negative ones.

Long-term use of stimulants, including tobacco, generates irritability, sleep problems, appetite problems, and a moodiness or jumpiness that can interfere with performance in a number of areas: academic, athletic, artistic, and social.

If you yourself are a smoker or have been, you know only too well how difficult it can be to stop. This will likely make you more sympathetic to your teen than a nonsmoker can be! But you can use this experience to help your teen—though what worked for you may not work for your teen. The important thing is to get started on a program to stop smoking.

What Parents Can Do

Dealing with drug use, or potential drug use, is perhaps a parent's worst nightmare. Scared for the safety of our children, both now and in the future, we run the risk of resorting to threats and blame. By now, you should know that this type of approach will get you nothing but trouble. So what can a parent do? Lots.

Be Prepared to Admit Your Own Errors

Many parents used drugs during their own teenage years; many did not. Many of those who did use drugs found the experience to be benign and even rewarding. Others found the drugs to be injurious to their emotional or physical well-being. Regardless of the parental experience, it is rare to find a mom or dad today who is comfortable with their kids' use of drugs. The difficulty for those who did use, of course, is that they run the risk of being called hypocrites when they warn their own children against drug use. But that label is neither accurate nor fair. A hypocrite says people ought to act one way, and then acts in a contrary way himself. Recognizing the errors of your past and being afraid when you see someone about to repeat them is not hypocrisy. It's simply changing your mind (your belief) on the basis of newer, more credible empirical evidence.

I once went on one of those Hollywood movie studio tours. An entire wall of the studio lobby was filled with glamorous shots of movie stars from the 1930s and 1940s. Many peered provocatively at the camera through a stream of smoke coming from the cigarette posed artfully in their hand or mouth. Clearly, in those days, smoking was seen as classy and benign. Even after Humphrey Bogart died from smoking-induced lung cancer, people refused to accept the harmful realities of smoking.

Think of other hazardous things that we once thought were safe: asbestos, radium watch dials, X-ray machines in shoe stores, opium (or laudanum). While no one would argue that smoking is a thing of the past, tobacco is now widely recognized as harmful, and smoking tobacco is no longer publicly acceptable, let alone admirable or sexy. Moreover, no one calls ex-smokers hypocrites when they advise their kids not to pick up the habit. So don't fall into that trap when your kids ask if you tried drugs. Be honest. Tell them that you did, and that you didn't know how dangerous it was. Now you do.

Recognize the Attraction

Rather than make your kids feel stupid or ashamed for being attracted to drugs, let them know that you understand their attraction. In fact, there are three very powerful reasons teenagers use drugs. If parents can't acknowledge these reasons, we risk losing credibility in our concern:

1. **Drugs feel good:** If drugs didn't feel good, no one would use them. Everyone wants to feel good, whether because it eases anxiety or simply provides euphoria. It's worth remembering that there's nothing shameful or abnormal about this attraction.
2. **"Everybody" uses drugs:** Normative, empirical estimates suggest that the majority of teenagers do *not* use drugs—but it can sure seem to your teenager that "everyone" is using. Again, it's not abnormal or wrong to want to be part of the group.
3. **Curiosity:** I wrote earlier about how curiosity—the need to know— is such a powerful and normal human motivator. Let your kids know that you aren't blaming or shaming them for their curiosity.

Having acknowledged the attraction of drugs, parents now must provide the other side of the argument. You must convince your teen that once he puts drugs into his body, he is placing himself in a situation where there will, indeed, be a "price to pay," whether he wants to or not. The best thing you can do is make sure your child knows what that price is. Unfortunately, however, many parents and their kids do not know those costs. That can and must be remedied.

But what if the kids know the costs? After all, not too many tobacco smokers can feign ignorance. The sad truth is that people often keep doing something even when they know the dangers. This can mean one of three things:

■ They do not believe the bad thing will happen to them.
■ They don't want the bad thing to happen, but they are willing to pay the price because they are desperate for the pleasure and escape.
■ They want the bad thing to happen.

The first reason is fairly common and can be dealt with via good, democratic parenting. The second and third options point to the need for professional intervention.

Educate Yourself

To illustrate the possible dangers of drugs to your teenagers, ask them what they think would happen if they went into a store to buy a computer and pretended not to know anything. They'll probably say that the salesperson would try to take advantage of their ignorance, lie to them, and cheat them. Now ask your kids what they think a drug dealer would do when he discovered they don't know anything about drugs. Your kids will quickly recognize that knowledge is their best protection.

Educate yourselves, and demand that your kids also get a good education on this topic. This means reading and researching. Make sure your kid has all the facts. Although it's difficult, try to keep the emotional aspect of your concerns and fears in the background—though your teens must know that you *are* concerned. By knowing how drugs affect the brain, as discussed above, you are already better informed than your teen! Share this information with your kids.

Earlier in this chapter, I included some quotations from the book *The Health Effects of Cannabis*. I did that so you'd have at least two expert sources (this book is the other) to back up your arguments about drugs being harmful. When I'm talking to teenagers about drugs and they insist that a drug like marijuana is really safe and even benign, I ask where they got their information. Usually, they say that "this guy" told them. I wish I could meet "this guy"! He's pretty elusive, though, because wherever I go—Toronto, Chicago, Laguna Beach, Miami—"this guy" has always been there ahead of me. I ask them where "this guy" got his Ph.D. and how he gets his information. This often brings to light a few articles that were "downloaded from the Internet." I explain to them that virtually anybody can have virtually anything published on the Internet. My information, on the other hand, is derived from professional scientific investigations, published in refereed scientific journals. The results are both valid and reliable.

When their arguments are challenged in this way, kids may become frustrated. Voices may rise and doors may slam. But if parents present their evidence in a context of concern and even fear for their kids' health and safety, the impact will be more effective than if the context results in making the kids feel stupid. Parents faced with opposition may have to back off a bit, but at least they can be sure that their concerns were heard. For the kids' part, their job will have been made clearer: to make their parents feel "safer."

Recognize the Symptoms of Drug Abuse

Regardless of the reason(s) behind a teenager's drug use, the starting point for parents is to find out what they are dealing with. How can you tell whether your child is using drugs, and if so, is it a "normal" experimentation or a serious case of abuse or addiction? It can be hard sometimes to distinguish between the everyday ups and downs of the normal adolescent and the changed behavior of the drug-using adolescent. There are some signals you can watch for, though.

▌ **Performance:** Be alert to a dramatic deterioration in any of the following areas of your teen's life: academic, occupational, athletic, artistic, ethical. If your straight A daughter starts to bring home D's or your basketball star son ends up benched three games in a row, pay attention.

▌ **Use by friends:** If you know your teen's friends are using drugs, the chances are good your teen is using drugs too. You may think that because your teen is up front with you about his friends' use of drugs and assures you "But I don't do it," you're being told the truth. Don't be so sure. And it's almost never true when kids tell you that the drugs you found in their drawer or in the garage were not theirs, but that they were only holding them for a friend.

■ **Secretiveness, need for money:** Taken together, these are classic warning signs. What parents might identify as secretiveness on its own could well be a teen trying to claim some space for herself and to mark out her own territory, and that should be respected. But when it goes hand in hand with a new need for money—especially when there is no related purchase such as a new pair of jeans or a new CD—you should go on high alert.

■ **Defense of a known drug user:** The debate over the decriminalization of marijuana is quite open these days. If your teenager is talking about this in general terms, that is probably a sign of a healthy interest in the topic. This is different from strongly defending drug use in general, or a given individual's use of the drug. Use your judgment. If she becomes hostile or defensive when the topic comes up it can be a warning sign that she's rationalizing her own drug use. Use your new knowledge about the myths of marijuana (above) to engage your kids in the debate.

■ **Mood swings:** Teenagers are notorious for mood swings. They can reflect any number of things from social pressures to love. Trust your gut on this one. Nobody knows your kids better than you. If you think something unusual is going on, show them that you see this and that you care. Make it clear that you are ready to talk about even the most personal and difficult of topics—and that you are prepared to intervene in their lives if needed. For example, if they are being bullied, you can speak to someone at school. If they have emotional problems, you can set them up with a confidential counselor or therapist. By avoiding the stigmas of blame and shame, you give your kids a chance to open up and discuss these things safely.

Get at the Root of the Problem

It's pretty obvious that people take drugs to change how they feel. But there is an equally compelling reason that teens take drugs: to change how they look—and I'm not talking about their bodily features. I'm referring to their social "image," or how they look to their friends or those they want to impress. When a 12-year-old girl decides to try a drug with her peers, it might be that she simply wants to appear cool so as to be accepted in that group. The powerful need for acceptance in a peer society can often override an individual's better judgment or the morals they learned in their familial society. It's important not to trivialize this need when you're discussing issues concerning drugs with your teen.

CASE STUDY

Tim was 14. His parents came to see me after they smelled smoke on his clothing. They told me they had confronted him with their suspicions. At first, he denied it, claiming that he'd been in a smoky room with his friends. His parents gave him the benefit of the doubt. Even when they discovered the cigarettes in his jacket pocket (and he said he was just "holding them" for one of his friends), his parents weren't sure what to believe. But when a friend called to say that she had spotted Tim smoking with some kids outside a shopping mall, they knew they had to do something.

With my help, they decided not to come down hard on Tim but, rather, to approach the matter democratically. The first order of business was to agree on their goals. At the outset, Tim's dad took what might be called a harm-reduction approach. Since he couldn't be with Tim every moment of the day, he expected Tim at least to respect the family by never smoking in or around their home. He also expected Tim to give an accounting of where his allowance was going, because he was not prepared to finance his son's smoking habit. Tim's mom took an abstinence approach. Regardless of where, when, or on whose budget Tim was smoking, she wanted it to stop. She argued (and I agreed with her) that her husband's approach would send the wrong message—that it was all right for Tim to smoke as long as it wasn't on their property or costing them any money. I told them that Tim needed to understand that they would not be comfortable with his smoking under any circumstances.

Next, they did some research. They got statistics from the federal government's department of health to get their facts straight. As a result, they were able to counter the following pro-smoking arguments:

1. *"I won't get sick. I'm only going to smoke for a few years. I won't get hooked; I'll stop before any real damage is done."* Nicotine is a highly addictive drug, and it is never easy to quit. Even before things like cancer and heart disease kick in, the lowering of oxygen capacity by the inhalation of various gases in cigarette smoke is a significant threat to athletic, artistic, and academic endurance.

2. *"It's a free world. It's my body, and if I get sick it's my problem, not yours."* In Canada, about 45,000 people die annually from smoking-related diseases. If the cost of hospitalizing and treating one of those 45,000 people were approximately $1,000 per day, that translates to 45,000 times 1,000, or $45 million a day! At those prices, I'll never agree that it's Tim's "right" to smoke. The truth is, it's not a "free country" if doing what you want impinges on the freedoms of others. As long as taxpayers are footing the bill for the treatment of smokers' diseases, Tim's smoking is everyone's problem.

3. *"I'm only hurting myself."* Tim's parents read a story about a mom who came home after work one day at about 5 p.m. Her seven-year-old son usually ran to greet her, but he didn't do that on this day. She knew he was home because his things were in the hallway. She went upstairs to his bedroom. The door was (uncharacteristically) closed, and she heard her son crying. When she opened the door, he shoved his head under his pillow. "What's wrong?" she asked. "You're going to die!" he sobbed. "No!" she said. "Why do you say that?" "Because you smoke! A doctor came to my school today and showed us a gross picture of what smoking does to your lungs and he said that people who smoke die." The mom had only one choice. She quit smoking then and there. This story gave Tim's parents a way to convey to their son how much his smoking hurt those around him.

4. *"It relaxes me."* As I said, the use of stimulants—including tobacco—results in irritability, sleep irregularities, and moodiness or jumpiness. These symptoms become exaggerated when the drug begins to leave the body (withdrawal). By taking more of the drug into the body when withdrawal is inducing irritability, the smoker does create a momentary relaxation. But the key word is "momentary." The moodiness is bound to return, which perpetuates the addictive cycle. Tim's parents now had a potent argument. They pointed out that he had

been making judgmental errors and losing his cool more on the play-ing field since the smoking started. Given how passionate Tim was about his athletic performance, this was an extremely relevant exam-ple of how the harmful effects of smoking go well beyond a far-off threat of cancer or heart disease.

5. *"It's cool to smoke."* Very few people report that smoking tobacco makes them feel good physically. In fact, increased use of the stimu-lant nicotine generally makes the smoker feel more and more anxious. So it must be that holding a cigarette makes a kid think that others will see him in a way he wants and hopes to be seen. And that way is "cool." This makes that cigarette a sort of camouflage or a mask—a "cool mask." Tim's parents could now ask their son, "Who puts on a mask, and why?" Masks are meant to hide our true features. Would an obese person put on a costume that makes her look obese? Would a bald person wear a disguise that makes him look bald? Would a person who is already cool need to put something on that makes her appear to be cool? Because they knew their son better than anyone else in the world, they knew that his smoking was, at least in part, derived from low self-esteem. So they didn't say, "Who do you think you're fooling? All you look like is an uncool kid trying to look cool." Instead, they spoke of how they were aware that to him, look-ing cool with his peers was obviously very important. And if he had started smoking and been willing to get into such trouble over it with the people he loved most, it could only mean that Tim must feel genuinely uncool without it. They used that knowledge to their advantage by communicating with him about how he felt about himself. And they pointed out the ways in which he really was cool, not just with them, but with his peers, too.

By combining these arguments with their consistent message about how much his smoking scared and hurt them, Tim's parents brought him around to the realization that what he got out of smoking was not worth the price he'd have to pay. ■

10 The Big Three, Part III: Relationships, Intimacy, and Sex

The need to connect with other people is fundamental to the human condition. Moreover, we all recognize that sexuality is a normal and healthy part of being human. Parents genuinely want their teenagers to develop safe and healthy attitudes and practices about sex. Perhaps it's more accurate to say that while parents want their kids to enjoy sex as adults, they don't want them to have sex as teenagers. Many parents fear that by admitting to their kids that they want them to have good and healthy sexual experiences, they will encourage them to become sexually active at too young an age. I can assure you that talking to your kids about sex from an early age does not lead to increased sexual behavior, and certainly not to unsafe sexual behavior.

Although North American popular culture appears to have sanctioned early sex, there does not seem to be any corresponding increase in the longevity of relationships or in emotional security levels among our youth. Indeed, we hear more and more about the emotional dissatisfaction that goes with being unattached. Popular media never glorify the single life. The most popular characters in movies or on television are always looking for that "perfect" relationship, and casual sex doesn't appear to be satisfying to anybody except the clownish caricatures depicted in sitcoms and "reality" dating shows.

The Foundations of a Healthy Sexual Journey

I believe that today's frenetic urgency to connect is the direct result of the very popular but very damaging impact of casual sexuality on a young person's social and emotional development. I believe this is because the sexuality that our kids see around them is often portrayed without the benefit of context. That is, healthy foundations are not in place when most kids begin their sexual journeys. Nor, in my opinion, are these foundations regularly introduced to teenagers (or adults, for that matter) in standard sex education classes. Those curricula focus on the easier matters of anatomy, physiology, and safety. Please don't misunderstand. Those issues are important and must be addressed. But without the foundations I am about to discuss, teenagers will be poorly prepared for the voyage. These foundations are ethics, intimacy, commitment, sensuality, and passion.

Ethics and Morality

Unlike "moral" behavior, which changes across generations and cultures, ethical behavior remains constant (see Chapter 6). Ethics can be best understood in terms of the "Golden Rule," which encourages us to treat others as we would be treated ourselves. In the 21st century, we consider many things to be moral that would have been considered immoral a few decades ago. When I'm giving a lunchtime talk to a group of women, for example, I point out that the entire exercise would have been considered scandalous at the beginning of the 20th century. Here I am, a married man, speaking behind closed doors to married women. Many of the husbands of these women do not know where their wives are at that moment. The women are often clad in skirts that previous generations would have considered much too short, or else in pants, which would have been considered unacceptable. In many of the cases, the women are wearing makeup and have dyed their hair to make themselves more sexually attractive. All this was once considered to be the mark of depravity. Yet, today, this situation is considered to be completely moral by most members of our society.

The morality of the society in which each generation grows up is not the same as the one in which their parents grew up. Our kids will have to live and work in their own society, just as our generation lives and works by the morals we have created. By keeping the moral rules of their parents' society, today's kids might have to break the moral rules of their own society. And they would do that at great risk, since they face the possibility of being rejected by a society whose rules they refuse to keep.

Ethics is another matter, however. How your teen treats his or her partner is part of an ethical issue. If you find it difficult to enter into the discussion of sex, you might have an easier time discussing ethics. Ask your kids how they would feel if their partners

- cheated on them
- refused to practice safe sex
- had no respect for them
- never communicated how they were feeling
- were dishonest about their feelings or behaviors

Of course, these are rhetorical questions, focused on eliciting feelings of empathy. When your teenager says that she *wouldn't* like it if her partner did these things, explain that she should remember that if she hopes to have ethical and successful relationships. There's no need to preach or take a "holier-than-thou" approach. In fact, you can relate some examples of your own unethical relating, and tell of the harm that was done as a consequence. This has the desired effect of avoiding the need to blame kids for what is merely normal and human; only in this case, "normal and human" acts are also unethical and hurtful.

We know that teenagers have always acted in ways that provoke their parents. This is part of their effort to establish their own generational cultural identities. What's most important to remember is that what parents may consider immoral about dress codes is not immoral within the generational normality of the kids themselves. The worst mistake parents can make is to impugn the morality of their kids.

CASE STUDY

Aaron was a 17-year-old high school student who lived with his parents and younger sister. In the summer he worked as a camp counselor. At the camp, he met Samantha, a 20-year-old drama instructor who attended university in a city in another part of the country. The two fell in love and began a romance that quickly became sexual.

When summer ended, the two decided that, despite the difficulty, they would try to remain a couple. They corresponded regularly, and when the first opportunity presented itself, Aaron (at his own expense) arranged a short visit to Samantha's city.

Aaron's parents knew their son was staying with and having sex with the young woman in her home. They were somewhat apprehensive about it, but felt they could not stop their son from traveling to see his girlfriend. The trip went quite well, and Aaron returned home safe and sound.

Just prior to the next school break, Aaron announced to his parents that Samantha would be visiting him. Although nothing was said at the time, it was clear that Aaron and Samantha intended to sleep together in Aaron's room. In the morality of their society, this was acceptable behavior. In that of Aaron's parents, however, it was not. They told Aaron they could not allow the two of them to sleep together in their house and implied that it was immoral of them to want to do so. Aaron and Samantha felt this attitude was hypocritical, since the parents were aware of the nature of the relationship and had accepted it when the couple was in Samantha's home. Because neither side was able to see beyond the morality of their own generation, a satisfactory resolution in the higher "court" of ethics could not be found. Samantha felt insulted, demeaned, and unwanted. She cut short her visit with Aaron and never felt comfortable around his parents again. The relationship ended soon after. ∎

The problem here, of course, has to do with the confusion between morality and ethics. Aaron's parents should have realized that the young people were behaving in an entirely moral way, as defined by their own generation. Unfortunately, this generational morality went against their own generational morality and the moral climate in which Aaron had been raised. In keeping the rules of his generation, Aaron had little choice but to break the rules of his parents' generation. His parents should have been sensitive to this. While they were certainly within their rights to speak of their pain and anger, they should not have labeled the young couple as immoral.

For their part, Aaron and Samantha should have shown the sort of maturity that adults expect from people who think they are old enough to have sex. They should have realized the discomfort to which they were subjecting Aaron's parents. Knowing that they would not want to be put in such an uncomfortable position in an analogous situation, Aaron and Samantha should have seen their behavior as unethical. They should have raised the matter with Aaron's parents before assuming it was all right for them to sleep together in his parents' home. It is my opinion that in this case—and in every case, for that matter—"golden rule" ethics, which are higher in the hierarchy of rules than ever-changing morality, should have taken precedence. Morality should never have been brought into the equation. Aaron and Samantha should have offered to sleep in separate rooms in order to comply with the dictates of ethics.

What if a similar situation comes up in your own home? Here's a practical and successful way to approach the problem.

1. **Empathy:** Start by revisiting the Babysitting Analogy from Chapter 3. Remind your teen that she would be able to see dangers that her younger charge cannot see. This demonstrates to teens that their own behaviors can seem dangerous to more experienced parents.
2. **Empirical support:** Follow your expression of empathy with the empirical evidence that you've collected in your research of the matter.
3. **Ethics:** Use the principle of ethics versus morality. To a teenager with an emerging abstract brain, these principles ought to bring the discussion to a respectful and fruitful resolution.
4. **Behavioral modification:** If your son or daughter doesn't seem to "get" that they are making you uncomfortable, or if they seem not to care, they have probably not yet reached the maturity that comes with abstract thought. In such cases, no amount of talking will change things, and it might be necessary to invoke strict behavioral rules of positive and negative reinforcement.

Commitment

The term "commitment" has several different meanings in the English language. It can mean a promise to do something. It can mean that your personal freedom is taken away (you are committed to an institution, for example). It can also mean going beyond a point of no return—by committing yourself to a course of action, you are losing control.

You cannot be in a "committed" relationship unless you are prepared to accept that all these meanings apply to your relationship. You give a promise, you lose a certain amount of freedom, and you give over some control to your partner. These are ideas that kids can understand and apply to presexual or nonsexual relationships. Once they understand the concept, they have a huge advantage when the time comes to commit to a romantic, sexual relationship.

How do you help your teens understand this crucial concept? Talk to them about the meaning of a promise. If you and your spouse are separated or divorced, your kid may wonder why two people made a solemn promise—wedding vows—to each other if they couldn't keep it in the end. Here are some questions you can pose that will get your kids thinking about what "commitment" means to them. If you can make these questions more applicable to your kids' actual lives, then do so:

▌ Why do people break certain promises? Is it because they never meant to keep them, or is it that they really didn't know what they were getting into?

▌ If you play in a band and the band gets a job playing at a local coffee shop, you'd feel great. But what if another band that is better than yours asks you to join them? And what if they practice when you are supposed to be playing with your old band at the coffee shop? How does this relate to not being free, or to not being able to control the circumstances of your life?

Ask your kids what is the ethical thing to do in each of these cases. It would be best if they could see, without any prompting, how these situations apply to themselves, since that would be the optimal way for them to incorporate the appropriate message. If they do not see this on their own, give them some timely hints until they seem to grasp the meanings of commitment and how this applies to all areas of life.

Intimacy

A person under attack will cover up, usually by adopting a fetal position. This is an instinct that results in the protection of the body's most vulnerable parts: face, throat, abdomen, and genitals, some of which many people call the "private parts." We expose our private physical parts only to those we believe will not hurt us. In that respect, sexual intimacy must find its basis in trust.

The same is true of emotional intimacy. We all have what we could call private *emotional* parts: fears, angers, loves, hatreds, etc. They are true parts of ourselves, yet we keep them hidden from everyone, except those with whom we have our most intimate relationships. That is because we are confident of not being hurt—in other words, we trust. *The strongest obstacle to good relationships is the inability or unwillingness to trust.* This is especially true if trust has been betrayed in the past. Yet in order to move forward, people must learn to trust all over again. This, by definition, involves risk. To reinforce this, just remind yourselves that the words "intimacy" and "intimidate" come from the same derivative, having to do with getting "under one's skin" (the inner parts of which are called the "intima"). How is trust re-established after it has been broken? The first step is for the person who has lost trust to give up their anger and pain.

In Chapter 4, I discussed the question of apology. I said that many people require an apology from the person who hurt them in order to be able to forgive them. But what if the apology doesn't come? Or isn't sincere when it does come? Can the person who was hurt still forgive? The answer is this: They *must* forgive. They can do so by abandoning their need to establish who started it. They must take responsibility for their own contribution to their pain. Talking to your teen about trust can be especially difficult if a divorce has taken place in the family. All the people involved, adults as well as children, may well be wary about trusting. Discussing this openly and honestly, even though it may stir up feelings of hurt and anger, is the only option.

In Chapter 4, I discussed the issue of re-establishing a child's trust in their parents following a divorce. The appropriate response for a parent to the "but you got divorced" accusation is dependent on the emotional and cognitive maturity of the child or teenager in question. It also depends strongly on the parent-child relationship and their mutual comfort with intimate discussion.

Sexual intimacy is, of course, a healthy part of a romantic relationship. But it is only the tip of the iceberg. The rest of the iceberg deals with the sort of intimacy that characterizes all the other relationships we have— with friends, business partners, roommates, siblings, and so forth. Talking to kids about the concept of intimacy in a nonsexual context prepares them for the sexual context when the appropriate time comes.

CASE STUDY

A dad wanted to introduce the topic of non-sexual intimacy to his ten-year-old son. Once, when they were on a camping trip with another man and his son, he saw the perfect opportunity. It was bedtime; the men would share one tent and the boys the other.

In the relaxed atmosphere created by the trip, the dad told his son about a problem he had had as a boy. When he was a baby, he used to suck his thumb all the time. As he got older, he learned to control this when he was awake, but his older brother told him that when he was sleeping, his thumb would "find its way" to his mouth. He was horrified! Then, when he was ten, a camping trip was arranged. He knew he'd have to sleep with other boys but dreaded being seen sucking his thumb. So he made himself stay up all night. He simply couldn't face the humiliation. Of course, it wasn't long before he had to stay up in so many situations that his problem came to the attention of his parents, who gave him the chance to talk about his fear of ridicule. They encouraged him to trust another boy—someone he felt was his friend—with the story. In the end, he did confide in someone. Pretty soon, he was sleeping properly, and within a few months, the thumb sucking stopped altogether.

When the dad confessed to his son, he opened the door for the son to reciprocate by discussing anything that was embarrassing to him. Since the dad had given him permission to be imperfect, the son was able to expose himself in an atmosphere of trust. He learned that intimacy is not possible without risk and that true intimacy requires trust. ■

Sensuality

Before discussing passion, we must talk about sensuality. And before we can talk about sensuality I'd like to tell you how the brain gets bored. Let's say you and I were having a quiet conversation over a cappuccino one afternoon. Suddenly, I pulled out a gun and fired it into the wall across the room. You would certainly jump! Maybe you'd scream, or run for cover, or hide under the table. After a while, you'd realize that nobody had been injured and you'd begin to calm down. You still wouldn't know why I'd done it, but you'd realize that you were safe.

If we had been measuring your physiological reactions to the whole incident, we'd have seen what we call the typical "fight or flight" constellation of responses, including a shift in brain function from calm to vigilant, an increase in heart rate and blood pressure, increased perspiration, etc. These reactions last for a while, but once it's clear there is no further need to respond, all physiological functions go back to their "resting" levels.

Now let's say I pulled out the gun and fired it again. This time, your brain wouldn't react as strongly. A brain can do things like remember, anticipate, and reason. Because of the first incident, your brain "knows" that I am capable of such an action, and that no harm comes of it. The fight or flight responses of your brain would be much less intense.

If I pulled the gun a third time and fired it, you might not even look up from your cappuccino. It would all be pretty usual or even boring to you. Although the brain is still aware of what is happening out there, there's nothing really new or different going on. So the brain remains relaxed in a kind of resting mode. At the cellular level, this is called neuronal habituation. At the behavioral level, it's called boredom. And boredom is passion's killer. As I mentioned before, in order to engender passion, we have to talk about sensuality first.

The Sensuality Grid

By using the following approach, you'll see how using your senses can lead to appreciation, interest, and passion. Try this exercise yourself first. Once you get a handle on how it works, do it *with* your kids.

First, construct in your mind a grid consisting of five rows and three columns like the one below. Let the five rows represent the five physical senses, and the three columns represent increasing levels of involvement. This will result in 15 "boxes" that you can fill with a check mark when you begin working on that level of involvement with that particular sense.

	LEVEL I	LEVEL II	LEVEL III
	Awareness	Appreciation	Passion
Vision	_____	_____	_____
Hearing	_____	_____	_____
Touch	_____	_____	_____
Taste	_____	_____	_____
Smell	_____	_____	_____

Level I: Awareness Through Observation: Think about which of your senses offers you the most pleasure. If you can't decide, that's okay—just choose one of the senses. At this level, you need only to make yourself increasingly aware of your surroundings by using that particular sense.

If you chose *vision*, I would expect you to keep your eyes and mind open. Look at everything, and try to notice things you never saw before. Walking down the street, look at the architecture in buildings, people's faces, how the lines on the sidewalk were placed, the design of the city buses, the way ads were created. In a park, look at the shape of trees and the pattern in the bark on their trunks; look at the different breeds of dogs; look at how clothing was designed. During a business meeting, look at the details on a man's tie or a woman's scarf; notice how a desk was manufactured or some flowers were arranged. At an art museum, take a good look at a master's work. Do you notice anything different between two paintings by Claude Monet? Observe the colors and the brush strokes. Just become more aware of visual surroundings.

If you chose *hearing*, keep your ears and mind open. Listen for sounds that you've let slip by in the past. On the street, listen to the cars and trucks; listen for human voices in all their emotions. At home, when listening to music, try to figure out what instruments are playing (Is that two guitars or three? Is that a clarinet or an alto sax?). See if you can tell what a person is feeling by listening to the tone of their voice. As with vision, take in all the sensory information you can.

Wherever you are, you are always *touching* something. Most of the time, you're not arrested for touching that something. For the sake of propriety, let's restrict our discussion to the things you're allowed to touch when in public. When in private, you're on your own. (Remember, this is the chapter on passion and sex.) So place all your awareness into the tips of your fingers. Touch is the sense that claims the largest brain area; the skin (our touch organ, in addition to many other functions) is the largest organ in the body. (In fact, most people choose "touch" as their favorite sense.) Be aware of textures and changes in temperature or the passage of air across the skin. Remember that touch can be both didactic (to tell you what's out there) and emotional. Examples of "emotional" touch are itch, pain, tickling, and, of course, anything erotic.

For *taste*, try to be aware of the flavors passing over your tongue. Can you distinguish among various herbs and spices? Can you gauge if the difficulty you have eating a certain dish is because the cook put in too much garlic or ginger for your taste? Expose yourself to new flavors. Each time you go to the grocery store, make a pledge to buy at least three things you haven't tried before. Try different restaurants, opening yourself to the foods from other cultures. This opens new worlds for you and your family.

Wherever you are, you can always *smell* something. It's the oldest sense we have. Remember that single-celled animal, the amoeba? The "awareness" of its surroundings with respect to what was good for it and what was bad was based on its ability to respond to chemicals dissolved in its environment. That was the beginning of the sense of smell. I think it's the most emotional sense in many ways and the most fascinating.

As a student of emotional disturbances, I became very familiar with the brain regions known in their archaic terminology as the rhinencephalon or "smell brain." Today's more common name for this region is the "limbic" system. It is the seat of emotional function (and dysfunction) and is also very caught up in the process of memory. Indeed, if you were to examine the brain from below, you'd see how the regions subtending smell, memory, and emotion are anatomically linked in a visible triangle. The functions of the members of this triangle are also inexorably linked.

Just think about all those times when an unexpected scent can bring back vivid and emotional memories. When I was a kid growing up in Montreal, I'd often play ice hockey with my friends after school at the outdoor ice rinks—the weather was often freezing but we didn't care. The games usually went till about 5:30, and then we'd all walk back to our various homes. We were tired, sore, and wet, but mostly hungry. Just about five minutes from my house, I'd pass a bagel bakery. The windows were usually all steamed up, but the smell coming from inside that bakery was pure heaven. Today, whenever I pass a bakery, I get the involuntary flashback to my childhood, and I can remember the smell of wet wool and hockey tape as if I'd been out on the rink with my friends that very day.

Level II: Appreciation Through Research: If you've spent some time learning how to observe the world more carefully and completely through your senses, you're probably feeling more awake and informed. But the awareness you get by observation is limited. The next step is to build on what you've been experiencing by doing some research or investigating. Take a music appreciation course, or attend a lecture series on just about anything—Persian rugs, ancient architecture, comparative religion, the history of professional wrestling. Whatever you take, you'll begin to appreciate it a lot more.

Level III: Passion Through Involvement: Now you really appreciate things! You've developed an interest in things, and you're more attuned. The next obvious step is to become more *involved*. For this, you need to make an even greater investment. Remember that a financial investment (say, in a bank) is the best way to begin earning interest. When it comes to different aspects of the world around you, the obvious way to build interest is to start "doing it."

Who's passionate about sports? An athlete! Who's passionate about cooking? A cook! Gardening? A gardener! Why is that? Because only if you've tried to grow orchids can you appreciate the skill of a great orchid grower. Only if you've tried to make a certain kind of play in hockey can you really appreciate the skills of the best pros. Only if you've tried to bake napoleons can you appreciate the skill of a great pastry chef.

Now how do we take the exercise you've been through and transfer it to your kids? By challenging them and getting involved with them. Start with the first level, where they just observe—it could be noticing the wrinkles on someone's face, the sounds of other kids playing in the park, or the way the towel feels as they're drying themselves after a bath. I know you think they won't go along with this, but don't give up. Find something. You can do it. This is how you and your teenagers can begin to see each other in new light. You'll know you're succeeding if you hear yourself or your teen saying, "I never actually noticed that before!" If your teenagers are normal, they will soon experience a very essential aspect of this process. Based on what they observe, they will become *curious*. They will want to know more. That "need to know" has presented itself throughout this book as the most human of motivations. Remember, *an interested person is an interesting person.*

Parents can model this sort of curiosity by example. Whenever you see your kids wondering about something, pick up on that curiosity and encourage them to explore further, by means of what scientists call research. The Internet is a wonderful research tool, but remember what I said earlier about information as opposed to knowledge. Searching the Internet can provide a great deal of information, but not all of this information can be trusted (as with the contradictory and biased "information" about marijuana, for example)! Still, it provides a great jumping-off point to talk about what's reliable and what's not.

Awakened sensuality is behind some of the most valuable assets a person can have: curiosity, a questioning mind (including questioning the status quo), empowerment, involvement, etc. These assets are found in most successful students, artists, and athletes. Passion arouses passion, and comfort with physical sensuality always makes for more varied, more profound, and better sex.

Passion

Let's get one thing straight right from the start: No one has to *learn* how to have great sex. Try as we might to hide it, the fact of the matter is that we're animals, and if you've ever been to a zoo, you know that animals know how to do it, and do it well. But you may also know, either firsthand or from talking to friends, that often the passion has gone out of a marriage or long-term relationship. This usually means the sex isn't going well for adults. What's happened? Either one partner is biologically or psychologically abnormal or sexual habituation has occurred. Biological abnormality includes things like erectile dysfunction or vaginal pain; psychological abnormality runs to issues like sexual perversion or irrational fears. In my experience, abnormality is almost *never* the culprit when there are sexual problems. The problem is that sexual habituation (call it boredom if you like) has occurred. This usually depresses both partners, because they really do love each other, and they miss sex. So it's only natural that they might hope for an explanation of their dysfunction that would lead to a quick and face-saving fix. Otherwise, they have to face the truth, which is that they've lost sexual interest in the only partner they're permitted, ethically and morally, to have sex with. To use their words, "The passion is gone." It's particularly poignant when only one of the partners feels this way. But here's good news:

■ If passion isn't there now, it can be restored.
■ Once the passion is restored, great sex will return.

Providing Teenagers with Passion

Passion doesn't begin with sex. I say this because if we can restore deadened passion or create passion where it did not exist, we can also create the capacity for passion in our kids. This will provide them with an essential component of healthy sexuality. I repeat: It doesn't have to begin with sex itself. It begins with teamwork.

Start by getting your kids involved as early as possible in activities where they must interact with others in a cooperative manner. They will learn to depend on others, and have others depend on them, in order for the goals of the activity to be met. The best word for such an activity is "teamwork"; some examples of organized team-based activities are sports, theatrical productions, and debating tournaments. It is often best to get kids involved in activities that are organized by adults other than their parents because the kids will soon learn that the demands of adults are normal in society and the kids will not see their parents as being unusually demanding.

Another advantage to adult-organized teamwork outside the home is that the kids will begin to affiliate with the larger society to which they belong. They will also see their involvement as being a larger contribution to a larger cause.

The concept of risk must also be present. Teach your kids that failure to come through when other people depend on them might result in some sort of harm to themselves or to the others. And yet, we've seen that there can be no chance of intimacy, sexual or otherwise, unless a person is willing to place him- or herself in a position of vulnerability (where they are "exposed"). And intimacy is a close cousin to passion.

What Parents Can Do

As with the other "Big Three" topics we've covered, the best possible parental approach to a teen who's experimenting with sex is based on principles that should, by now, be very familiar: open and honest dialogue, modeling, and a democratic approach to problem solving.

Talking to Your Teen About Sex

If you haven't been fairly open in discussions about sex with your children up to now, you're going to find it hard to get this talk going. However, you may find that the kids are less embarrassed about it than you are! If you don't let them know this is a topic you're willing to discuss, you're doing them a real disservice—especially the boys. Girls generally know about menstruation before they get their periods and have had a conversation with at least their mother about the onset of their first period. But boys rarely talk with either parent about ejaculation, for example. If you ask a random sample of men about their first experiences with ejaculation and women about menstruation, you'll find that the women usually remember how old they were when they got their first period and where they were, whom they told, how they felt; women usually feel good about the advent of their first period. The men will have tended not to talk to anyone about the event except that they felt embarrassed and ashamed and weren't sure what was happening. This exercise illustrates the different ways in which men and woman deal with sex. Women begin their sexuality in an atmosphere of information, communication, and pride. Men often begin their sexuality in an atmosphere of doubt, silence, and shame.

Let your kids know what your own values and experiences have been with regard to sexuality. You want your teen to be open with you—you need to be open with them, as well. It's not necessary to go into detail, but you can let them know just enough so they can see why you have the attitudes you do. Don't be put off by your teen appearing to reject the opening you're providing. You have shown that you are willing to talk—in a few days or weeks or even months, the teen may feel ready to talk.

This approach will work with issues as diverse as homosexuality, teen pregnancy, and abuse. Discuss with your kids the components of mature love that I discussed earlier—intimacy, commitment, passion, and sensuality. Some other topics you might bring up include the more traditional subjects of sexual education. You may find that discussing them is a good way to enter into the talk on sex.

▌ Is pornography (including Internet pornography) a victimless crime?
▌ What constitutes harassment and abuse?
▌ Is it wrong to masturbate?
▌ What are the morality and ethics of discussing sexually transmitted diseases with sexual partners?

Finally, kids have heard a lot about safe sex. To them it means wearing a condom or taking other precautions, designed to ensure the physical safety of sex. Ask your kids what they think *emotionally safe sex* means.

The same applies to each of the potentially harmful elements of modern society that face us and our kids. Trying to protect people by restricting contact with the "toxic" factor is what we call a "supply-side," or "prohibition," approach. It involves either restricting the availability of products such as violent video games by placing age restrictions on them. Or separating skin from viruses with the use of condoms. Or making drugs or alcohol illegal or taxing them to make their prices prohibitive. Prohibition also involves trying to restrict the comings and goings of our kids with curfews and other rules. But "supply-side" approaches have their limitations. And they must be complemented by another sort of protection—that afforded by what we call "demand-side" approaches. Put most simply, these are the tools we give our kids to resist the allure of the toxic elements out there. Let's face it, no product can stay on the market if nobody buys it.

Part IV: When Things Go Wrong

11 The Underachiever: Unable or Unwilling?

Most parents take their job seriously. In simplest terms, that job is to nurture a helpless and totally dependent child into a self-sufficient, independent adult. This maturational process is often referred to as a "life journey." Although many parents try to delay their teens' departure, they instinctively know that they cannot, *and must not*, prevent their children from making that journey. Nor can they accompany their kids. The best parents can do is to make the trip as safe as possible by equipping their children emotionally and physically to handle whatever might be out there.

One of the purposes of this book is to help you prepare your children for their life journey. You can do this by giving them the gifts of intelligence, courage, and love. Once they are confident that they possess these qualities, your children will be able to embark on their own road. The road's obstacles and threats—like drugs, and sex, and rock and roll—will be met with courage, wisdom, and confidence.

But, to further pursue the metaphor, there are children who may not begin their journeys at the appointed time, despite everyone's best efforts. Many teenagers are reluctant or afraid to begin the maturational process. They seem unable or unwilling to set out. They retain childlike characteristics, such as defiance, irresponsibility, and selfishness. They seem unmotivated. They are the ones who, among other things, bring home report cards that refer to "failure to live up to their potential." These are the underachievers.

Having said this, it would not be hard to find parents of teenagers who complain about bedrooms that resemble trash heaps, noontime wakenings, and opposition to family expectations as evidence of underachievement. What's worse, most "experts" would argue that such teenagers are perfectly normal. So is underachievement in teenagers "normal"?

To answer that question, it's essential to agree on the boundaries of normalcy. This will be hugely helpful to parents who want to know how to respond to their children's behavior with effective guidance and fair limits. After all, what if a parent fails to intervene when her child underachieves, only to discover later that something really *was* wrong? And what if a parent assumes that his kid is abnormal because he isn't working up to his potential in school? He might haul him off to a series of professionals for help, only to find out that nothing "abnormal" is going on. No parent wants to make these mistakes.

To help you sort this out, this chapter will distinguish between what clinicians consider to be clinically normal and abnormal. You'll discover that moody doesn't necessarily mean depressed or suicidal, and that being picky about body image does not necessarily mean anorexic. Moreover, you'll learn that when those behaviors *do* extend into the clinically abnormal range, there are interventions—both familial and professional—to deal with them effectively.

The Unable Teen: True and Pseudo-Disabilities

A person who is *truly unable* to do better at something is not suffering from a lack of effort. This inability can result from a problem at birth, or an injury or disease that occurs during the individual's lifetime. The ensuing handicap is what I call a *true disability*. No amount of nagging, psychotherapy, or compassionate support will change the situation. In these cases, the disability must be diagnosed and, if possible, remedied.

But there are other kinds of disabilities, as well. Sometimes, for a variety of reasons, able-bodied and able-minded kids *give the appearance of not being able to do better*. Please understand. These kids are not aware that they are doing this. (An analogous situation that most people can identify with is stage fright. The actor knows the lines perfectly, but subconscious psychodynamic factors such as the anxiety of performing in front of "all those people" make him "freeze." To the audience, he might appear to be a terrible actor, or at least one who isn't trying very hard—in short, an underachiever.) When these individuals fail to live up to the expectations of parents, friends, and educators, not to mention their own expectations of themselves, they are not being consciously oppositional.

I refer to the underlying cause of their situation as a *pseudo-disability*. Like true disabilities, pseudo-disabilities require diagnosis and treatment. Competent psychological assessment procedures almost always uncover an explanation. Let's take a closer look at each of these situations.

True Disabilities: Kids Who Can't

Let's say you never knew that when the human spinal cord is severed, a person becomes paralyzed below the location of that injury. Seeing a woman with such an injury in a wheelchair might confuse you. After all, she seems to have two perfectly good legs. If you told her that she should just try harder to walk, she'd explain that there is something wrong with her central nervous system. This changes everything. Now, the blaming and shaming of the paralyzed woman turn into understanding, compassion, and efforts to help her cope. In the same way, many "underachieving" kids have something wrong with their brains—something that is not readily apparent to the uninformed. What these kids need is the same sort of understanding, compassion, and coping strategies.

Learning Disabilities

Many instances exist in which individuals give the impression of greater potential than they actually possess. In most cases, they are not doing this intentionally, maliciously, or even consciously. Rather, they might have a neurologically based limit to their abilities. They might be capable of verbally receptive learning but less capable of demonstrating that learning, which could manifest itself in behaviors such as

■ "freezing" when watched or judged

■ becoming anxious when they feel the pressure of time

■ having difficulty with thoughts that seem to race ahead of their ability to speak or write them down

■ exhibiting intelligence, but not being able to satisfactorily show what they know

CASE STUDY

Benjamin was about to enter high school. Since the earliest grades, Benjamin's report cards and his teachers' comments expressed the sense that he was not doing as well as he could. This had always baffled his teachers because when they spoke directly to him, he showed good comprehension. He had a spark of understanding in his eyes that made them believe he was a very intelligent young man. His parents felt the same way, for the same reason. Even Benjamin knew he was pretty smart. When he did not to do so well, his teachers tried harder. But when he continued to do poorly, they began to believe that he didn't care, and they turned their attention to their other students. This led Benjamin to believe that the teachers didn't like him. In a way, he was right. But when he brought home the "Benjamin isn't working up to his capacity" report cards, his parents had trouble accepting his explanation of "lousy teachers" and "lousy schools." They spoke to the teachers, who denied treating Benjamin negatively. Because his parents saw the same thing happening at home, they began to accept that Benjamin wasn't trying. Even Benjamin began to think that he wasn't trying. All this could have been avoided with psycho-educational testing to determine if Benjamin's problem(s) stemmed from a true disability.

To be continued ...   ■

The most common test used by psychologists and educators in cases like Benjamin's measures an individual's cognitive capacity or intellectual intelligence. It is commonly referred to as an IQ (intelligence quotient) test. Intelligence tests are often divided into two major sub-groups of tests: those that reflect the functions of the more verbal, logical left hemisphere of the brain, and those that reflect the functions of the more spatial, artistic right hemisphere. Each group of sub-tests produces its own score. And when one of the sub-group scores is significantly higher than the other, it is taken as a sign that there could be trouble.

Such discrepancies do not necessarily mean that a learning disability exists. But when they occur, further testing is a good idea, because that discrepancy might reflect an organic weakness such as a learning disability, an attention deficit disorder, or a perceptual weakness.

If that's the bad news, the good news is that regardless of whether such discrepancies and disabilities are discovered in the earliest grades or well into the teen and even adult years, something can almost always be done to improve the situation. Intervention and treatment plans can be put into place; in most cases, these plans can follow the individuals beyond their high school years into their university and post-university lives. It is never too late.

CASE STUDY

Benjamin's story, continued

Benjamin's overall intelligence was measured to be well above average. But his left hemispheric potential measured significantly higher than his right hemispheric potential. His academic weakness became apparent when he used both hemispheres simultaneously (which is what we all do all the time). Think how hard it would be for a runner who had two legs of very different strengths. Even if the better of her legs was able to run much faster than the average person's, her speed would be determined by the slower leg, which simply couldn't keep up. What's worse, if she tried running with both legs going at their best, she would trip and fall. On an intellectual level, that's what had been happening to Benjamin.

From these findings, it was clear that Benjamin's learning capacity should be investigated further. He was sent for additional psycho-educational testing. Once the true nature of Benjamin's problem was discovered (in this case, a learning disability), school officials were able to respond with an individualized remedial plan that enabled him to show what he had learned. With these measures in place, Benjamin began to have successes in school. That in turn led him to enjoy it more and try harder ■

Attention Deficit Disorder (ADD)

Much has been written and argued about whether kids who have trouble attending to tasks, or who are hyperactive or impulsive, actually suffer from a true (biological) disability. Although a full discussion of this topic is outside the boundaries of this book, I will say that all empirical findings suggest that Attention Deficit Disorder (ADD) and Attention Deficit Hyperactive Disorder (ADHD) are true biological disorders.

Excellent diagnostic tools are available to take the guesswork out of a diagnosis, and parents who wonder about their kids should have them tested by qualified experts. The following selection of symptoms is taken from the *American Psychiatric Association's Diagnostic and Statistical Manual of Mental Disorders*, Fourth Edition (DSM-IV). In order for a diagnosis of ADD or ADHD to be made, these symptoms have to be seen in at least two different settings, such as at school *and* in the home, or in the home *and* in outside social or athletic activities.

Inattention Symptoms
- the making of careless mistakes
- difficulty with sustained attentiveness
- failure to follow through or to complete schoolwork or household duties
- forgetfulness
- easy distractibility

Hyperactivity Symptoms
- excessive talking and fidgeting
- difficulty remaining seated when that is expected

Impulsivity Symptoms
- difficulty waiting turn
- frequent interruptions of others
- blurting out answers before the question is completed

Whatever the diagnosis and (where necessary) regimen of medication, parents should be aware that other concomitant therapies are available and highly recommended. These might include counseling, behavior modifica-tion, or EEG feedback programs.

Emotional Blindness

In Chapter 4, I related how scientists sewed shut the eyelids of newborn kittens or monkeys; when the kittens' eyes were reopened, the kittens acted as if they were unable to see, despite having what appeared to be perfectly healthy eyes. I noted that if the human brain fails to experi-ence certain emotional stimulation during critical periods of its devel-opment, the individual might be left with emotional blind spots, perhaps for life. These individuals will be incapable of recognizing social cues and expectations. Their failure to respond socially in an appropriate or normal manner might land them in some socially difficult situations. The emotional isolation that ensues—which is the result of an undiag-nosed neurological disability—would be as real and as devastating as visual blindness, paraplegia, or any other physiologically based handicap.

If you suspect that something like this is going on with your child, you should seek professional assessment and therapy.

Prefrontal Cortical Injury

One of the most important changes in the brain that accompanies the tran-sition from childhood to adolescence is the rapid development of the prefrontal cortex, also called the executive part of the brain. This is the part of the brain involved in judgment. If this part of the brain is damaged very early in life—through injury or abuse—the results could go unnoticed until adolescence.

The impairments caused by such injury include reduced control over behaviors and emotions and reduced control over cognitive and commu-nicative activity. These are true disabilities that can easily be misidentified as character flaws.

What Parents Can Do About True Disabilities

If you suspect you are dealing with a true disability, the best and safest approach is to call in the professionals. Clinical psychology offers valid and reliable assessment instruments (including the intelligence tests mentioned earlier), and these ought to be used to diagnose such cases. There are tests for personality patterns, mood and anxiety disorders, attention deficit disorders, addictive disorders, and many others. The right therapeutic intervention can be applied only after solid diagnostic information is obtained.

Pseudo-Disabilities: Kids Who Can, but Appear Like They Can't

As I wrote earlier, many kids who are otherwise capable of achieving appear to be unmotivated. It's not as if they want to do poorly; indeed, many of them are perplexed and even tormented by their lack of progress. Yet for reasons they and those around them do not understand, they give the appearance of being unable to do better. It's as if they are behaving according to the following conundrum: If I do well, I'll get certain rewards, including better grades at school and better relations with my family; but if I do poorly, I'll get other rewards that are even more important to me. To most people, this seems counterintuitive, and even indicative of some sort of mental illness. After all, is it possible that there are rewards more compelling than doing well in school and getting along with your family? Indeed, many such rewards exist for our kids— I'll get to those in just a moment. First, we have to address the related issue of underachievement that reflects the absence altogether of meaningful rewards.

Lack of Motivation

When I was an undergraduate, my first psychology experiment involved a rat running down a "T" maze and learning which way to turn to get food. Simple. I placed the rat in the base of the maze and watched. Nothing. The rat simply stayed there. Didn't move. My first experiment as a psychologist, and it failed.

A teaching assistant came to my rescue. "What's his motivation?" she asked. "Why should he go anywhere? What's in it for him?" "Food," I answered. "Right," she said. "So why isn't he moving?" "Not hungry, I guess," I replied. "That's it," she said. "Go back to his home cage and remove his food for a day. We'll try this again tomorrow."

Well! What a difference. Now the rat was all moves. Sniffing. Rearing.

Running. Exploring. This was one motivated rat! And, of course, he learned where the food was rather quickly.

When parents tell me their kids don't seem to be motivated in school or around the house, I remember my teaching assistant's words: "Well, what's in it for them?" In other words, what do they really want—and are you sure you're not already providing it? Think about it. Are you placing the "food" at the base of the maze, and then wondering why they don't run off to search for more? In this age of affluence, material wealth abounds. And parents naturally want their kids to have things, especially if they themselves grew up in a more economically restricted time. But be careful. It may well be that your kids aren't doing things because they aren't "hungry." Ask yourself if your teen's lack of motivation is just another way of saying "I have everything I need *without* working, so why should I work?"

But if "lack of motivation" is really the absence "hunger," what forms might that hunger take?

Curiosity Revisited

The hunger for food and water is paramount for the survival of any species, as is the hunger for sex (see Chapter 1). In my opinion, there are two additional and very powerful human motivators, each of which is also closely related to individual and social survival:

- the hunger for knowledge (curiosity)
- the need for affection (love)

These two motivators are closely related in human mythology. For example, the Pandora myth makes curiosity the defining human characteristic. In the biblical Adam and Eve story, the symbolic representation of both curiosity and love (the Tree of Knowledge of Good and Evil) is paramount in defining what many would call "normal" about the human species: curiosity (discussed at greater length in Chapter 6). The logical conclusion is that it is fundamentally abnormal for humans to lack motivation.

CASE STUDY

Eighteen-year-old Sonia was about to leave her parents' home and enter university when she developed anxiety symptoms. She knew she was being irrational, but she could not shake the feeling that she wouldn't be able to take care of herself while away.

I discovered that Sonia's parents, when they were just barely out of university, had fled an Eastern European satellite of the (then) Soviet Union one week after their marriage. And though they didn't know it, Sonia's mom was pregnant. Sonia's dad had some relatives in a large Midwestern U.S. town and, at their urging, he went there with his bride. As often befalls new immigrants, they discovered that the work credentials they had earned back home were not recognized in their new land. They were forced to take jobs well below their capabilities. Still, they were glad to do so, especially when Sonia and, two years later, her younger brother were born.

Sonia's parents were intelligent and ethical people. They made sure that both their kids grew up with good values and principles. They monitored their school progress and enrolled them in artistic and athletic after-school programs.

As time went by, both parents were able to climb the occupational (and economic) ladder. Eventually, they started a business that brought affluence they could never have dreamed of in their homeland. Three forces combined and led them to shower Sonia and her brother with the things money could buy:

- pride in their financial prosperity
- North American social pressure to acquire material things
- their need to see that their children never faced the sort of insecurity and deprivation that they had

Like most parents, Sonia's mom and dad responded to their first-born's every wish. They met all her needs, beginning with her demand for attention, from the time she was a newborn through her teenage years. (By the time her brother was born, they knew better, and he was left to fend for himself more than his sister. Naturally, he resented this as a child, feeling his parents preferred his sister. Only later did her brother realize that his parents were not doing Sonia any favor.)

By seeing that Sonia never lacked anything material, they imparted to her a sense of entitlement and expectation that prevented her from relying on her own devices. She developed a personality of dependency and had little confidence in her own abilities.

Some of the anxiety she experienced when faced with leaving home dissipated as she mastered the necessities of paying her own utility bills, stocking her own refrigerator, and getting herself from here to there in her new town. But her lack of self-confidence in her academic and social abilities subsided only after months of counseling at the university student health center.   ■

In situations where parents reward their kids with all the things they need (or *believe* they need) before the kids actually *do* anything to earn those things, the kids truly will be unmotivated. These kids have been termed "cornucopia kids" by Dr. Bruce A. Baldwin, because everything they want is provided for them, and they don't have to work for it.

I can't even count the times I've heard parents say the following:

- ▌ "He's content to sit around the house for a whole day doing nothing!"
- ▌ "She'd rather not eat if it means she has to get up and prepare a meal for herself!"
- ▌ "If I can't give him a ride, he'd rather miss a soccer practice than take the bus!"

Yet to say "Kids today are just lazy" is simply a restatement of the fact that they lack motivation. I don't accept the notion of laziness as an explanation for a lack of motivation. Instead, it is lack of motivation that underlies laziness. There are certainly situations in which a teenager will seem to be lazy, but look deeper. It's likely that, in his opinion, there is no point in doing anything. If he asks the question "What's in it for me?" and comes up with an answer of "Nothing," he won't act.

Motivated to Do Nothing

What about those other individuals I referred to earlier, the ones who appear not to be motivated, but who in fact are very motivated to do nothing? This relates to kids who appear to sabotage themselves by working, subconsciously, for rewards that outweigh the more traditionally valued rewards associated with good school, family, and social achievement. It is crucial for parents to understand this. It means that these kids must be responding to hidden factors that cause them to sacrifice some of their future "conventional" happiness. This is the price they are subconsciously driven to pay in order to gain some more important "nonconventional" reward. It is essential to uncover those rewards if we are to be able to help these troubled kids. What I describe below are some (but not all) of the factors that could be at work in these cases.

Avoidant Personality Disorder

Symptoms of avoidant personality disorder include enduring social inhibition, feelings of inadequacy, and extreme sensitivity to negative evaluation. Avoidant personality is characterized by a strong refusal to become involved in any endeavor unless there is a guarantee of success. A formal definition includes "fears of criticism, disapproval, or rejection," but I believe these teens are *certain* they *will be* rejected. Such adolescents see this expected rejection as too steep a price to pay, so they remove themselves from school and social involvements that would contribute to their overall integration and fulfillment. They pay a very high price in order to avoid paying what for them is an even *higher* price.

Fear of Failure

Expectations can be daunting. How would you feel if you truly believed that, no matter how hard you tried, you would fail to measure up to someone's expectations? Whether it's a boss, a spouse, or even a child, you'd likely feel discouraged and somewhat daunted. Teenagers grapple with these feelings all the time—at home, at school, and with their peers. Faced with the possibility of failure, it sometimes seems easier not to try at all. After all, it is socially more acceptable to rationalize not doing something than to admit to having tried but failed.

For many years, I've acted as consulting psychologist at some pretty high-end private schools. These schools (some of which are residential) are expensive, but the student body is made up of kids from a wide range of economic strata. Some of the kids are from families that simply reached into their pockets for spare change to pay the tuition, but others are stretched to the limit. Regardless of their economic background, these kids are under enormous pressure to succeed—to meet their parents' lofty expectations and to justify their place at the school.

Let's say a kid tries but just can't make the grade. Let's say her parents are both lawyers, or doctors, or politicians. Let's say she thinks there's no way she can ever accomplish what they've accomplished. But she's surrounded by teachers with high expectations, and she knows her parents are counting on her to do well. Under these circumstances, admitting her doubts about her own abilities would be very embarrassing indeed. So, instead of trying and failing, she simply doesn't try. This might not look so good to the parents or to the school officials, but it might look pretty good to her and her peers. Compare the next two dialogues:

"I hear you failed math."
"Yeah. I never studied."
or
"I hear you failed math."
"Yeah. I really tried hard, too."

Even though she sacrifices the conventional reward of good grades (one she might not have been able to achieve even if she had tried), she gains the nonconventional rewards of self-relaxation (not having the anxiety related to studying and feeling stupid) and approval from a group ("the 'Wrong Crowd'") that will reward her for being like them, i.e., "rebels." Finally, even though she might not be getting the sort of attention from her parents she would like (approval), at least she is getting some sort of attention, and this might be better than no attention at all.

Fear of Success

When teenagers excel in certain areas (say science or football or singing), it's natural for their friends, families, and school career counselors to encourage them to pursue that activity. This encouragement comes out of love and with the best intentions. And there is little doubt that if the kids *were* to pursue such careers, they would probably continue to perform very well. For many people, this might be considered a success.

But what if a teen isn't ready to commit to a particular career? What if she needs time to decide what she wants to do? What if she already knows she doesn't want to be an accountant, a lawyer, or an architect? What if the encouragement from her loved ones turns into pushing, and what if that pushing is perceived as bullying? In situations like this, a teen may feel as if she is traveling on a train that's headed to a place she doesn't want to go. Now she has a problem. She knows that as long as she's successful at whatever she's being pressured to be, she will continue to be pushed along that track to success. What are her options? Well, she can begin to fail.

CASE STUDY

Eighteen-year-old Hanna was a straight-A high school student with an early acceptance to a prestigious university. Her father and grandfather ran a successful accounting firm. Hanna grew up with strong pressure to go into the family business. But Hanna didn't want to be an accountant. In fact, she wasn't even sure she wanted to go to university. She dreamed of a career in the arts. She wanted to try her hand at playwriting. But she believed this would be frowned on by her family and considered a frivolous waste of her talents.

All through high school, she couldn't find the courage to confront her family with her problem. She was afraid of insulting them or hurting their feelings. Worse, she was worried that they might become resentful or angry. Meanwhile, she continued on a track leading to a career in the family business. As final exams drew closer, she inexplicably "shut down." She began to fail courses. She even skipped some essential classes and exams. At one point, she was close to being kicked out of school on disciplinary charges.

When Hanna was given the chance to tell her side of the story in confidential therapy sessions, she gained the confidence to speak up for herself. Things began to improve dramatically. She completed high school and deferred her entry into formal postsecondary education. She got a job at a small community newspaper and began to report on local human-interest stories. She wrote a play based on her experiences. The play was entered in the town's literary competition and won second place.

Hanna's family began to comprehend her passion and to respect and trust her desire to pursue writing as a career. Hanna knew that she needed formal training and wanted the advantages of a university degree, so she entered a fine arts program where she thrived. ■

Family Affairs

I've seen countless kids get kicked out of boarding school when something traumatic is happening at home: it could be divorce or the serious illness or death of a parent. Often they feel they are needed back home to help take care of family business. But broaching the subject with their parents might not be permitted. In the case of a divorce, one parent might fear that the teen's presence could lend too much emotional support to "the other side." In the case of an illness or death, the parents might feel guilty about letting their kid miss out on a great opportunity at school. For the teenager, there might not appear to be any acceptable way to achieve their goal of returning home. So they force the issue by getting booted out of school on behavioral grounds.

Ethical Considerations

I wrote earlier about Hanna, who held herself back because she was concerned that her life was heading in a direction she had not chosen.

She wasn't completely aware of her own motivation. Indeed, she might have felt guilty about not wanting to please her parents, so she suppressed awareness of her true motivation. Because of this nonconscious aspect, we can say that Hanna suffered from a pseudo-disability. In other words, without knowing that they are doing it, people will apply a minimum of effort if they do not believe in what they are asked to do. For example, many businessmen and -women are subconsciously uncomfortable when they discover that in order to be successful, they must act unethically and cheat the system or their clients. If they do badly in their job, they might appear to be underachieving.

I'll never forget the 17-year-old downhill skier who suddenly went from Olympic-level competition to consistently losing her races. She had devoted endless hours of grueling practice and training to be on the team. Her parents had spent a lot of money and put a lot of pressure on her to win; the last thing she wanted to do was disappoint them and let herself down in the bargain. But she began to see that other members of the team were becoming nasty in their drive to win. They undermined their own teammates with emotional and social pressures. It went against everything she believed about fair play and sportsmanship; she refused to be a part of it. She couldn't bring herself to deal with her conflicting emotions on a conscious level, though, so she subconsciously sabotaged herself. As with most cases of pseudo-disabilities, she paid a price for something that was worth more to her than winning on the slopes.

Not Wanting to Look Too Good

I was once called in to interview a young man who was about to be expelled for participating in an act of vandalism. He was a senior student at an exclusive boys' school, and his expulsion meant that he might not be able to graduate with the honors he had expected. He was part of a small group of boys who began the episode as a prank directed at a very expensive girls' school. The prank turned ugly when the vandalism took on misogynist tones.

When I interviewed him, his remorse was evident from the start. He had always complied with the school's rules, and, in fact, had earned a reputation as a boring nerd. He told me that, just once, he had wanted to be bad—to show everyone that he was one of the guys.

He wrote a letter of apology to both his school and the girls' school. Moreover, he offered to do community service in the form of some gardening and light maintenance work during the summer months at the girls' school. Finally, he gave speeches at both schools on the topic of misogyny.

The minister's daughter who stays out all night at a friend's place and doesn't call home, the school principal's son who gets drunk and gets in trouble with the authorities, and the police officer's kid who cuts class are all underachieving in one area in order to gain points in another.

Passive Aggression

Teenagers are sometimes very angry about real or perceived wrongs. Perhaps they are angry with their parents for divorcing or at their siblings for being better than they are at something. Acts of revenge in such situations are neither the noblest nor the most effective way of handling anger, yet very few of us can say we haven't considered it. When kids feel this need to strike back, it's often combined with feelings of powerlessness—against parents or school or society in general, and they may begin to act in a way that psychologists describe as passive aggressive.

Passive aggressive behavior manifests itself when a person reacts to events in an aggressive or obstructive way—by doing nothing. For example, a teen who feels his parents are bugging him too much about his less-than-spectacular grades in school might promise to buckle down and then do absolutely nothing. What's been accomplished? His promise has raised his parents' hopes and gotten them off his back, at least temporarily. But his refusal to follow through on his promise really seals the deal. He has, in effect, set his parents up: he sent their expectations crashing simply by failing to live up to them. This is a very effective way to avenge perceived wrongs, but it is also very destructive to the teenager engaging in it.

CASE STUDY

Jake was 12 when his parents split up. It was a messy divorce. The father was a physically large, very wealthy, and powerful man. The mother's best friend and her family had been very close to Jake's family—so close Jake used to call the adults "aunt" and "uncle." They even spent vacations and holidays together. It wasn't unusual for Jake to see his "aunt" at his house when he came home from school. You know where this is going, don't you? That's right. Jake's father had an affair with his mom's best friend.

The divorce was acrimonious. Jake lost his "aunt," his "uncle," and his pals. His mom was absolutely furious—not to mention injured, alone, and financially in a much more precarious place than before. I won't paint Jake's dad entirely in black. To do what he'd done, he must have been a pretty damaged man himself. He, too, was hurt by the whole thing, but much less so. He seemed to maintain his wealth, his job, his status, and he even seemed to gain social points in the circles where "trophy" wives are valued.

Jake was livid. He couldn't believe that his father and his new wife were "getting away" with what they'd done. He decided, subconsciously of course, that he would dedicate his life to making them pay for their crime. He did this by systematically raising their hopes for him. He allowed them to pin their dreams on him. And then, just when he knew he had them, he let them down. Repeatedly. After promising to do better, he got involved with drugs and alcohol—in a big way—from the time he was 14. After promising to do better, he dropped out of one expensive private school after the other. After promising to do better, he got in trouble with the law. Put most simply, he never let them relax. And this hurt them terribly.

Of course, his aggression was never overtly (or actively) directed at his father and stepmother. He was being aggressive by (passively) *not doing* what he would have had to do in order to live up to the constantly renewed expectations. In this way, a relatively powerless individual was able to punish his father and stepmother. Unfortunately, he also punished himself. ■

What Parents Can Do About Pseudo-Disabilities

Parents of children with pseudo-disabilities have a number of options to help them assess the problem and cope with it.

"Talking" psychotherapy is a common approach, although it may fail to identify the underlying problem—especially if the individual is unaware of what that might be. In such cases, an "insight-oriented" approach might be preferred. This is often applied in tandem with the use of "projective" tests, such as the Rorschach (inkblot) Test. Tests like these allow therapists to take a look at the subconscious roots of the problem. Another powerful way to access the subconscious is clinical hypnosis.

As I have detailed above, these investigations usually reveal one of two possible explanations for the underachievement: Either the individual truly lacks motivation, or they are motivated by a need not to apply themselves.

If a true lack of motivation exists, the teen in question will usually respond well to some form of directive counseling. In my practice, directive counseling refers to specific instructions. This means that my clients will have to do some "homework." Depending on the diagnosis, my directions will vary. In the case of pseudo-disabilities, my goal is to do away with the client's casual or depressive rhetorical question "Why bother?" and replace it with a passion to get involved. In other words, if a person won't do something because there's nothing particularly "valuable" in it for him, we must make something valuable available in return for his efforts.

THE PAYOFFS FOR WORK

Ask anyone what they get for the work they do, and they'll probably think of money first. And why not? In our society, it's necessary. However, just like everything else in a market economy, money costs. You can have it if you're willing to pay. So make sure your kids have a chance to grapple with two questions: "How much money do I need in order to find fulfillment?" and "What am I willing to pay for that money?"

Once you've discussed these issues, you can turn your kids' attention to the fact that there are other rewards for work, like a sense of contribution. Think about your own work. If you work hard and do a good job, who benefits? If you see the primary purpose of your efforts being that you will become wealthier, you have chosen money as the main reason to work. If, on the other hand, you work hard and do a good job and make money, but you need someone else to benefit as well as you, you will have made contribution to society a focal "payoff" for your efforts, and this has tremendous value. This is particularly true if the contribution you make to society is in line with what you feel passionate about.

And passion itself can be a major payoff for working. If your kids aren't sure what they're passionate about, ask them: "What makes you angry about how things are in the world?" Some of the answers I've received to this question from teenagers are war, cruelty, poverty, environmental decay, and racism. The next question is obvious: "What are you going to do about it?" I promise you, if you encourage your kids to choose a career that enables them to heal—even in a small way—one of the world's wounds, you can rest assured that they will always find satisfaction and reward in the work they do.

Parents can help tremendously on this front. Ask yourselves: "What am I doing for my kids that they ought to be doing for themselves?" When kids are very young, it's good to help and protect them when they can't do these things for themselves. Helping a kid in elementary school with her science project will provide a sense of accomplishment and teamwork. It will give her the strength to ask for help when she needs it. These are strengths she will keep throughout life.

When your kids become teenagers, however, it's good to look for ways to let them try things, even if they might fail. I've had to advise parents *not* to go to the school with notes explaining that homework was not done because their son was away at a cousin's wedding. The son *knew* he was going to be away, and the homework could have been done if he'd planned his time better.

Simply put, parents need to know that rescuing young kids is the right thing to do; rescuing older kids is wrong. Obviously, every child is different, and no one can tell you when the appropriate time to stop rescuing your own kids comes. Use your judgment here. If you give them what they need all the time, they'll never learn how to get it for themselves.

The Unwilling Teen: Defiance and Hostility

So far, this chapter has dealt with teenagers who mystify their parents (and often themselves) by performing below their potential capacity. In Chapter 3, I wrote that some degree of opposition (rebelliousness) is expected, healthy, and even necessary in the development of a teenager's sense of empowerment. But what about brazenly defiant kids who refuse to comply with family, school, or other social expectations? What about the 16-year-old who fails to show up or openly defies the special education tutor his parents hired to help him with his homework or study habits? What about the 14-year-old girl who sneaks out after curfew to meet her friends and have a smoke? What about the 15-year-old who uses the most profane language and openly ridicules his parents when they express their concerns about his unapologetic use of marijuana?

In some cases, teenagers who underachieve do so not because they *can't* do better, but because *they choose not to*. Some of these kids act out of hostility, and their defiance is deliberate and aggressive. These are the oppositional or antisocial ones. Others are what might be called "conscientious objectors." They are acting on the belief—whether accurate or not—that by doing something that is expected of them, they will be acting against their own convictions.

How's a parent to cope? First and foremost, you need to know what you're dealing with. What follows is a look at some of the ways in which psychologists and psychiatrists categorize hostile defiant behavior, taken from the DSM-IV.

Oppositional Defiant Disorder (ODD)

To be diagnosed with ODD, a person shows a recurring pattern of "negativistic, defiant, disobedient, and hostile behavior toward authority figures that persists for at least 6 months." This can include losing one's temper, arguing with adults, defying adult requests and rules, blaming others for their own mistakes, being touchy and easily annoyed, being angry and resentful, and being spiteful and vindictive. These kids rarely see themselves as having a problem. They regularly feel justified and blame their behavior on "unreasonable demands."

I know, you're going to say: "Hey, that's *all* teenagers," and you may be right. But remember, ODD is diagnosed only if it seems to occur more than seems "normal." Statistics tell us that less than 20% of teenagers qualify for a diagnosis of ODD. To get a handle on this, ask yourselves these questions:

▌ Is the behavior having a significant negative impact on your kids' school, home, and social life? If the impact is not significant, you're probably not dealing with ODD.

▌ Do your kids display this behavior with everybody, or mostly with people they know well? Very often, parents who feel their kids are horrible around them are surprised to hear that when they're at school or at a friend's home, they behave very well. So why do they save their worst behavior for those closest to them? The theory is that these kids are worried that showing their true anger and frustration to people who aren't absolutely committed to them will lead to abandonment. With their close family, there is usually unconditional acceptance. They know they can be at their worst and, usually, not be abandoned. But they must be careful. As they get older, their "worst" gets worse. Remind them that, when they were little, they could hit you as hard as they wanted and not do any real damage. Now that they're older, though, those same hits pack more of a punch. The same is true psychologically. They may not know their own emotional strength. And no matter how unconditionally parents love their kids, there will come a time when they simply cannot stand the pain any longer.

Conduct Disorder

ODD is very often a precursor for conduct disorder, which is defined as repetitive and persistent behavior that violates the rights of others, seen over the course of a year. This kind of violation can include aggressiveness to people or animals, including bullying, cruelty, confrontational theft, and sexual assault. It can also relate to destroying another individual's property, stealing, lying, or other forms of deceitfulness. Finally, serious violation of rules—such as school truancy or running away—is frequently seen in conduct disorder.

Antisocial Personality Disorder

Now we're getting into some serious criminal territory. If your kids are repeatedly doing things that are against the law, and they either could be or already have been arrested, they can be said to have an antisocial personality disorder. These kids lie or deceive for their own profit or pleasure. They rarely plan ahead. They get into lots of fights. They care little for the safety of others. They are consistently irresponsible. And they seem to have no conscience.

I remember asking one such teenager why he stole another kid's winter coat. Without hesitation he said, "He had it. I wanted it. It's his fault if he wears a coat like that. He's just asking me to take it from him."

Conscientious Objectors

Sometimes teenagers are defiant for reasons that do not require psychiatric diagnosis. These kids know they are breaking the rules; they are doing so to make a point. Their reasons for underachieving have nothing to do with lack of capacity or lack of motivation. For example, some kids are simply uncomfortable "performing." Oppositional and defiant ones are aware of this and tell you so. But others have a hard time realizing, accepting, or explaining this to themselves or those around them. They might not have confidence in their own belief system or else they are afraid of appearing weak or preachy. Hanna, for example, shut down because she was afraid of overtly insulting or disappointing her family. Jake felt angry yet power-less about his parents' divorce, and he shut down in an effort to punish his father. Both Hanna and Jake may not have been conscious of it at the time, but they did what they did in order to be true to their inner values.

Other examples of this "principled" reticence to perform include

▐ competitive teenage athletes who refuse to use performance-enhancing drugs and who would rather drop their sport than be forced to cheat
▐ teenagers who drop out of expensive prep schools because they don't like what they perceive to be the snobbish attitude of their schoolmates
▐ adolescent artists (actors, dancers, sculptors) who will not participate in certain competitions because those competitions are sponsored by the manufacturers of tobacco or alcohol products
▐ teenagers who do not want to enter certain jobs or university programs because they feel those programs would lead them to careers that either don't make the sort of social contribution they would like to make, or they do make the sort of social contribution they abhor

These individuals might well be called "conscientious objectors." Unlike Hanna and Jake, however, in these cases the underachiever has a pretty accurate view of why he or she does not want to perform well.

Finally, there are individuals who *inaccurately believe* their objections are conscientious. Inaccurate beliefs have come up in our discussions many times, and they always lead to trouble. In this case, a teenager might believe

- "Nobody likes me at that school anyway, so why should I try?"
- "Studying is for losers!"
- "The teachers are jerks!"

How can parents respond intelligently to such hyperbolic outbursts? I know you might be tempted to say something like "Oh come on, that's ridiculous!" Such a response only makes kids who are already at a loss feel even more stupid. By all means, let them know that you see how upset they are and that you are willing to help. But don't engage them beyond this when they're irrational. It's better to wait till they calm down a bit. Then you can introduce the possibility of a more acceptable explanation of what's been going on. This takes away the negative labeling that kids resent so much and offers them hope of a real solution.

CHARTING YOUR PROGRESS

I hope this book will provide you with all sorts of ideas on coping with your difficult teenagers. But what if you've been trying to use these ideas, and nothing seems to be happening? Try to imagine a line graph that gives a score to each day. If something happened that day that made you think things were working, place that day's score at one measure above the day before. If something happened that made you think that things were not working, give that day a score one measure below the previous day's score. If you can't tell, leave that day's score the same.

As time goes by, you would hope to see an improvement. After two or three months, you will see a trend in the graph, which will clearly indicate how you are doing. If things are not improving after a few months and the line is clearly on a downward slope, it is time to call in a professional.

What Parents Can Do About Unwilling Teens

Earlier in the book, I wrote that even though we humans aren't always aware of what our beliefs are, we still act on the basis of those beliefs. Remember the setting-sun exercise from Chapter 2? The point of that exercise was to show people the beliefs they hold and act on are likely to be quite different from the beliefs held by others around them. Moreover, as the exercise showed, there is a very good possibility that they are wrong in their beliefs. If those beliefs make teenagers unwilling to meet family and social expectations, the sooner these kids realize they might be wrong the better off they'll be. And this is the beginning of the end of the problem.

Behavioral Intervention

When kids are too immature or too defiant to change their own minds, behavioral modification may be in order. This allows parents to respond consistently to undesired behavior(s) with the systematic use of positive and negative rewards in order to shape behavior(s) in a more positive direction.

Earlier in this chapter, I mentioned my first laboratory experience using a rat and a "T" maze. In that case, food was the reward offered in exchange for desired behavior. A reward is defined as a reaction to a behavior, which increases or perpetuates that behavior. If you want to stop undesirable behavior, you don't reward it, right?

 But be careful. "Listen" to this next exchange, and see if you can spot the problem for the parent:

> Kid: "You're not gonna tell me what to do."
> Parent: "Don't open your mouth to me!"
> Kid: "Why not? I have no respect for you!"
> Parent: "I told you not to talk that way to me!"
> Kid: "I'll say whatever I want, you bitch!"

Let's translate this into *behavioral* language:

> Kid: *"bad thing"*
> Parent: *"response"*

Kid: "more of the *bad thing*"
Parent: "response"
Kid: "still more of the *bad thing*"

In other words, even though the parent thinks she's not encouraging this sort of language from her kid, her responses are perpetuating or increasing the undesirable behavior. Without knowing it, this mother has been *rewarding* the very behavior she wants to eliminate. You may have seen this in toddlers—remember those tantrums? They were a great way of getting your attention and they always worked.

Walk Away

Any parent will say that walking away is an easy thing to say and a tough thing to do. I know this, but do it anyway. The mom in the example above, who reacted to her kid's obnoxious behavior by yelling, was offering positive reinforcement that perpetuated the unwanted behavior. By walking away, she is actively and purposefully withholding the rewards that she once used to reinforce the undesirable behavior.

In psychology, we did experiments with rats that rewarded the animal with food when it learned to press a lever. Then we took the food away. The rat continued to press the lever until it finally realized that pressing the lever was useless. This change in behavior is called "extinction," meaning that the behavior stops. Similarly, if the mom walks away, the kid's behavior might first become more exaggerated and intense, but eventually it will stop.

Remember pinball machines? You could jostle them a bit to get more action on the ball. But if you pushed too hard, everything went wrong. All the lights went out. The balls dropped to the bottom reservoir, and a small word appeared on the display: "Tilt." That's how you should react when your teen is giving you a hard time. Let them jostle you a bit. But if they push too hard, tilt. Just shut off all your lights. And walk away.

Silence Is (Sometimes) Golden

Here's another example of a behavioral approach to irresponsibility. Say you go to a parent-teacher meeting, and the teacher tells you your kid would do so much better if he only handed in all his work or applied himself more. You're aggravated because you've been nagging him about this very thing. Here's how the process goes:

Kid: Does no studying for the exam
Parent: Nags kid about not studying
Kid: Fights with parent
Parent: Nags more
Kid: Fails the exam

As in the previous example, nagging turns out to be a *reward*, because it *perpetuates* the behavior, even though the behavior was undesired.

Also, this scenario doesn't give the kid a chance to make the appropriate association between his own behavior and the *results* of that behavior. Just like the rat who learned that the last thing he did (press the lever) caused food to appear, this kid is learning that the last thing that happened (fighting with his parent) is what resulted in his failing the exam. He attributes this fight directly to the thing that happened before the fight began, which was the nagging. He rarely gets far enough in his analysis to realize that his own lack of studying was the cause for the nagging in the first place. So here's a better plan:

Kid: Does no studying for the exam
Parent: (Silence)
Kid: Fails the exam

Now, when the kid looks back over events, he is forced to associate not studying with failing. Otherwise, he'll blame his parent, not take responsibility, and be forced to depend on forces outside himself to change if he is ever to get where he wants to in life. In this scenario, his parent robbed him of the opportunity to be responsible for his own actions and achieve the independence that comes with that.

In order for this to happen, however, you must back off and say nothing when you see that your teen isn't studying. It's similar to walking away when your teenager continues to argue and refuses to see to his or her responsibilities. Many parents feel that in the first case this would be akin to abdicating parental responsibility when they allow their teens to fail. You may think it's your job to nag and cajole; this is a form of rescuing. But your job really is to *teach your child to take responsibility for his or her actions*. Parents also feel that by walking away when their kids are disobeying, they are letting their kids "get away with murder." This is not so.

Take a Time-Out

Instead of letting the kids think that the matter is over when the parents walk away, parents should tell their kids that this is not the time to talk about it, and that there will be consequences later. An example of inappropriate punishment is yelling at kids when they come home late and intoxicated. What's the point? That's a discussion that should occur later, when the individual is able to participate responsibly and accept appropriate consequences of inappropriate behavior.

Moreover, I warn against rescuing teenagers from the negative and even painful consequences of their own mistakes. Rescuing prevents adolescents from experiencing the pain of growing up, pain that is necessary for the change in behavior we refer to as learning. Rescuing will only render teenagers helpless in future situations because they will not have learned any strategies for responsible action.

12 Beyond Teenage Angst: Adolescence and Mental Illness

Parents who love their kids want them to become happy and healthy adults—it's only natural. But so much adolescent behavior seems alien and troublesome to adults. It's not that we can't remember what it was like to be a teen, it's more likely that we *do* remember and fervently hope our own children won't have to go through what we did!

We worry that the moodiness we see in our kids goes beyond normal teenage angst. Everyone has read stories about teen suicides where the parents never even knew their children were depressed. Were these kids sending out cries for help? If so, what were they, and how could the parents have missed them? We also see our kids struggling with shyness and feelings of isolation. Are they simply too anxious? If so, can this be assessed and treated? Adding to *our* anxiety is the knowledge that serious mental illnesses like schizophrenia present themselves in the late teen years. We worry that our teens' often bizarre behaviors might signal the onset of something serious.

In this chapter, I'm going to discuss some of the emotional and mental disorders that afflict teens and offer guidelines to help you identify when you should talk to experts. It is clearly beyond the scope of this book to discuss all mental illnesses that can affect teenagers; I'll restrict my comments to those disorders that appear most frequently in my clinical practice. Before we begin, though, let's revisit the question of incorrect beliefs.

Incorrect Beliefs: Nature or Nurture?

Let's start by revisiting an idea I introduced earlier: Everything we do in life is based on our beliefs. What we believe is based, in turn, on how we perceive and remember things. If our brains are working normally, we perceive things accurately, and we're fine. But if our brains aren't working correctly, our perceptions will be inaccurate. The result is misperceptions that lead to beliefs that are different from reality. If that's the case, there's trouble.

Because the brains of the mentally ill do not work normally, these people have spurious beliefs. When they act on those incorrect beliefs, their behavior is called "abnormal." For example:

▌ The depressed teenager *believes* that he has nothing to offer. He feels the world would be a better place without him. He feels he is just a pain in the butt to those around him. His family and friends don't share his belief. But if he cannot be convinced he is mistaken, he might end up committing suicide.

▌ The schizophrenic *believes* the voices he hears are real. No one else hears the voices, but when the voices tell him to give away all his possessions and live by himself in order to avoid being detected by aliens, he acts according to those beliefs.

▌ The obsessive-compulsive woman *believes* that if she does not wash her hands 30 times an hour, something bad will happen to her children. She cannot say what the bad thing could be; only that it would be bad. Nobody else believes this, but she is compelled to act on the basis of her belief.

▌ The anorexic girl *believes* that she is obese. The scale in her bathroom indicates that she is losing weight. But because she is acting on her belief by not eating, she risks starving herself to death.

Each of these mental illnesses is based on a belief system that most of us would consider to be wrong. But no logical "talking" therapy can reverse the beliefs.

THE LIMITS OF NORMAL

We've seen that the "normal" teenage brain is not the same as a "normal" adult brain. We also know that because of the workings of their *normal* teenage brains, many teenagers are unable to do certain things, such as inhibit impulsive behavior. If the result of this is that many teenagers get into trouble with their parents or other "authority figures," can they be excused because they are only doing what is "normal" for them? We've begun to hear lawyers argue that their teenage clients are not to be held responsible for their crimes because they were "suffering" from "teenage brain syndrome" (something not yet recognized by the clinical community). It will be interesting to see how this debate resolves itself.

Here's where things become complicated. In *most* cases, the incorrect belief is the result of a brain dysfunction. However, current thinking in the psychiatric and psychological communities would have us believe that other cases of abnormal behavior are the product of physiologically normal brains having *learned* to behave abnormally. This, of course, is a restatement of the "nature or nurture" debate. This ancient discourse has been partially settled by scientific evidence that proves that many mental disorders—including schizophrenia and depression, which were once thought to be the result of poor parenting, social pressures, or even spiritual distress—are really the result of genetically determined chemical imbalances in the brain.

But what about eating or personality disorders? So far, science has not been able to link them to specific brain dysfunction. Is that because such dysfunction does not exist, or because it hasn't been detected yet? I'd bet on the eventual discovery of a biological basis for these disorders, too. For now, we must satisfy ourselves with the certainty that, regardless of the underlying cause, these mental disorders still reflect incorrect belief systems and must be treated as "true disabilities." What are some of these disorders? Let's take a look.

Mood Disorders

Most psychologists refer to a mood as an emotion that is sustained over a period of time. In other words, it stays with a person throughout the day and colors all aspects of the person's experience. If the emotion is negative, such as sadness, anger, or irritability, it is easy to see how we would call this a mood disorder. But any sustained and pervasive emotion, including elation, which results in the interference with family, social, and occupational (including school) functioning, can be included among the mood disorders.

Depression

Just about everyone can think of a time when they felt depressed. This usually occurs when something bad is going on: someone is sick or dying; love is unrequited or rejected; a friend moves away. These situations leave people feeling dark and hopeless. But most often, even though something is very wrong, these people are still able to recognize their own strengths and appreciate the good things going on in their lives. Moreover, if the bad situation improves dramatically, so does the mood.

But nearly two out of three North Americans are familiar with another type of depression, either because they feel it themselves or because it has struck someone close to them. This type of depression feels as dark and hopeless as the first, but it seems to occur independently from life's stresses, and it clouds every aspect of the person's experience.

Both types of depression are characterized by loss of pleasure and interest. Both may also feature loss of appetite or increased appetite; loss of sleep or excess sleep; feelings of helplessness or hopelessness; feelings of worthlessness; "melancholia"; and a feeling that there's not much point in bothering to take care of hygiene, education, family, health, or finances.

Clinicians take both forms of depression very seriously. They are both referred to as clinical depression and are treated with therapy. The first type has had several descriptive names over the years—the blues, a deep funk, a broken heart, the winter blahs, reactive depression—but I prefer situational depression. The second type usually reflects an imbalance in the brain chemistry. It is another example of what I referred to in the previous chapter as a true disability.

What makes matters more complex is that the two forms of depression are not mutually exclusive, and each can affect the other. We know, for example, that life's stresses can interact with existing or underlying biologically based depressed feelings. Also, common sense dictates that some depression is normal and even desirable in life. This is why, apart from the distinctions I have raised, it may be very difficult for parents to determine whether their teenager suffers from a biochemical imbalance, is depressed because of situational factors, or both. If you are concerned about your teenagers' depressed mood, have them seen by a qualified professional for a valid and reliable diagnosis.

"Normal" Depression: Situational and Adaptive Depression

Is depression ever normal? Of course! It is entirely appropriate and adaptive (good for our survival) to feel sad when sad things happen. In fact, we might wonder what was wrong with someone who *didn't* experience mild depression under these conditions. As odd as it may sound, depression, and the pain that causes it, can be good for you at times.

To get your kids thinking about this issue, ask them if they'd choose to never feel physical pain again, if they could. Those who refuse have already learned a valuable life lesson: They know that while pain is not pleasant, it is a necessary part of life. It tells us to stop doing whatever we were doing when the pain started, and it teaches us not to do the same thing when we find ourselves in the same situation in the future. If we didn't feel pain, we'd be at great risk.

Abnormal Depression: Loss of Pleasure, Loss of Interest

What happens when this normal reaction to life's troubles refuses to let up, even when efforts are made to pull out of it? In these cases, the individual in question may develop a "why bother" attitude: Why bother with family, friends, work, hobbies, or interests? Why bother getting up in the morning? Why bother living?

People suffering from this type of depression don't seem to care if something bad is going to happen. They appear to have given up hope of preventing it. They don't seem to care if they get sick from smoking, or fail in school, or get pregnant. They seem to ask: "Why bother to put in the effort? No one would appreciate it, and it wouldn't get me anywhere, anyway." These beliefs are, of course, mistaken—and this is because their brains are not working properly. As I said above, accurate beliefs depend on the normalcy of brain chemistry.

Loss of Pleasure

What's going on in the brain during depression? The answer can be discovered in the words of depressed people themselves when they answer their "Why bother?" question like this: "Even if I did try to pull myself out of it, it wouldn't get me anywhere. It wouldn't work because I wouldn't feel any better."

In this, they may be right. When there is a chemical imbalance in the systems of the brain related to reward, the inability to experience pleasure is very real. Here's how it works.

The ability to experience pleasure seems to depend on the biochemical balance in certain brain systems. In Chapter 9 I described how these systems were discovered in Canada in 1954 when scientists inserted tiny metal electrodes into the brains of rats. Stimulating those brains electrically at the electrode tips seemed to elicit an extraordinarily pleasurable effect on the rats. When the rats learned to deliver this pleasurable stimulation to their own brains, they did so repeatedly for hours.

The 1960s and 1970s witnessed a veritable frenzy among neuroscientists, the goal of which was to trace the anatomy of the brain systems underlying this pleasurable reaction. Much was learned. Particularly fascinating was the finding that the brain's reward systems extended to the prefrontal cortex. This meant that executive decisions to inhibit impulsive tendencies and make responsible decisions would be rewarded, but of course, this reward would apply only to responsible behavior after the prefrontal cortex assumed its fully developed capacities.

Having identified the anatomy of these systems, scientists turned their attention to the chemical identity of reward system brain cells. They found that the chemical neurotransmitters most often related to brain reward mechanisms are noradrenaline and serotonin. They surmised that an imbalance of those chemicals causes a malfunction in the brain's reward system(s) and that this resulted in the individual's inability to experience pleasure.

Imagine the impact on the individual whose reward system is either entirely absent or functioning at a level far below normal. Think back to my discussion of the behavioral modification approach in the preceding chapter. Every time we do something that is followed by a reward, we tend to repeat that behavior. Moreover, we remember the reward and repeat the behavior when the opportunity to do so occurs. We do this because we expect to be rewarded again. Let me give you an example.

Your teenager writes a terrific report for school or puts in hours of practice before an athletic or artistic performance. If the teacher rewards the great report with a good grade or if the performance is received with applause and adulation, the effort will have been "worth it." Your teenager will be motivated to repeat the effort in the future. That reward is called positive reinforcement. But if there is no recognition of the effort, the teen may develop a "why bother?" attitude—a warning sign of possible impending or existing depression.

Antidepressant medication aims to regulate the levels of serotonin and noradrenaline in the brain, thereby restoring an individual's ability to experience pleasure. The answer to the "why bother?" question becomes "Because if I bother, I can begin to feel better."

This is a huge advance in the treatment of depression. But antidepressants are not perfect. They do not cure or necessarily bring about an end to depression. Also, because of concerns that the use of some antidepressants may be associated with an increase in suicidal ideation or attempts among teenagers, some government regulatory agencies have ruled that they not be used to treat adolescent depression. So the story is still being written.

If you believe your son or daughter is depressed, have them examined by a professional who is well versed and experienced in the theory and treatment of teenage mood disorders. Make sure they are very familiar with all the medications available, and that they understand the potential dangers associated with their use.

Loss of Interest

I've said that people who are depressed seem to have lost interest as well as pleasure. Their attitude is often characterized by the rhetorical question "Why bother?" Is there a way of changing the rhetorical to an empirical question? In other words, if we can get the depressed individual to see that there is a reason to bother, is the loss of interest reversible? If so, would this alleviate clinical depression? I believe so. In Chapter 6, I discussed self-interest in some detail. In monetary terms, interest is the gift you get from the bank for making deposits. It's no coincidence that *the gift you get for investing in yourself is self-interest*. And if you have this vested self-interest, it means that you *care about yourself*. To the therapist, this means changing the mind of the depressed individual and encouraging them to do what they may feel least like doing. Some examples of this might be reconnecting and getting back on better terms with family members; volunteering among people who are desperate for affection; seeking comfort in faith; respecting their bodies by eating better and getting some exercise.

This is much more easily said than done. But it must be done in order to answer the newly empirical question "Why bother?" Because you "bother," you will feel better.

Suicide

Although there are many reasons a person might decide to take his or her own life, the vast majority of suicides are the consequence of deep depression. If you are concerned that your teen could become suicidal, here is some important information:

■ Most suicidal people send out cries for help. Never treat such warning signals casually (no matter how often they happen). Always respond with concern. And always be ready to intervene by seeking medical help.

■ If you feel that someone may be contemplating suicide, ask them directly, using very clear wording. Don't say, "You're not thinking of doing something silly, are you?" The person might be offended or feel that you were trivializing their intentions. Instead, ask, "Are you thinking of killing yourself?" When people are thinking about suicide, they usually admit it.

■ People who are serious about suicide usually have considered the means of carrying it through. Ask if they have a specific plan. If they do, there is cause for alarm.

■ If they admit to suicidal intentions, tell them that you'll do whatever it takes to prevent it. Let them know that you don't agree that the world would be better off without them. Tell them how deeply and personally you would be hurt by their death (use the word "death," not "loss" or "passing").

■ Finally, if you know that suicide has been on someone's mind, treat a sudden reversal of mood with extreme concern. A change from despair to composure or serenity might mean that the person has decided to act soon.

What Parents Can Do About Depression

As we've seen, people care about themselves once they become self-invested, and teenagers are no exception to this rule. Self-interest acts as armor against situational depression. It is also a strength available to a depressed individual who may have been biochemically depressed, and who (via medication) is ready for therapy or counseling.

Parents can act proactively by modeling diversification and balance in their own lives and encouraging their kids to do the same. For example:

■ Parents who commit to family relations and friendships lead the way for their kids to do the same. Those relationships will be in place for kids when challenges arise.

■ Parents who are well rounded with regard to how they spend their time (interests, hobbies, careers, friends) show their kids the benefits of this approach. If one thing falls through, there are other places to go and people to see.

■ Parents who are well-grounded in their moral, ethical, and spiritual beliefs usually lead the way for their kids to have similar grounding.

■ Parents who model and encourage communication about feelings as part of their normal day-to-day lives find it easier to approach their kids when they see that something is wrong. As a result, their kids will be more willing to talk about their own problems.

This last point is particularly helpful if there seems to be a need for professional help. If that help results in a prescription for medication and talk therapy, encourage your kids to give the medication a chance to work. Speak to them about how important it is not to give in to feelings of stigmatization. And encourage them to stay the course in counseling.

Depression is not the only mental incapacity that affects teenagers. I have given it a lot of attention here because it is the disorder that most resembles "normal" adolescent angst. However, for many teenagers and their families, many other mental illnesses can be equally devastating.

Bipolar Disorder

Bipolar disorder is a condition in which people bounce back and forth between months of depression and months of manic behavior. Whereas depression is characterized by a lack of interest and withdrawal, mania is characterized by an accelerated lifestyle. Manic individuals have little need for sleep, "down time," or relaxation; their speech and action appear accelerated. Social, financial, and sexual indiscretions are also common in the manic phase.

Like most mental disabilities, bipolar disorder is the result of biochemical imbalances in the brain and can often be normalized with medication. As always when serious psychological disabilities are suspected, parents should have their teenagers seen by a qualified professional with the first goal being to obtain a valid and reliable diagnosis.

Anxiety Disorders

Many of us feel overwhelmed by anxiety at some time or other—usually because there's just too much to do in our over-busy lives. It should come as no surprise that teens are just as prone to this type of disorder as their parents. They experience distress, which may be expressed in lack of sleep, inability to concentrate, nervousness, etc. As with most mental disorders, it is commonly believed that anxiety disorders are biologically based and genetically predisposed. Nevertheless, all the anxiety disorders are affected by environmental and personality factors. In other words, some people are more resilient to stress than others.

A number of different anxiety disorders have been identified. They share many symptoms but can differ significantly in their presentation, course, and treatment. Let's start with the most basic.

Generalized Anxiety

People with generalized anxiety disorder experience persistent and consistent worry over many areas of their lives for at least six months. Generalized anxiety is accompanied by at least one of three groups of symptoms:

- Musculo-skeletal symptoms include muscle pain, such as headache or lower back pain.
- Visceral symptoms include stomach problems, perspiration, heart palpitations, and increased heart rate or blood pressure.
- Cognitive symptoms include a sense of impending doom and the flooding of the mind with competing thoughts. When these symptoms become intense, panic is felt.

Anxiety and the Brain

Picture a barber with only one chair in his shop. If 20 people try to squeeze onto the chair at once, all demanding a haircut, the barber will not be able to satisfy anyone. He will feel overwhelmed. In a similar way, our brains cannot attend, simultaneously, to all the things most of us have going on in our lives. Teens might find themselves coping with friends, school assignments, sports, family commitments, and more. Like the barber, they must "tell" most of their thoughts to go sit down and wait their turn. But how?

Our brains allow this to happen via an elaborate system of inhibitory cells that keep important but extraneous thoughts outside the realm of consciousness. The chemical transmitter used by those inhibitory neurons is called gamma-amino-butyric acid (GABA). When GABA seems not to be doing its job, a chemical booster may be needed. Minor tranquilizers (like Valium or Ativan) work by boosting GABA's efforts in the brain, thereby inhibiting the extraneous thoughts from demanding conscious attention. When one issue can be dealt with at a time, all issues will eventually get their needed attention.

A word of caution about tranquilizers: These drugs are in the same pharmacological family as alcohol, and they do have a potential to be abused. For this reason, qualified clinicians will prescribe them only in conjunction with crisis counseling during times of acute stress—for example, if a teen is dealing with the recent suicide of a friend, being dumped by her boyfriend, or having to make friends after a family move. In these cases, the anxiety can be overwhelming, but it is tied to a specific event and will almost certainly not last forever. Indeed, the longevity of this sort of anxiety might be measured in days or weeks, not months or years. The tranquilizer helps the individual get through these stressful times, but once a feeling of stability has been reached and the crisis has passed, the person must stop taking the tranquilizers.

The Anxious Teenager

Teens sometimes find it hard to see which issues can go to the back of the line and which must be dealt with right away. Should they get their homework done before talking on the phone with their friends? Should they spend time with their close same-sex friends or pay more attention to their newly interesting friends of the opposite sex? Those decisions depend on a grasp of future potential consequences. For that understanding, teenagers must often rely on a prefrontal cortex that is still incompletely developed. This uncertainty regarding priorities can lead to feelings of being stupid, overwhelmed, and even panicky.

Parents and other adults may see teen behavior as impulsive and self-serving. When they point this out to their kids, whether (rarely) through calm discussion or (more frequently) through angry confrontation, the kids are made to feel stupid, shamed, and controlled. And those feelings often lead kids to rebel and cling defiantly and even more tightly to ill-informed or ill-fated decisions.

Phobias

The feeling of being swamped can also be caused by a phobia, which is anxiety that is related to very specific stimuli (snakes or bugs, for example) or very specific situations (being alone, being in an enclosed space, heights). Sometimes the situation is less concrete. Many parents have seen what is called "school phobia" in their kids. Moreover, this school phobia can be related to separation anxiety. Phobias respond well to behavior modification techniques. These procedures begin by exposing the phobic person to the identified stimulus or situation in a very minimal way. Once this minimal level of exposure is met with relative calm by the phobic person, he or she is gradually exposed to successively prolonged or more intense exposure to the stimulus or situation. Eventually, full exposure can occur without producing any symptoms of anxiety.

Panic Disorder

Everybody knows what it feels like when they reach for their wallet and realize it's not there, or when they realize they're lost in a dangerous place. These are very serious situations. When something serious happens, the sudden shock of recognition is quite normal. But sometimes people react in a serious way when the situation isn't quite so serious. Misplacing a homework assignment or forgetting to confirm a date can lead teenagers with panic disorder into a tailspin of anxiety, self-doubt, and self-recrimination. When this has a clear impact on the teen's schooling or family and social life, it should be looked at professionally. Though it is not classified as a mood disorder, panic disorder often responds well to antidepressant medication.

Obsessive Compulsive Disorder (OCD)

CASE STUDY

Nathan was in Grade 11. He could never complete his written exams because he'd get the feeling, just before starting his first essay, that he had not followed the proper ritualistic procedure. This meant counting the spaces on the answer sheet 20 times before beginning to write. Invariably, he would question the accuracy of his just completed count and begin counting again. Special consideration and the presentation of oral exams allowed Nathan to complete high school and university and to be effective in his chosen occupation. ■

When uninvited and very negative thoughts invade a person's peace of mind, we refer to them as obsessions. People who suffer from obsessions often cannot complete life's most simple tasks. They either repeat those tasks from the beginning or else accompany them with rituals in order to prevent what they can only describe as an impending disaster. Both behavior modification and antidepressant medication are recommended to treat OCD.

What Parents Can Do About Teenage Anxiety

When dealing with anxious teens, parents must exercise wisdom. Pointing out mistakes—regardless of how obvious they seem—will only make kids feel nagged, and they will rebel. Worse, in their immaturity, they are likely to transfer the responsibility for their failure onto (what they see as) unreasonably demanding and overprotective parents.

If, on the other hand, kids are allowed to make their own choices, the dynamics change. If that choice hurts them (remember the hot-stove example from Chapter 4?), they might feel stupid, but at least they have the opportunity to learn from their mistake. They might also learn the valuable lesson of taking responsibility for the consequences of unwise decisions.

The wise parent will be there to support and praise the teen for having taken responsibility. Beyond this, parents can help their kids draw up a list of priorities, identifying where deadlines can be renegotiated and offering to arrange professional help if it's needed. That support may take the form of confidential counseling, tutoring, or mentoring. If this does not take away the underlying anxiety, talk to your family doctor. In some situations, professional help may include psychiatric therapy and medication.

Schizophrenia

Schizophrenia is without doubt the most prevalent and therefore well known of the dissociative disorders. In North America, it occurs in one in every 100 individuals—and it appears to be genetic. The Greek term *schizo* means "split." This meaning leads to perhaps the most prevalent misunderstanding in psychology, because a great many people believe that schizophrenia is a technical term for what is commonly called split (or multiple) personality disorder. In the latter disorder, however, the individual's personality appears to be split into two or more distinct parts. In schizophrenia, the split refers to an individual splitting away or dissociating from reality. Another term for this separation from reality is *psychosis*.

Schizophrenia usually appears between the ages of 18 and 20. It is characterized by a precipitous change from normal to abnormal functioning. It will include "positive" signs, including hallucinations and delusions of paranoia or grandeur, and "negative" signs, including marked slowing down of movement and poverty of thought.

What Parents Can Do

As parents, you must intervene whenever you consider what your kids say or do to be bizarre and inexplicable. As with all mental illnesses, valid and reliable diagnosis by a competent physician is the place to begin. If schizophrenia is diagnosed, medication, counseling, family support, and intermittent institutionalization are often coordinated in treating the disorder.

As a general rule, if you are concerned that your teen is suffering from a mental illness, you must learn more by contacting your local mental health organization, your family doctor, or both. Share what you learn with your teen. You may find that your fears are unjustified as you learn more about these conditions, but if serious disorders do exist, you can prepare for dealing with them; you'll also have opened lines of communication and understanding with your kids.

Eating Disorders

According to the DSM-IV, there are two specific diagnoses of eating disorder: anorexia nervosa and bulimia nervosa. In both disorders, more than 90% of the sufferers are females. The anorexic individual looks at herself in the mirror and, as with all mental illnesses, sees something quite different from reality. Usually, this means that she sees someone who needs to lose weight. She then compensates by refusing to eat and thereby fails to maintain a normal body weight.

CASE STUDY

Jill was a pretty normal kid until she turned 14. She had friends, did well in school, and got along with her family. After her 14th birthday, her friends started to notice that Jill wasn't eating very much when they went out together. They dismissed it as the result of a normal desire to slim down.

One day the group decided to go to a county fair. The fair had the usual attractions, including a Hall of Mirrors. All the girls wanted a turn in front of the mirror that made them look obese. Each took her turn, giggling and teasing as they went. Then Jill stepped in front of the mirror. First she froze. The she turned pale, started to cry, and ran off sobbing. When Jill's friends finally caught up with her, they got her to explain what had happened. "Oh my God," she cried. "I've never really seen myself in the mirror before. It was always some stranger. But with this mirror, I finally saw myself as I really am!"

The girls convinced Jill to go with them and talk to her parents. It was revealed that Jill had been starving herself for a few months without anybody knowing. She readily went for professional help and, after some time in therapy, managed to overcome her anorexia. ■

Whereas Jill chose the most common approach to weight loss (self-starvation), the teen may use other methods in conjunction with it—abusing laxatives or diuretic medication, purging (self-induced vomiting), and excessive exercising.

Sadly, any weight loss that accompanies these methods does not reduce the fear of weight gain, and the methods continue despite significant decrease in weight. Anorexic individuals may be concerned about their overall weight or body shape, or about specific body parts such as thighs, or butts, or breasts. They look in mirrors an awful lot. They view weight gain as a sign of weakness or a failure of self-control. Anorexic individuals often become depressed, irritable, or socially withdrawn. They may lose libido and have difficulty sleeping.

Teenagers with bulimia nervosa present a very similar set of behaviors to anorexics. However, they do not restrict their food intake, and they are usually able to maintain their weight at or above a minimally normal level. They are, however, excessively concerned about body weight and shape. They typically binge eat. That is, they eat an amount of food that is unarguably more than would normally be eaten in a given situation. Often, they binge when feeling particularly low or stressed out. To qualify for the diagnosis, a person must binge eat and engage in inappropriate compensatory behaviors at least twice a week for at least three months. Contrary to intuitive or popular belief, people with bulimia eat reasonably balanced diets and do not necessarily crave sweets or other carbohydrates. Following the binge, bulimics use inappropriate ways to prevent gaining weight. They too will purge, over-exercise, use laxatives, etc.

What Parents Can Do About Eating Disorders

While many mental disorders have biological bases, they can be mitigated by emotional strength. And by following the principles outlined in this book, parents will give their kids just that. In the case of eating disorders, kids who are raised in such a way as to have empowerment, good self-esteem, lots of friends, balanced lifestyles, and good parental involvement in their lives are more resilient in combating the depression and anxiety that accompany the disorder than kids who do not have these strengths. As well, parents should be aware of their own attitudes about body size and shape. Do you place too much emphasis on the importance of being thin? Have you become too casual about your own obesity? Either of these attitudes can contribute to undue concerns on the part of their kids.

Unfortunately, many parents find out too late that their kids have emotional problems. It should go without saying that parents must carefully watch their kids' eating pattern and their weight. Any concerns they have should be conveyed to both their kids and to their kids' physicians. Responsible physicians will call the kid in for a private, sometimes confidential talk.

Narcissistic Personality Disorder (NPD)

According to the DSM-IV, a personality disorder is "an enduring pattern of inner experience and behavior that deviates markedly from the expectations of the individual's culture, is pervasive and inflexible, has an onset in adolescence or early adulthood, is stable over time, and leads to distress or impairment." Earlier, I spoke of the avoidant and antisocial varieties. This next one has all the usual patterns of these disorders, but relates to the monster that many parents fear they might have created: the spoiled brat.

The cardinal features of narcissistic personality disorder are grandiosity, need for admiration, and lack of empathy. Persons suffering from NPD can be snobbish and will brag and overstate their abilities. They act as if they are privileged and display a sense of entitlement when it comes to how they should be regarded or how they ought to be treated. They don't really care too much about the needs or feelings of other people, and they may become impatient when they have to sit and listen to someone else's problems.

Do you find yourself thinking "That's my kid!? After all, even the DSM-IV states that "narcissistic traits may be particularly common in adolescence and do not necessarily indicate that the individual will go on to have Narcissistic Personality Disorder." Remember the "cornucopia kids"—they are given everything, so they lack motivation to get it for themselves. This could easily extend to an attitude of entitlement, whereby they begin to believe that they are somehow special and deserve all the things they have. It becomes more serious when this leads to a significant impairment in how your kids manage in the home, at school (or work), and in social situations. Most kids will grow out of their normal adolescent narcissism.

What Parents Can Do About NPD

To get an idea of how likely a person is to grow out of a narcissistic phase, I usually use a literal analogy. I ask the kid to remember a particularly loved article of clothing from when they were younger. Say it was a jacket. That jacket looked great back then, but how would it look now? It wouldn't fit, it would look silly, and they would be ridiculed for wearing it.

Once you've got basic agreement on this fact, you can explain that this is how they look when they try to hold onto childish ways of behaving. It doesn't fit. It looks silly. If your kids respond with a modicum of comprehension, they'll almost certainly come out of their teenage narcissism on their own. If not, professional help is required.

Conclusion:
Teach Your Children Well

As your teenagers emerge from the scarier parts of adolescence and start to show signs of being more comfortable with themselves and others, the dynamics of your relationship will change. You're dealing with individuals well on the way to maturity. Soon you'll be watching them set out on the greater journey that will be the rest of their lives. As parents, you want to encourage and support them on this journey. Building on the experiences you and your teens have been constructing, you can continue by giving them the sense that they are competent to make decisions that will affect their lives. By implementing and adapting the ideas in this book, you will empower your teens and help them become independent and responsible young adults.

Empowerment is a word that gets thrown around a lot these days but its familiarity to the point of cliché doesn't lessen its importance. Whether you're a teenager or an adult, not having power is associated with just about every emotional and behavioral problem you can name—drug abuse, depression and suicidal feelings, anger and violent lashing out at "dictatorial" authorities, bullying or teasing peers, shyness, social isolation, and so on. On the other hand, empowerment leads to involvement, owner-ship, self-confidence, and so much more. So how you define and use power in your home will be of paramount importance in determining whether your kids develop a sensible, realistic, and responsible sense of empowerment. As you've seen in the preceding pages, I'm a great believer in sharing power with your kids. Remember the discussion about democ-racy—sharing power doesn't mean you're abdicating your responsibility!

Learning how to share power isn't easy. But if you want to empower your children, you must do exactly that. Here are some reminders for parents who want to have a family that is democratic and thus empowered:

- Listen to your kids. Even if you have no good answers to what they're asking you, make them know that they are smart for having asked. And let them know that you too are perplexed by the same questions.
- Give your kids a sense of representation. Kids are busy with their own agendas and they usually don't want to "rule the roost." But they do want to be part of the ruling of the roost.
- Your kids will take ownership of the rules that they helped formulate.
- Don't worry if there are two parents in the home and they don't agree on the rules. Show kids that when adults don't agree, they use the art of compromise to reach an agreement. Your teen will soon pick up what it means to negotiate—for starters, it means you're listening to him!
- Finally, remember that there are many different levels of rules and that ethics occupy the top of the hierarchy. And although views about sex, religion, politics, and so forth are quite likely to differ across generations and cultures, ethics never change. Keep this in mind when you negotiate the details of the rules being set. Another way of saying this is "pick your fights."

All too often the truth is that parents really *don't* trust their kids. At some point, though, we *have* to trust them. We have to trust them to make their own decisions and to make their own mistakes. We have to trust them to follow through on what they said they would do. The tools I've outlined in the preceding pages will help you become the confident and trusting parent of your adolescent. I hope you'll take away with you the confidence to trust your teen, the understanding of the importance of modeling and being an honest mirror, and the confirmation that your parenting instincts have been right. Don't forget to trust your own instincts—you might have seen some of the same solutions in these pages that you've used yourself. But many parents feel as if they're stumbling around in the dark and don't trust their own skills.

I appeal to you as parents and as citizens to teach your children well. Make them aware, by your own attitudes and actions, that all humans are of equal value and deserve equal respect and opportunity. Show them that doing the "right thing" applies well beyond the boundaries of their own selves. Extend their sense of responsibility to embrace the larger society in which they live. By doing this, you give your kids what you want most to give them. Independence. It will be their greatest gift.

Index